CANNIBAL
DEMOCRACY

To Reginald,
It was a great pleasure to
meet you and exchange ideas
on our panel. I admire the
passion and integrity of your
approach to your work —
an inspiration!

L.

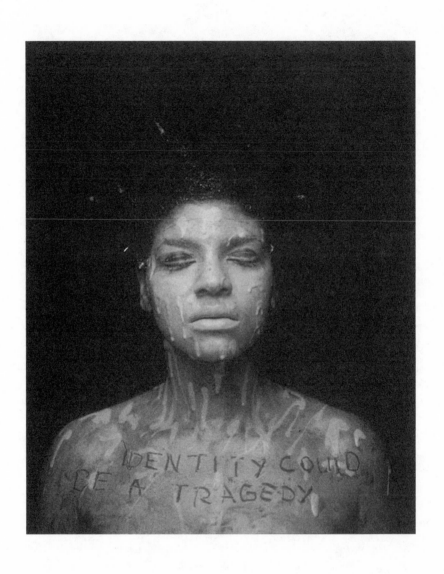

CANNIBAL
DEMOCRACY

Race and Representation
in the Literature of the Americas

ZITA NUNES

CRITICAL AMERICAN STUDIES SERIES

University of Minnesota Press
Minneapolis
London

CRITICAL AMERICAN STUDIES SERIES

George Lipsitz, University of California–Santa Barbara, Series Editor

The University of Minnesota Press gratefully acknowledges the financial assistance provided for the publication of this book from the Graduate School and the Department of English at the University of Maryland.

Frontispiece: María Magdalena Campos-Pons, "Identity Could Be a Tragedy," from *When I Am Not Here / Estoy allá . . .*, 1996. Color Polaroid triptych. Courtesy of R. H. Norton Trust, Norton Museum of Art, West Palm Beach, Florida (99.92.1–3). Printed with permission of the artist.

Poetry by Mário de Andrade in the epigraph to the Introduction and in chapters 1 and 2 appears courtesy of Família Mário de Andrade. Poetry from "Tra" by María Magdalena Campos-Pons in chapter 5 is reprinted with permission from the author.

Portions of chapters 1 and 2 were previously published as "Race and Ruins," in *Culture/Contexture: Explorations in Anthropology and Literary Studies*, ed. E. Valentine Daniel and Jeffrey M. Peck (Berkeley: University of California Press, 1996); copyright 1996 by the Regents of the University of California; reprinted with permission. Portions of chapter 4 were previously published as "Phantasmatic Brazil: Nella Larsen's Passing, American Literary Imagination, and Racial Utopianism," in *Mixing Race, Mixing Culture: Inter-American Literary Dialogues*, ed. Monika Kaup and Debra J. Rosenthal (Austin: University of Texas Press, 2002); copyright 2002 University of Texas Press; reprinted with permission. Portions of the text were previously published in "'Loving Our Children to Death': Identification and the African Diaspora," in *Dislocating "Europe": Post-Colonial Perspectives in Literary, Anthropological, and Historical Studies*, ed. Manuela Ribeiro Sanches (Lisbon: Universidade de Lisboa, 2005); reprinted, translated, and abridged in *Mostra Pan Africana de Arte Contemporânea*, ed. Solange Oliveira Farkas (São Paulo: Associação Cultural Videobrasil, 2005), 22–27.

Published by the University of Minnesota Press
111 Third Avenue South, Suite 290
Minneapolis, MN 55401-2520
http://www.upress.umn.edu

Library of Congress Cataloging-in-Publication Data

Nunes, Zita.
    Cannibal democracy : race and representation in the literature of the Americas / Zita Nunes.
      p.   cm. — (Critical American Studies series)
    Includes bibliographical references and index.
    ISBN 978-0-8166-4840-5 (hardcover : alk. paper) — ISBN 978-0-8166-4841-2 (pbk. : alk. paper)
    1. United States—Race relations—Historiography. 2. Brazil—Race relations—Historiography. 3. Caribbean Area—Race relations—Historiography. 4. American literature—African American authors—History and criticism. 5. Brazilian literature—History and criticism. 6. Caribbean literature—History and criticism. 7. Metaphor. 8. Cannibalism in literature. 9. Race relations in literature. 10. Democracy in literature. I. Title.
    E184.A1N86 2008
    305.896'07—dc22   2008018324

Printed in the United States of America on acid-free paper

The University of Minnesota is an equal-opportunity educator and employer.

15 14 13 12 11 10 09 08   10 9 8 7 6 5 4 3 2 1

For
Manuel J. Nunes, MD
and in memory of
Valentina St. Aubyn Nunes and Maria Silva St. Aubyn

Contents

Acknowledgments

I AM HAPPY to have the opportunity to acknowledge the many colleagues, librarians, staff, friends, and family who accompanied me in the writing of this book. Their guidance, assistance, and support have been invaluable.

I am grateful to George Lipsitz for his careful reading of my manuscript and his inclusion of my book in the Critical American Studies series. I thank Richard Morrison, executive editor, and the staff at the University of Minnesota Press, including Adam Brunner, Emily Hamilton, Laura Westlund, Rachel Moeller, Renie Howard, and Sallie Steele.

I am fortunate to have a mentor in Carla Peterson, who meticulously read the manuscript at a crucial phase and offered helpful advice. I thank Houston Baker, Eric Cheyfitz, Colin Joan Dayan, Brent Hayes Edwards, Emory Elliott, Farah Jasmine Griffin, Sandra Gunning, Biodun Jeyifo, David Lloyd, Natalie Melas, Priscilla Wald, and Mary Helen Washington. Each read and commented on the manuscript, sometimes more than once, giving me with their insightful comments the chance to improve what I had written. Their scholarship—and their generosity in supporting my own—has served as an enduring source of inspiration.

This project benefited from the unstinting help of librarians at the University of Maryland, especially Patricia Herron and Susanna Van Sant; the Library of Congress; Cornell University; New York University; the Moorland–Spingarn Research Center at Howard University; Schomburg Center for Research in Black Culture of the New York Public Library; the Oliveira Lima Library at Catholic University, especially Thomas Cohen and Maria Angela Leal; the W. E. B. Du Bois Library at the University of Massachusetts, Amherst; the Instituto de Estudos Brasileiros of the Universidade de São Paulo; the Biblioteca Nacional (Rio de Janeiro); and the Fundação Joaquim Nabuco.

I thank Manuela Ribeiro Sanches, Telê Porto Ancona Lopez, Heloisa Buarque de Hollanda, Orna Messer, Camilo Penna, Muniz Sodré, Beatriz Kushnir, Solonge Farkas, Nina Maria de Carvalho, Elias Rabha, and Robert Stam for their guidance and support of my project. I am especially grateful to Carlos Augusto de Andrade Camargo and the family of Mário de Andrade, who could not have been more generous in making his work available to me.

María Magdalena Campos-Pons welcomed me into her home and studio, making her work available and spending hours with me discussing it. I will not forget her extraordinary generosity. I similarly thank Keith Piper, who was also very forthcoming, and Salah Hassan, who introduced me to both of these artists and served as an important source of information and support.

I also thank all of my colleagues and students at the University of Maryland, College Park. They have contributed to an intellectual environment that has enriched me and my work. John Auchard, Jonathan Auerbach, Charles Caramello, Kent Cartwright, and James Harris have my gratitude for having read the manuscript and given me valuable support. I also express my sincere appreciation to Betty Fern, Isabella Moulton, Irene Sanchez, and Betty Wienecke for their help.

I have been fortunate to receive funding from Fulbright, the Social Science Research Council, the University of Maryland, Cornell University, and Columbia University, which allowed me to conduct research and to write.

I thank my friends, Tonita Lipscomb Abrahams, Nancy Castro, Ramez Elias, Kathryn Gravdal, Bill Hinchberger, Pedro Martins, Orin McDougall, Lucianne Mello, Abdul Nanji, the late Maruska Freire Rameck, Rebecca Reichmann, Alan Thomas, Deborah White, as well as my family—my siblings, Frederick, Maria Valentina, James, and Mark; my niece and nephews, Justin, Christopher, Kathryn, and Felix, and Ty, all of whom, with Lauren and Linda Nunes, were with me as I mailed the final version of the manuscript; and my stepmother, Dea Soren. This book is dedicated with love and gratitude to my father, Manuel Nunes, M.D.; to my late mother, Valentina St. Aubyn Nunes; and to my late grandmother, Maria Silva St. Aubyn (Vovó).

Preface

*The "scare quotes" used to signal our understanding that "American" is a
misnomer . . . also signal the failure of too many of us to "rethink" what we
thought we already knew in the context of what we all know that we do not
know—how to reconceptualize a field that is clearly no longer mappable
by any of the traditional coordinates . . . but that also resists the reconfigu-
ration called for by its own historical and geographical expansion.*

—Carolyn Porter, "What We Know That We Don't Know:
Remapping American Studies"

IN *Cannibal Democracy,* I uncover and account for a web of American
contact zones that constitutes a new archive. Through this web circulated
and continues to circulate a remarkably consistent set of concept-metaphors
derived from cannibalism, informing the way race relations in a democracy are
apprehended and theorized. My book takes up this set of concept-metaphors,
the persistence of which is suggested by its objects of study, and tracks the
metaphors' circulation through the work of a number of American writers.
Many of these writers—like Mário de Andrade, Charles Chesnutt, W. E. B.
Du Bois, Gilberto Freyre, Nella Larsen in the earlier period, and Toni Morrison and Wilson Harris in the later period—will already be familiar to the
readers of this book. They and their less well-known counterparts from the
United States, Brazil, and the Caribbean will be presented throughout my
book in a less familiar transnational context to argue for the significance of
this context to interdependent debates about black citizenship in democratic
societies. Among the writers whose work disappears when the national takes
precedence is José Clarana. His career is exemplary in demonstrating the
importance of placing the transnational at the center of American Studies in
a way that challenges the national as the central category of analysis, revealing in its place "a web of contact zones."[1]

In 1918, apparently at the request of its editor, W. E. B. Du Bois, José Clarana published "A Letter from Brazil" in *The Crisis:* "In acceding to your request that I send you 'one or two letters about the color problem in Brazil,' I keep within the limitations of my capacity and comply with your admonition that I 'make them as short as possible,' by writing one letter with the simple statement that there is no color problem in Brazil." One year later Clarana's book, *Os estados unidos pela civilisação e a civilisação dos Estados Unidos* (*The States United by Civilization and the Civilization of the United States*) appeared in Brazil. A translated and vastly expanded version of *The Crisis* article, the book countered the article's central argument by criticizing Brazil's lack of response to racial violence in the United States and the racist roots of this apathy. Since the English text is included in its entirety in the Portuguese version (except for the assertion that there is no color problem in Brazil), I wanted to know more about Clarana in order to properly contextualize these conflicting texts and their audiences.

When I set out to gather more information about the author, I found myself faced with an interesting puzzle. I learned that José Clarana was a pseudonym. *Os Estados Unidos* is catalogued at the New York Public Library under the name J. B. Clarke. Clearly, the original cataloguer had information that linked José Clarana to J. B. Clarke. Further research showed that Clarke was also the compiler of *A Memento of the Emancipation Proclamation Exposition of the State of New York* (22–31 October 1913)[2] that the Schomburg Center for Research in Black Culture has in its collection and which is dedicated "To Arthur Schomburg, With the compliments of the compiler, J. B. Clarke." The Schomburg Center's copy of *Os Estados Unidos* was originally dedicated (in handwriting identical to that on *A Memento*) in English: "To *the Crisis* New York, with the compliments of the author. Rio de Janeiro, 21-10-1919" and rededicated, in the same handwriting: "From *The Crisis* to a more appreciative recipient, the author's esteem. Brooklyn, Nov. 25, 1920." Arthur Schomburg's signature appears beneath the epigraph on the dedication page. I inferred from this page that Clarana/Clarke initally made a gift of his book to the *Crisis* and later took it back himself to make it a gift to Arthur Schomburg. The copy of *Os Estados Unidos* at the Library of Congress, which was acquired from the Pan American Union on 3 October 1925, is dedicated in English and in a hand that corresponds to the copy at the Schomburg: "To Mr. John Barrett, with the compliments of the author, who has heard him talk and has read his writings on panamericanism. Rio de Janeiro, 21-10-1919." Clarana/Clarke also made gifts of *Os Estados Unidos* to the mayor of Lexington, Kentucky (at the University of Kentucky), to the renowned U. S.–based Brazilian academic, Oliveira Lima (at Catholic University), and to the Cornell Library.

I found that Clarana had published, under this name, yet another article in *The Crisis* on Brazil.[3] Jessie Redmon Fauset published an article in *The Crisis* on the Brazilian abolitionist José do Patrocinio, which she coauthored with a Cezar Pinto, who also may have been Clarana/Clarke.[4] Robert M. Levine and John J. Crocitti speculate in *The Brazil Reader* that Clarana may have been the Brazilian sociologist Gilberto Freyre.[5] This seemed impossible to me, given that Clarana published his first article in *The Crisis* in 1913 and Freyre would have been thirteen years old at the time. Furthermore, the unusual perspective of the argument in *Os Estados Unidos*, critical of Brazil's lack of response to racial violence in the United States, also argues against their suggestion.

An entry in Howard University Library's card catalogue led me to a notice in a December 1916 society column in *The Crisis*. The notice regarded a James Bertram Clarke, a Cornell graduate, who was to depart for Brazil as a representative for "a United States commercial concern."[6] The 1922 Cornell alumni directory contained registration information for James Betram Clarke, (Cornell 1912), cross-listed as Jaime Clarana Gil.[7] Armed with this new information, I found that, in 1923 under the name Jaime Clarana Gil, Clarke had published *America the Peacemaker,* an evaluation of the League of Nations. On the entry for the Schomburg's copy of this book was a local note stating: "In ms. on t.p.: James B. Clarke, colored." In the course of searching for the manuscript referred to in the note, I came across a reference to William Edgar Easton's 1911 play, *Christophe: A Tragedy in Prose of Imperial Haiti.*[8] The information for Easton's play in the card catalogue, including that it had appended to it two essays, "A Job for Uncle Sam" and "An Hour with Harriet Tubman," by James B. Clarke, was crossed out. Clarke's name was typed above Easton's and the notation: "American Negro author" typed below it. An examination of the book showed that it includes not only these two texts but also a photograph of Clarke and a biography of him by Easton.

Clarke turns out to embody the American Negro as the Negro is translated in very contradictory ways, across nations and languages. Born in 1888 in St. Vincent, British West Indies, Clarke was educated at the St.

Vincent Grammar School. In his writings, he says that he came to United States in 1905, probably from Brazil, since the matriculation record at Cornell University lists his address as rua Municipal, 9, Rio de Janeiro, Brazil. Fluent in and a teacher of French, Spanish, and Italian, he was clearly a speaker of Portuguese and English. When Clarke interviewed Harriet Tubman just before her death, she noted that his speech testified to his West Indian origins.[9]

As a student between 1908 and 1912, Clarke made himself known at Cornell. In 1910, he was initiated as an early member of the Alpha Phi Alpha fraternity, the black fraternity that was founded at Cornell in 1905. While at Cornell, Clarke published an article in the *Cornell Era,* titled "Race Prejudice at Cornell" and circulated "a letter addressed to the President and the Board of Trustees appealing to them not to establish racial discrimination at Cornell by excluding colored girls from the women's dormitory."[10] This stand and its successful outcome — a public statement by the president of the university barring discrimination on the campus — brought him widespread attention and certainly solidified his connection to Jessie Redmon Fauset, who would be the literary editor of *The Crisis* from 1919 to 1926. She had graduated from Cornell in 1905, majoring in languages as would Clarke, who had included her experiences with racism without naming her in the article on race prejudice at Cornell. He was also the associate editor of the *Cosmopolitan Student,* the publication of the Cosmopolitan Clubs of America, an organization of international students from all over the world founded at Cornell and active from 1904 to 1958. After his 1912 graduation from Cornell, Clarke worked as a Spanish teacher in the Brooklyn public schools, along with Arthur Schomburg and wrote for *The Crisis* and other publications, before moving to Brazil in 1916 as indicated by the social notice in *The Crisis.* This commercial interest was probably associated with one of the black colonization syndicates that had gained momentum during the period. These syndicates sought to promote migration of black professionals — doctors, lawyers, dentists, businessmen, to Brazil, where they presumably could exercise their professions without fear of discrimination. The dedications on *Os Estados Unidos* show that Clarke returned to Brooklyn in 1919, after which he continued to publish articles, the book on the League of Nations and letters on pressing issues of the day.[11] The last reference I have for him is a 1923 letter signed Jaime Gil to the *New York Times* on "Race Feeling in France."[12]

In addition to the articles on Brazil, Clarke as Clarana wrote for *The Crisis* on the nineteenth-century Cuban poet and revolutionary Placido,[13] on education,[14] and the racial identity of the Louisiana creoles he had visited.[15] He wrote extensively on Haiti and Cuba, perhaps even residing in these two nations. He collected and published documents related to the Emancipation Proclamation and raised money for a fund to allow Harriet Tubman to transform her house into a retirement home. He was a member of the Society of Social and Political Sciences. His article on international aspects of the color problem appeared in the September 1913 issue of that society's journal commemorating fifty years of Negro progress alongside those of Kelly Miller, W. E. B. Du Bois, and Booker T. Washington, among other prominent scholars.[16] In short, Clarke/Clarana/Gil's United States connections read like a *Who's Who* of the early twentieth century: Harriet Tubman, Booker T. Washington, Arthur Schomburg, W. E. B. Du Bois, Jessie Redmon Fauset, Kelly Miller, William Edgar Easton, and given his propensity for travel and networking, surely many more. He apparently was equally well connected in Brazil and in the Caribbean. Clarke/Clarana/Gil's life and work — his writings in English and in Portuguese (and I have no doubt that further research will show that he published in French and in Spanish as well), his engagement with issues of race and democracy, his publications in highly respected sites, and his complex international politics — reinforce in a particularly dramatic way the reality of the transnational network under examination in *Cannibal Democracy*. The use of pseudonyms and the fact that some aspects of Clarke's arguments do not translate completely from one language or country to another is an indicator of the tension between the national and the transnational. My work on James B. Clarke suggests that the tension between the national and the transnational represented by the problem of translation need not always be seen as a barrier to be overcome. In some cases the impossibility of completely translating the term *negro,* (even as the same scripted term signified differently in English, Spanish, and Portuguese) was used strategically to advance national and transnational agendas that "spoke" differently in different contexts in deference to local concerns. In other words, Blacks in Brazil needed their image of the United States as much as Blacks in the United States needed their image of Brazil to articulate and negotiate the contradictions inherent in representing blackness in democratic societies.

In her widely cited article from which my epigraph is taken, Carolyn Porter suggests that shifting the terrain of American Studies from the national to the transnational necessitates not only a change of archive, but also of methodology. For this reason, *Cannibal Democracy* has what could be seen as an unconventional organization. On one level, this book's organization contains within it a residual genealogy, one that, in many ways, corresponds to the last decade's reorientation not only of American Studies, but also of African American/African Diaspora, Latin American, and Comparative Literary Studies. *Cannibal Democracy* originally was to be about Brazilian literature, which had been the subject of my doctoral dissertation. As I began the process of revising my dissertation for publication, I was teaching courses on the Harlem Renaissance and on Latin American and Caribbean literature. I soon began to note in the texts I was teaching not only persistent references to other nations in the Americas, particularly where issues of race and citizenship were in play, but also that resonances of the metaphor of cannibalism and the remainder sounded in different times and places. I eventually came to see the metaphor of cannibalism as a mobile metaphor that inheres in attempts to conceptualize the relationship between race and democracy extending far beyond Brazil and that the original national focus was insufficient. While the idea of the remainder is derived from the theoretical model of cannibalism elaborated by the Brazilian modernists during the 1920s, I came to see that the prevailing narratives of identity formation throughout twentieth-century America share a dependence on the metaphor of incorporation. Collectively, these narratives present the individual, the social, and the political as a body that ingests; and, from the position of the incorporating body, the construction of a national/racial identity through a process of assimilation presupposes a remainder.

As my project developed, I also realized that any discussion of the content of the metaphor of cannibalism as it related to race and democracy had to take into account the structure of metaphor itself. In their groundbreaking 1980 *Metaphors We Live By*, George Lakoff and Mark Johnson challenge the traditional view of metaphor expressed in the equation *A is B*. They argue that metaphors are rooted in concepts and not merely in the words we use, that metaphors contribute to and structure understanding, and, therefore, constitute an unavoidable aspect of human thought processes. They also maintain that the conventional definition of metaphor obscures the fact that "metaphorical structuring . . . is partial not total."[17] The unending

struggle — unending precisely because the source and the target of the metaphor cannot be the same or they would be the same thing — inherent in this
process requires, in the terms of my study, a remainder. Metaphors work,
according to Lakoff and Johnson, because the similar aspects, or, again in
the terms of my study, the incorporated aspects of the source in the target,
are highlighted and the remainder remains hidden. Metaphor, therefore, is
the very figure on which the discussion of the relationship between race and
democracy logically should rest since all attempts to conceptualize the con-
struct of race fall back on metaphors of color or blood or taint. In addition,
the structure of metaphor mirrors the structure of cannibalism, which, in
turn, structures the relationship between race and democracy. Significantly,
all share a resisting remainder that is disavowed in the interest of coherence
and stability.

On a second level, the book's organization derives from the need to
"rethink" as yet unresolved questions related to representing difference in
democracy. These old but still unresolved questions — questions that have
become more rather than less urgent — have echoed throughout the Americas since the late nineteenth century. In addressing these questions, I did not
want to argue by accretion. I wanted to go beyond a collection of separate
readings of texts from distinct regions and also to avoid producing a study of
influence or one that would endorse one national model over another. In the
introduction to *The Black Atlantic: Modernity and Double Consciousness*,
Paul Gilroy addresses the double consciousness and cultural intermixture
that, for him, distinguish those of the African Diaspora. He looks to African American thinkers to challenge what he calls the "narrowness of vision
which is content with the merely national." According to Gilroy, these thinkers "were prepared to renounce the easy claims of African American exceptionalism in favour of a global coalitional politics in which anti-imperialism
and anti-racism might be seen to interact if not to fuse." My examination
of the interactions among writers and artists of the Caribbean and of North
and South America indicates how complex these coalitional politics can be.
Our understanding of their complexity, however, requires a new approach,
one that addresses the methodological, theoretical, historical, and ethical
dimensions of the transnational relationship. I believe that only by looking
at all these aspects together, each aspect coming to the fore at different points
to analyze its significance, can a new accounting of the stakes and outcomes
of these coalitional politics take place.

The introduction to *Cannibal Democracy* outlines the historical and geographical parameters as well as the methodology of my argument. It introduces the two central themes of the study that provide the inspiration for the title of my book: cannibalism and racial democracy. In the following chapters, I examine these themes in relation to texts and images from Brazil and the United States.

Chapter 1, "United by Anthropophagism," and chapter 2, "Bringing in the Dead: Nostalgia and the Refusal of Loss in Gilberto Freyre's *Casa Grande e Senzala*," together elaborate, in relation to Brazil, the theoretical model derived from the concept metaphor of cannibalism. Chapter 1 focuses on Mário de Andrade's novel *Macunaíma* and on "A medicina dos excretos" (Excremental Medicine), the second essay from the collection titled *Namoros com a medicina* (Flirtations with Medicine). I argue that Mário de Andrade's texts try but fail to find a place in this world for their black and indigenous characters, suggesting that identification with an ideal of Brazilian (racial) democracy requires a choice that would remainder blackness as a marker of a viable social and political position. Andrade's work enacts the contradictions of being represented, at one and the same time, as Black and Brazilian.

Chapter 2 examines how Freyre's reliance on metaphors of incorporation to describe the relationship of black and indigenous peoples and cultures to Brazilian history and identity both secures and resists the notion of racial democracy. I argue that this resistance is conveyed through the persistence of excremental remainders in Freyre's prose. The remainders convey the unresolved tension between the constituent terms of racial democracy.

Chapter 3, "The Foreigner and the Remainder," analyzes references to Brazil in selected works by W. E. B. Du Bois and Charles Chesnutt, in light of the concept metaphor of cannibalism and the remainder from a psychoanalytic perspective. I argue that their texts call attention to the violence of identification, permitting me to explore the ethics of a relationship to the remainder.

The strict association of Freyre's name with the concept of racial democracy has obscured its earlier circulation in the United States and in Brazil. Chapter 4, "The New Negro and the Turn to South America," analyzes the representations of Brazil and the United States in the black press of each nation in the decade before and after the First World War, as well as the public debate of values that eventually would be resumed in the idea of racial democracy. This chapter ends with a consideration of Nella Larsen's *Passing,* and Jessie Redmon Fauset's *Plum Bun.* In these works, Brazil (or Latin America) plays a significant role in the exploration of what gets left behind or remaindered when one passes racially and/or across borders.

The last chapter, "The Remainder Is a Reminder: Cannibalizing the Remains of the Past," jumps ahead sixty years to shift from a consideration of the politics of comparison to a consideration of the politics of diasporic identities. It should be clear that *Cannibal Democracy* does not pretend to be a continuous history of the use of the concept metaphor of cannibalism nor is it a continuous history of race and race relations. Its focus is the tracking of a metaphor as it plays out in discussions of race and democracy at the opening and close of the twentieth century. Although it would be possible to make a historical argument validating the gap in sixty years between chapter 4 and chapter 5,[18] an argument that would justify the chronology of my book, this section, while acknowledging the continuity of the issues regarding black citizenship, is more concerned with addressing directly the ethical questions that have shadowed my argument up to that point. Chapter 5 is, therefore, more speculative than the preceding chapters. The novels and images that I analyze in this chapter suggest a way of thinking through the dyad *incorporation/introjection* in favor of a process that can acknowledge, without endlessly taking in or overcoming, the remainder. As I demonstrate in this chapter, the dyad *necrophilia/necrophagia,* which derives from the work of John Akomfrah, Kobena Mercer, Nicholas Abraham, and Maria Torok, seems to offer more creative possibilities for the relationship of the remainder to the *demos.*

The epilogue does not suggest a resolution — or, better, an "outside" — of the issues of the metaphorical models of knowledge, of the liberal citizen subject, or of the psychosexual underpinnings of modern racism that *Cannibal Democracy* engages. My argument throughout emphasizes that metaphors of incorporation that structure both the seemingly benign goals of integration and "racial democracy" on the one hand *and* the goals of separatism, often experienced as less benign, on the other, imply, logically, a remainder. I propose that it is more fruitful to think about what is left over rather than what is left out from or foreign to a process of unification or incorporation. In my epilogue, I suggest that the Carib bone flute, as described by Wilson

Harris, is a figure for this possibility. In the work that follows, I propose that we shift the field of cultural inquiry from a project that seeks a new or autonomous modality of inclusion (which, whether consolidated inside or outside, would be doomed to repeat, in the attempt to unify, the very act of exclusion it protests) to a project that articulates a relationship to the remainder, as such, a relationship that would not require complete identification or understanding.

Introduction

We urge in Brazil and Central America that the people of African descent no longer be satisfied with a solution to the Negro problem which involves their absorption into another race, without allowing Negroes as such full recognition of their manhood and their right to be.

—W. E. B. Du Bois, "The Negro Takes Stock"

PRECISA—SE BRASILEIROS
Assim está escrito no anúncio vistoso de cores desesperadas pintado sobreo corpo indeciso do nosso Brasil, camaradas.

WANTED: BRAZILIANS
This is what is written on the furiously colored eye-catching advertisement painted on the shifting body of this, our Brazil, my chums.

—Mário de Andrade, "Cartaz"

IN 1989, the attention of a passerby in Rio de Janeiro would have been drawn to a striking poster affixed to a wall. This poster, one of many plastered throughout the city's poorer neighborhoods, showed three nude, brown-skinned torsos—one, the lightest in color, apparently a woman as indicated by the salience of the breast; the other two were less easily categorized. The three bodies were layered from the left to right with the *mulata* closest in terms of perspective to the surface plane and, therefore, to the viewer of the photograph. In the center of the photograph, superimposed on the torso in the middle was a white box containing racial designations, each followed by a question mark: "branco? preto? pardo? amarelo? indigena?" (white? black? dusky? yellow? indigenous?).

The poster, a response to the summary of census data that had recently been made public, carried two phrases: "Não deixa a sua cor passar em branco" (Don't let your color pass [fade] into white) and "Responda com bom s/Censo" (Answer with good sense). In addition to the reference to

1

"passing" familiar to English speakers, this first phrase also called attention to the then-imminent first direct presidential election in three decades. The candidates were Fernando Collor de Mello, the candidate favored by the wealthy and by business interests of the right, and Luis Inácio da Silva (Lula), a labor leader (and president, as of January 2003) favored by unionists and the left. Soon after the election of Fernando Collor, the *Folha de São Paulo,* one of Brazil's most prestigious and widely read newspapers, published a response by a very well-known journalist and essayist to a complaint of racism he had received from a reader. The reader objected to comments made in an earlier article, in which the journalist had described the new president as "tall, handsome, white — white in the western mold" ("Ele é alto, bonito, branco, branco ocidental"). The journalist defended himself by claiming that in attaching a value to Collor's whiteness, he has done nothing to distinguish himself from the vast majority of Brazilians. In fact, when, as part of an opinion poll, respondents were asked to describe the ideal president, 89 percent said that he should be white. The journalist stated that people of color were as "palatable" to him as any other but to consider Brazil a Third World country and to seek to forge links with Africa (as the other candidate, Luis Inácio da Silva, had proposed) would require that "we [Brazilians] turn ourselves away from our cultural heritage which is the West . . . [and] the United States" (Nós nos afastamos da nossa herança cultural que é o Ocidente, os EUA). In highlighting Brazil's status as a Western nation, the journalist makes a distinction between *heritage* as that which is forged and guaranteed by law and custom, and the *residue* (in this case the link to Africa), as that which is disavowed to make the forged identity seem natural. The context of the election clarifies another significant aspect of the phrase: "Não deixa a sua cor passar em branco" (Don't let your color pass [fade] into white). The vote in the national elections was compulsory for all eligible citizens. The only way to opt out of the election was to "votar em branco," which means, colloquially, to cast a blank vote or, more literally, to vote white.

The second phrase, "Responda com bom s/Censo" (Answer with good sense), plays on the homology in Portuguese between sense and census. A broad coalition of respected organizations[1] underwrote this campaign in response to the 1980 census, in which 5.8 percent of the population declared itself black, 38.6 percent brown (mixed race), and 55 percent white. According to the pamphlet that accompanied the poster, the goals of the campaign were to convey a positive message to people of African descent regarding color and ethnicity, to raise their cultural and political profile, and to gather data relative to the socioeconomic status of people of African descent in an effort to combat the effects of the "ideologia de embranquecimento" (ideology of whitening).[2] Thomas Skidmore, in his influential *Black into White: Race and Nationality in Brazilian Thought,* calls this ideology, based on the theory that through miscegenation the nation would eventually become white, a uniquely Brazilian one. He maintains that it was embraced, with few exceptions, by the elite, following the abolition of slavery in 1888 and the declaration of the republic in 1889.[3] A brief review of Brazilian history will help to contextualize this ideology.

In 1500, Pedro Alvares Cabral sailed from Lisbon destined for India with a fleet of thirteen ships and a crew of 1,300. He landed near present-day Porto Seguro, Bahia, on the northeastern coast of the territory that would become Brazil. Claimed by the Portuguese Crown, this land was then occupied by a culturally and linguistically diverse and decentralized indigenous population estimated at six million people. The first Portuguese settlers arrived in 1531, displacing the indigenous people. Three years later, King João III of Portugal, in response to British, Dutch, French, and Spanish threats to Portuguese control of the coast, divided the area into hereditary captaincies distributed among his supporters to facilitate administration, and in 1549, the city of Salvador, Bahia, became the seat of the colonial government. Sugarcane plantations were established and slave labor was extracted from the indigenous peoples who had lived in the area. Their resistance to forced labor and their loss of life due to harsh conditions turned internal slave trafficking into a lucrative business, managed by Portuguese planters and carried out by *bandeirantes,* or scouts, usually the sons of indigenous mothers and Portuguese fathers. The *bandeirantes* raided ever further into the interior of the territory in search of people to enslave and, in the process, secured areas far from the coast for the Portuguese Crown. The internal slave trade was supplemented, and by the seventeenth century, largely but not completely replaced, by the transatlantic slave trade. Enslaved Africans, indigenous peoples, and occasionally European women and laborers, rebelled against the violence and oppression of the plantation system by running away and founding communities called *quilombos* that resisted military challenges mounted by forces in the interest of the Crown.

During the course of the slave trade (the first shipment is generally dated in 1538), Brazil received 40 percent of the total number of Africans brought by force to the Americas (as compared with North America's 7 percent).[4] In the last decades of the seventeenth century, the rate of importation of slaves increased as gold was discovered in Minas Gerais, a region west of Rio de Janeiro, drawing speculators and vast numbers of enslaved Africans who were forced to work under brutal conditions in the mines. This economic shift south from the northeast was accompanied by a similar political shift as Rio de Janeiro became the seat of power not only of Brazil (the colonial government had moved there in 1763) but also of the entire Portuguese empire. In 1807, to escape the invasion of Napoleon's army, the Portuguese Prince Regent left Lisbon for Brazil and established Rio de Janeiro as the capital, making Brazil the only American colony ever to serve as the center of a European monarchy. In 1822, the prince's son, who had remained in Brazil to rule the colony when his father returned to Portugal, declared independence and named himself Dom Pedro I, the first emperor of Brazil.

During the nineteenth century, after independence, coffee replaced sugar as Brazil's most significant export. Coffee producers demanded large numbers of enslaved workers. The coffee plantations were located primarily in São Paulo, and economic and political power again shifted, this time to the aristocracy of this region. In 1850, the Queiróz Law abolished the transatlantic slave trade, which unofficially continued along with a legal internal trade. In 1871, the unevenly enforced Lei do Ventre Livre (Law of the Free Womb) freed all children born to enslaved women, and the Saraiva-Cotegipe Law of 1885 freed all slaves who reached the age of sixty. In 1888, Brazil became the last nation in the western hemisphere to end slavery when the Regent Princess Isabel signed the Lei Áurea (Golden Law), instigating a reaction by slave owners, particularly among the coffee aristocracy, a reaction that resulted in the end of the monarchy and the establishment of the republic in 1889.

The majority presence of Africans and their descendants, who were visibly engaged in a wide range of occupations in both the public and private spheres preceding the Abolition, significantly affected social relations. As Mary Karasch has pointed out, many enslaved people worked not only in rural settings but also in urban settings as managers, salespeople, skilled laborers, craftspeople, and prostitutes.[5] In some cases, these forms of employment allowed for accumulation of capital and social and economic mobility for enslaved and free women and for racially mixed men.

By the mid-nineteenth century, according to Emilia Viotti da Costa, the population of Brazil consisted of 1,350,000 whites and 4,000,000 Blacks and mulattoes. That whites made up less than 30 percent of the population caused much concern for those among the elite anticipating the end of slavery. Reflecting this concern, Frederico Leopoldo Cezar Burlamaque, an abolitionist and doctor of mathematics and natural sciences, proposed the return of Africans and people of African descent in his 1837 study titled *Memoria analytica á cerca do commercio d'escravos e á cerca dos males da escravidão doméstica* (An Analytic Report regarding the Slave Trade and regarding the Evils of Domestic Slavery). Worried about "a segurança da raça branca" (the security of the white race), which was constantly threatened by a populous race of "inimigos domésticos" (domestic or internal enemies), as well as the simultaneous desirability and impossibility of constructing "uma Nação homogênea," (a homogeneous nation), Burlamaque wonders:

> Would it be proper that such a large population of freed slaves, of a race absolutely different from the one that dominated it, remain in the country? Won't there be great dangers to fear for the future if former abuses are remembered [and] if the freed slaves prefer the people of their own race, as is natural? Could a nation prosper, or even exist, if it is composed of foreign races that in no way could have any connection to each other?[6]

While European and American observers of Brazil considered miscegenation an insurmountable evil, Brazilian scientists, social scientists and government officials eventually proposed that miscegenation presented the best possibility for establishing a homogeneous national identity. This thinking would provide the roots for later elaborations of the ideology of *embranquecimento* (whitening) and of racial democracy. The process of miscegenation eventually would provide Brazil, in the words of Silvio Romero, an important nineteenth-century literary scholar, with an "espirito, um caráter original" (a spirit, an original character) that it did not yet have but that "virá com o tempo" (will come with time).

> My idea, then, is that the victory in the battle for our life will belong in the future to the white [race], but the white [race], conscious of the roughness of this climate, must take advantage of all that is useful that the other two races can offer,

especially the black [race], with which it has crossed most in order to secure this very victory. After having taken the help that it needed, the white race through natural selection will continuously increase until it shows itself as pure and beautiful as in the old world. This will happen when the [white race] is completely acclimatized to this continent. Two factors will contribute heavily to this result: on the one hand, the end of the slave trade and the constant disappearance of the Indians, and on the other hand, European immigration.[7]

Notable in this passage is that miscegenation with Blacks is treated as an inoculation that will help whites adapt to and overcome the tropical environment of the Americas, countering in this way widely held pessimistic views of miscegenation. Further encouragement for the whitening thesis was provided by calculations that speculated that the white race would incorporate the Black and Indian within four or five generations.[8] This incorporation would ensure a return to the (white) racial type as imagined by Romero — "as pure and beautiful as in the old world" — on which the Brazilian nation would be based. The attempt to produce the ideal Brazilian, embodied through the ideology of whitening, would take place as a repetition with a difference — a repetition of what would constitute the ideal (white) Brazilian and the elimination of threatening elements, defined as black. Because blackness was seen as a barrier to Brazil's achievement of modernity, blacks necessarily would be "the remnant bound to be left behind in [Brazil's] march toward progress" — in other words, a remainder.[9]

In the preceding paragraph, I have placed white in brackets to emphasize that I am analyzing how race is defined, idealized, represented. The quotations above suggest that in public racial discourse, whiteness is a desire, deferred to the future, clearly constructed; it is named and identified with its promise. Many historians and social scientists, based both here in the United States and in Brazil, have discussed extensively the ideology of whitening. Their studies implicitly, if not directly, compare the history of racialization in these two countries, as do the primary texts they analyze.[10] My intention is to investigate the *representation* of race in Brazil — both in the effort to analyze how this representation functions and changes as it circulates nationally and internationally, and to account for why it recurs so persistently. As we will see, despite very different national spheres and historical moments, the logic by which the remainder is produced in every attempt to project racial integration seems inescapable.

To help me make this point, I return to my discussion of the census. In

1911, João Baptista de Lacerda, the Director of the National Museum, who officially represented Brazil at the First Universal Races Conference, calculated that by 2012 Blacks would no longer exist in Brazil and that mulattoes would make up only 3 percent of the population.[11] On the one hand, Lacerda's assertion seems preposterous. Throughout the twentieth century, spaces for promoting and sustaining black people as black people have, in fact, existed; during the first decades of that century in São Paulo alone there were over a dozen regularly published black newspapers, and active cultural, social, and political organizations and movements such as the Movimento do Negro Unificado, Black Rio, movements for reparations and affirmative action, Teatro Experimental do Negro, Quilomboje (a writers' collective), escolas de samba, blocos afro, and so on, have helped to organize communities. *On the other hand, on the level of representation where race and democracy are linked and addressed by the census campaign, Lacerda's predictions have been fulfilled.*

When the census data were released in 1996, only 5 percent of Brazilians self-identified as black; those identifying as pardo (brown) rose from 38.8 percent to 42 percent, and those identifying as white were 52 percent (down 1 percent from the 1980 census, which itself demonstrated a decline relative to earlier censuses). Melissa Nobles, a political scientist who has examined this data, has proposed that self-identifying as any category other than black makes of the census form a way of escaping the stigmatization that one couldn't escape in one's daily life.[12] I would extend her point to argue that the census and the failure of the campaign to realize its goals can be seen as a symptom of the history of the official disappearance of Blacks and a fulfillment of Lacerda's prediction relative to blackness on a discursive and representational level. This history shows that people of African descent, as a condition of their belonging, must consent to have a voluntary and participatory role in the discursively produced Brazilian national identity—in other words, and on the level of representation, they must leave their blackness behind as a remainder. A familiar illustration of this would be the example of the nineteenth-century author Machado de Assis. As his fame and prestige grew, making him one of Brazil's foremost writers, portrait painters began minimizing his "mulatto" appearance.[13]

The census campaign suggests that both political representation and discursive representation within an ideal of racial democracy require a choice that would remainder blackness as a viable marker of a social and political position. The response to the 1990 census demonstrates that subscription to (racial) democracy requires for participation a choice that will remainder blackness, even as it produces blackness as a remainder that persists and, in persisting, resists. The constitution of Brazil as a racial democracy—a unity based on a concept of mixture—requires that "a set of institutions can be so well—and so thinly—conceived and so well-ordered that it fits, without excess, the selves that it presupposes and the subjects it engenders. [This] assumes that . . . well-ordered institutions will produce well-ordered subjects who are comfortable in (and also not resistant to) their subscription to practices of self-containment and self-concealment."[14] In relation to the constitution of democracy, then, the remainder is both necessary when it is perceived as the result of an exclusion and threatening when it is perceived as the result of a resistance.

My focus on the process of remaindering and on the figure of the remainder might seem a subtle shift of emphasis but it is in fact decisive and articulates a different perspective on the intractable problem of inclusion in democratic multiracial societies. Exclusion is almost always understood as what is left out of a given polity and seen as incompatible with democratic formations. Yet, as Carl Schmitt has proposed, democracy requires exclusions:

> Every actual democracy rests on the principle that not only are equals equal but unequals will not be treated equally. Democracy requires, therefore, first homogeneity and second—if the need arises—elimination or eradication of heterogeneity. . . . A democracy demonstrates its political power by knowing how to refuse or keep at bay something foreign and unequal that threatens its homogeneity. The question of equality is precisely not one of abstract logical-arithmetical games. It is about the substance of equality. . . . Since the nineteenth century it has existed above all in membership in a particular nation, in national homogeneity. Equality is only interesting and valuable politically so long as it has substance, and for that reason at least the possibility and the risk of inequality. . . . Finally, one has to say that a democracy—because inequality always belongs to equality—can exclude one part of those governed without ceasing to be a democracy, that until now people who in some way were completely or partially without rights and who were restricted from the exercise of political power, let them be called barbarians, uncivilized, atheists, aristocrats, counterrevolutionaries, or even slaves, have belonged to democracy.[15]

Schmitt observes that heterogeneity must be eradicated only if the need arises. Because foreigners as unequals can be tolerated or "belong" to the demos, they are interpellated[16] and, therefore, recognized as "barbarians" or outsiders. Notably absent from Schmitt's catalogue of foreigners are racial minorities; none among those listed need be associated with a particular racial group.

As I will argue more fully in chapter 3, the discourse of foreignness is not commensurate with the discourse on race, which is better understood in terms of the remainder than the foreigner. In her analysis of *The Crisis of Parliamentary Democracy,* Chantal Mouffe asserts that, for Schmitt, the opportunity to draw a dividing line between "us" and "them" is more important than the nature of the similarity that this line ensures.[17] She points out that in Schmitt's theory of democratic arrangements, the similarity that fuses the identity of a people could be produced by "reducing it to one of its many forms of identification" (40). This identification creates the line that "claims some for democratic citizenship while remaindering others."[18] I will argue that the conflation of the remainder with the foreigner, on the one hand, and the disavowal of the remainder, on the other, hide the underlying operations that require identification with a similar ideal of racial democracy as a condition for belonging. Racial democracy offers the promise of inclusion, cordiality,[19] and a lack of resentment through identification with the concept of *embranquecimento.* In other words, the identification would revolve around the desire for whiteness, and those who refuse this identification are remaindered. Even when the emphasis on whiteness is no longer foregrounded, as in the discourse on racial democracy, its roots in this way of thinking are apparent when one attends to the remainder.

Self-representation in the public sphere impacts on and overlaps with the "lived lives" of people of African descent in Brazil in important ways. There is, however, a gap that occurs when the "lived lives" of black people exceed the state's willingness or even capacity to represent them as Brazilian. This gap speaks to the tension between the discourses of race and democracy. It bears emphasizing that democracy has two aspects—as a form of rule, founded on the self-determination of the people, on the one side, and on the other side, a symbolic framework within which this democratic rule is realized. For example, there can be an actual democracy in which black people vote that exists alongside and in contradiction to the sphere of representation in a racial democracy.

In *Cannibal Democracy,* I explore this contradiction in relation to both the concept of racial democracy, which depends on an ideal of inclusion, and to the metaphor of cannibalism that informs and structures it. The texts I examine throughout my study, drawn primarily from the Harlem Renaissance and from Brazilian modernism, but also from contemporary literature from other areas of the Americas, self-consciously enact cannibalism on many different levels—both thematically and structurally, and, in addition, find in its logic the inspiration for theoretical explorations of issues of identity (individual, social, and political), democracy, race, aesthetics, and language. The overarching questions—who is eating whom? what is remaindered from that process and why?—inform this study.

Cannibalism is a useful model for democracy.[20] The metaphor of cannibalism appears repeatedly in conceptualizations of democracy, particularly where these engage with issues of race. The metaphor is especially conspicuous in discussions of "racial democracy." A description of a cordial Brazilian society based on a harmonious blending of race and culture, the notion of racial democracy is often associated with Gilberto Freyre, author of the very influential *Casa Grande e Senzala (The Masters and the Slaves)*. The ideas that would inform racial democracy, as a concept, if not a term, are not peculiar to the work of Freyre and had already interested many writers throughout the Americas—including but not limited to the Brazilian modernists and Harlem Renaissance writers—as well as political theorists, commentators, and journalists of the black press of Brazil and the United States, many of whom were in conversation with one another. For these writers, democracy as political form and as a culture is capable of accommodating everyone in its conceptual and territorial space, without remainders.[21] "Racial democracy," furthermore, presents itself as the ideal of democracy; yet, racial democracy seems at once a redundancy and a contradiction in terms. It would appear that in the relationship, the democracy in "racial democracy" somehow undoes the salience and importance of race; however, the very idea of race as modifying the democracy implies that without it democracy would not be as visible.

These two concepts—cannibalism as a cultural metaphor and racial democracy as a cultural ideal—may have been most explicitly articulated in Brazil during the first decades of the twentieth century, but they also underpin U.S. discourses on race and democracy in the same period. In this book, I examine the circulation of these concepts and their consequences. One of my points is that the figure of the remainder, which derives from the metaphor of cannibalism, is ubiquitous and persistent, indicating that the contradiction between the discourses of race and democracy has not been resolved. For precisely this reason, the metaphor of the remainder endures and exceeds any specific historical moment.

I was first drawn to the metaphor of cannibalism because of its centrality in considerations of Brazilian culture. The modernists' project as outlined by Oswald de Andrade in the "Manifesto Antropófago" ("Anthropophagist Manifesto") involved swallowing and absorbing what is useful in a culture. The cannibalism attributed to the indigenous population of Brazil served as a model for a redefined cultural relationship between Brazil and the outside world (defined largely as Europe)—a relationship in which foreign influences would not be copied but rather digested and absorbed as a precondition for the creation of a new, more independent national civilization. This aspect of Brazilian modernism has been interpreted as producing exemplary postcolonial works. The creation of a national Brazilian identity, however, takes place on two fronts. In relation to Europe, it provided for a radical questioning and reformulation of the hierarchies engendered by colonialism. In relation to the black, mulatto, and indigenous populations inside Brazil, the model of cannibalism provided the means to create (if only in theory and deferred to the future) a homogeneous and stable national identity.

In 1928, Oswald de Andrade published the "Anthropophagist Manifesto."[22] The manifesto gave theoretical expression to the various artistic practices that preceded and followed its publication. Oswald's manifesto appeared six years after the Semana de Arte Moderna (Week of Modern Art, February 1922), which officially launched the modernist movement. Like Oswald, most of the participants of the Week of Modern Art were members of the São Paulo's elite, the sons and daughters of the wealthy planters and industrialists. They had studied and traveled abroad, mainly to France, but also to Germany and the United States, and they both mined and disavowed the European avant-garde movements—primitivism, Dadaism, surrealism—that provided them with the tools to forge the specificity of Brazil. Looking to the supposed cannibalism of the Tupinamba people of Brazil, Oswald asks (in English) "Tupy or not Tupy?" and decides that cannibalism would be the appropriate model for defining a properly Brazilian relationship to the world.

Oswald de Andrade shares the credit for establishing the modernist movement in Brazil with Mário de Andrade (no relation). Mário is unique among the modernists, in that he was from a racially mixed family with more pretensions to a middle class status than money or property. Mário worked as a music teacher, poet, novelist, theorist, journalist, ethnomusi-cologist, folklorist, and photographer. The relationship between Mário and Oswald de Andrade was a productive, yet contentious one. In 1928, Mário published an undisputed masterpiece of Brazilian literature, *Macunaíma: O herói sem nenhum caráter* (*Macunaíma: The Hero without Any Charac-ter*). The novel traces the adventures of Macunaíma, a trickster figure from Taulipang folklore, as he moves from the forest to the city and back to the forest battling a giant cannibal for possession of an amulet symbolic of Bra-zil's national identity. Mário says:

> I decided to write [*Macunaíma*] because I was overcome by a lyrical commotion when, reading Koch-Grünberg [the ethnographer who collected the original tales], I perceived that Macunaíma was a hero without any character, be it moral or psy-chological; I thought this extremely moving—I don't know why—maybe because it was such an unusual fact, or maybe because it is very much in line with our times.[23]

While the novel revolves around acts of cannibalism, Mário was dismayed at its coincidence with Oswald's manifesto. He lamented, using the language of cannibalism, the fact that it is his bad luck that "saem sempre no momento em que fico *malgré moi* incorporado neles" (they [Oswald's manifestoes] always come out at just the precise moment [so that] despite myself I become incorporated into them) (30).

Of course, Oswald de Andrade's recourse to the model of cannibalism was a provocation against a staid establishment, calculated to offend bour-geois standards of good taste and conformity. His gesture was, necessarily, an ambivalent one, not only, as Mário intimates, because provocations of the bourgeoisie often are, especially when made by one of its members, but also because cannibalism is, in itself, a practice marked by ambivalence. This ambivalence is related to the fact that cannibalism possesses only through loss. The taking in of an other in order to preserve it paradoxically neces-sitates that it be permanently lost as an other. While incorporation may be conceived of as a strategy against loss (as in melancholia) or to pay hom-age to the desired qualities in an adversary, it requires violence to a loved or desired and feared object, leading to its destruction.[24] I do not want to review debates on the historical existence of the actual practice of canni-balism, because I am interested, like the writers I discuss, in its symbolic occurrences; yet, I do want to point out that in accounts of both symbolic and real cannibalism, the process is only visible through its remainders: the (unconsumed) bones and other remains.[25]

An examination of the first decades of the twentieth century reveals a remarkable constellation of usage of the metaphor of cannibalism in various spheres. Freud developed a psychoanalytic theory based on a model of cannibalism that would describe his findings on object relations, identification, and the establishment of the superego. In *Totem and Taboo* (1913), a work that would overtly influence Oswald's manifesto, Freud states: "By incorporating parts of a person's body through the act of eating, one at the same time acquires the qualities possessed by him."[26] Freud took the prevailing anthropological understanding of the logic of cannibalism — that it was motivated by the desire to incorporate the other's qualities — to describe the actions of the primal horde: "One day the brothers came together, killed and devoured their father and so made an end to the patriarchal horde. . . . In the act of devouring him, they accomplished their identification with him, and each one acquired a portion of his strength" (142). In *Three Essays on the Theory of Sexuality,* Freud employed the metaphor of cannibalism to qualify object-relations and to identify a stage in psychosexual development: "The first of these [stages] is the oral or, as it might be called, cannibalistic."[27]

For Oswald de Andrade, an act of cannibalism marked the first contact between the indigenous peoples and the Portuguese in the territory that would become Brazil, providing for Brazil's inaugural moment. In his manifesto and in the various and varying practices of the Brazilian modernists, cannibalism accounts for Brazil's relationship to Europe, its relation to its large population of African and indigenous descent, and its sense of formlessness deriving from its lack of a coherent national identity. The artists that I address, however, like the anthropologists and psychoanalytic theorists, do not consciously pursue the excremental logic of their model: that it must, necessarily, produce remainders.[28]

From the position of the eater, the construction of an identity through a process of assimilation presupposes a remainder, a residue. While this remainder can be deferred into the future as unresolvable, or repressed as a past to emerge as a threat to the desired stability and integrity of the repeatable present, the indigestible residue prevents a sense of completion and haunts the discourse on/of national unity, undermining the ideology of racial democracy, even as it makes it visible. Although the language of this passage may recall Raymond Williams's use of the term "residual" in *Marxism and Literature,* my use of the term is different. For Williams, there are residual bits of history that survive in the present.[29] I am not using the term *residue* to suggest survivals of any kind that would exist prior to or independently of a moment or a system. I suggest that the model of cannibalism clarifies the extent to which the remainder is the effect of a process. In relation to the eaten, this remainder can be seen either as a rejection of the eaten by the national body or as the resistance posed by the eaten to assimilation. Thus, the power of the remainder is that it is neither (or not only) a constitutive absence nor an "other," in that it is produced by the system rather than preceding it.[30] The ethics of the relationship of the remainder to the body that produces it is a point I will return to presently.

The Brazilian modernist period and the figures associated with it—Oswald de Andrade, Mário de Andrade, Anita Malfatti, Paulo Prado and Tarsila do Amaral—have provided a point of reference for scholars and artists in the decades that follow. There is a consensus, which has attained the status of common sense, about the impact of the modernist movement, specifically where it coincided with anthropophagism. From this point of view, the movement, in a radical departure from elitist views of art and culture, staged and promoted cultural, if not racial, mixture, a democratic mixture in which all could be accommodated, even represented, with no one left over. This mixture is the cultural expression of racial democracy. In this study, by attending to what does indeed get left over, the remainder—that which resists incorporation or is expelled—I will argue that the cannibalistic model betrays far more anxiety and conflict than its reception would indicate, with far-reaching implications for ideas of race and democracy.

Although there are significant differences between the work of the modernists and Gilberto Freyre—the modernists are associated with the southern, urban, industrial, internationalist, modern future of Brazil, and Freyre is associated with the northern, rural, slavery-based, regionalist, nostalgic, patriarchal past of Brazil—my interest in bringing together their writings, in what could seem a startling meeting, is motivated by their relentless reliance on metaphors of incorporation in their work.

Long before Gilberto Freyre described Brazil in the way that subsequently was associated with racial democracy, nineteenth- and early twentieth-century journalists and scholars in the United States promoted the view of Brazil that has become identified with him. References to Brazil were pervasive and, because of inevitable discussions of miscegenation, complex in their effects on and implications for programs for responding to racism. Articles on Brazil appeared in the *Amsterdam News,* the *Baltimore Afro-American,* the *Chicago Defender, The Crisis,* the *Crusader,* the *Tulsa Star,* the *Atlanta Independent,* and other publications by writers like Alexander Crummell, Charles Chesnutt, W. E. B. Du Bois, Alain Locke, Booker T. Washington, Carter Woodson, Roy Nash, and Kelly Miller. While I will discuss many of these writers and their works in more detail in the third and fourth chapters of this study, I want to anticipate here some of that discussion in order to convey a sense of the persistence with which Brazil, and more specifically the idea of Brazil, was and continues to be an enduring reference point for African Americans evaluating the nature of black citizenship in a democratic society.

Cannibal Democracy examines the discourse of race and democracy in the United States and Brazil, and each in relation to the other. Howard Winant has argued that, "the comparison of U.S. *herrenvolk* democracy and Brazilian "racial democracy" is justified . . . because in both countries the claim that the system was democratic served to deny racially defined groups their democratic rights." In making this point, Winant cautions against collapsing the histories of racialization in the two nations.[31] I am not interested in collapsing these histories but rather in highlighting their moments of convergence and divergence as they inform discourses of democracy. I am interested in exploring how, along with the metaphor of cannibalism that is always imbedded in it, the concept of racial democracy migrates back and forth between the United States and Brazil. Accordingly, *Cannibal Democracy* is a comparative work that pursues the movement of the concept of racial democracy and the metaphors of cannibalism and the remainder through the cultural discourses on race in these two countries that established each as a counter-model for the other. While chronologically some of the texts I address in the second section of *Cannibal Democracy* precede the Brazilian texts in the beginning two chapters, my motivation for discussing the Brazilian material first is twofold: it helps clarify the terms of the discussion and decenters the United States, making evident the extent of these discussions of black citizenship in the early decades of the twentieth century. These discussions occurred in the black press, at meetings, and within works of literature that have generally been read solely in terms of a national tradition, thereby overlooking critical aspects of these texts. *Cannibal Democracy* explores the tangled network of allusions to the figure of the remainder, which is signaled in African American writing from the United States with surprising frequency through references to Brazil (or a generalized South America) and/or the metaphor of cannibalism.

In the United States, the ideas underpinning the concept of racial democracy entered via debates about citizenship and black representation after the end of the Civil War and the failures of Reconstruction. Faced with "the race problem," black leaders struggled with the barriers to full citizenship — barriers that included the color line and racist violence — and solutions to overcoming them. Alexander Crummell asked in his 1888 speech, "The Race Problem in America": "What, then, are the possibilities of the future? Do the indications point to amalgamation or to absorption as the outcome of race-life in America?"[32] As I will demonstrate, a number of black intellectuals would turn to the example of racial mixture in Brazil to answer to this question, in the hope of mitigating or eliminating racial difference, or at least the appearance of racial difference, as a source of conflict or as a justification for the color line.

Crummell, however, both anticipates and rejects this position: "The race-problem, it will be seen, cannot be settled by extinction of race. No amalgamating process can eliminate it. It is not a carnal question — a question of breeds, or blood, or lineage. . . . It is a question entirely of ideas" (48–49). Furthermore, in these quotations and in the article as a whole, Crummell distinguishes between amalgamation and absorption, showing that these two terms express more than two words for the same idea. He notes that, "Amalgamation in its exact sense means the approach of affinities. The word applied to human beings implies will, and the consent of two parties. In *this* sense there has been no amalgamation of the two races. . . . Intermixture of the two races there has been — not by amalgamation that implies consent, but through the victimizing of black women" (45). In the following decades other thinkers, like Kelly Miller, dean of Howard University, would take this question of consent into a calculus of the possibility of racial mixture.

In November 1927 Miller wrote a follow-up to an article in which he had reviewed the debate between Alain Locke and Lothrop Stoddard on the subject: "Can America Absorb the Negro?" In the article, Miller claims that, contrary to most discussions of "amalgamation," the limit to racial mixture between Blacks and Whites already had been reached. Miller dates the coming of this brown race post slavery, calling attention to the euphemistic use of intermarriage to describe miscegenation. He decouples the two concepts, arguing that if amalgamation implies consent, legal reproduction through marriage and browning would happen only among black people, not between Blacks and whites. As a result of this process, "The white and the brown are to be the residual elements in our American population. The other non-white groups, such as indians [sic], Mexicans and Mongolians will dwindle away or be absorbed into the two major races" — eventually yielding, on the one hand, "a composite man who would pass for white," and, on the other hand, causing the variegated Blacks to blend into one uniform brown color.[33] In the course of his discussion of amalgamation, Miller recalls for his readers Theodore Roosevelt's 1913 report of his trip to Brazil in *Outlook* magazine, in which he reports (without endorsing) a Brazilian's arguments for the relative merits of racial mixture as a superior solution to the "race problem." For Miller, the speculative nature of this solution makes it as impractical as a return to Africa, advocated most publicly by Marcus Garvey.

Roosevelt's article, and especially the phrase — "This difference between the U.S. and Brazil is the tendency of Brazil to absorb the Negro" — was widely quoted in the black and white press of the United States after its initial publication in *Outlook* magazine in 1913. Roosevelt repeated for his readers what had been outlined to him as the Brazilian solution to "the race problem." If, his Brazilian interlocutor explained to him, the United States and Brazil had both inherited a large Negro population as a legacy of the abolition of slavery, Brazil's solution based on the absorption of the Negro was superior to and less dangerous than the segregationist course that the United States was undertaking.[34] This absorption or assimilation does not involve racial or cultural mixing, but rather the consumption of another. According to Roosevelt, "My observation leads me to believe that in 'absorb' I have used exactly the right expression to describe this process. It is the Negro who is being absorbed and not the Negro who is absorbing the white man" (409). Miscegenation, then, as described by Roosevelt is, in fact, a hierarchical process of whitening in which Negroes, as such, disappear into the mixture. The recurring trope for this process of absorption is cannibalism, a metaphor that accounts for the process of ingesting, the assimilation of what is ingested, and the reassertion of the identity of the ingester.

Roosevelt's insistence on the word absorption rather than amalgamation clarifies the politics of this strategy of incorporation. In what follows, I will tease out the issue of consent that underpins both democracy and whitening. Consent characterizes amalgamation and distinguishes it from absorption. The distinction between amalgamation and absorption, however, is strategically broken down in the discourse of racial democracy, making racial democracy less a contradiction in terms than a mutually reinforcing one, since democracy also derives its legitimacy from consent.[35] Racial democracy is able to maintain what seems to be a contradictory racial politics of absorption (whitening) by making this process democratic by requiring consent. In order to defend this assertion, I will turn to two examples that show how absorption and democracy in America are linked to prepare a foundation for a discussion of the stakes of this argument.

In 1919, Harvard anthropologist Philip Ainsworth Means made the link between absorption and democracy. After traveling extensively throughout South and Central America, Means received his B.A. (1915) and his M.A. (1916) from Harvard. He became a member of the Yale Peruvian Expedition of 1914–15 and in 1917 returned to Peru as a representative for the Smithsonian Museum of the American Indian. Means was the director of the National Museum of Archeology in Lima from 1920 to 1921, before becoming an associate anthropologist at Harvard's Peabody Museum.

Means introduces *Racial Factors in Democracy,* which he wrote in response to the First World War, by questioning the relationships among European nations and the United States and their colonies. He asks whether, in the wake of the war, the portion of the world that has set itself up as modern and the epitome of progress does not provide rather to "the Chinese and the Indians, and the other peoples to whom we are wont to consider ourselves superior, every right to smile ironically? . . . The Chinese and the Indians may well ask if the European War is to be regarded as another proof of that civilization that we are anxious they should adopt. How many of us can be certain that the horrified world will not answer by rejecting as false that progress of which Europe was so proud?"[36] Despite the interrogation, Means does not seriously question the superiority of "that portion of the world," but he does fear for the stability of its position in the future, especially if war (and communism) was to be avoided. Means suggests, as a resolution to this concern, the institution of democracy internationally, among nations as among people.

In an articulation that resonates with racial democracy, this democracy would be constituted through a process of what Means calls "race appreciation":

> Most of us have lost sight of the fact that civilization, above all our own, is always a mosaic of elements assembled from widely separated sources to form a coherent whole. As this has been true in the past, so it is destined to become more profoundly necessary in the future. Scarcely any aspect of our European culture exists which would not be improved by a judicious admixture of ingredients derived from other cultures and other races. Future civilization, to be permanent, beneficial, and logical will make itself as between country and country and as between continent and continent, and it will at the same time, become richer and more various in its composition, for elements now peculiar to one region and to one race will, if found worthy, become general throughout the world, being spread everywhere by the machines for traveling and for the dissemination of knowledge which are our special contribution. (166–67)

Means declares his indebtedness to the Mexican anthropologist Manuel Gamio for the concept of "race appreciation." Gamio was a proponent of *Indigenismo*, an official policy of recovering the Indian of the past, often with, despite pretensions, little regard for the Indian of the present. From 1909 to 1910, Gamio (like Freyre in the 1920s) studied with Franz Boas, who supervised his Ph.D. In recognition of excavation work done under Boas's direction, Gamio succeeded Boas as the director of the Department of Archeology of the International School of Archeology and Ethnology in Mexico City, and, in 1915, he became the Director General of the entire institution. In one of his most influential works, *Forjando Patria* (Forging the Fatherland), Gamio claimed that Mexico did not measure up to the modern nations of the world because it did not have a common language, a defined character, a homogeneous race, and a single shared history. He argued that the formation of "a powerful *patria* and a coherent, defined nationality" would come about through "racial approximation, cultural fusion, linguistic unification, and economic equilibrium."[37] According to David A. Brading "There is little doubt that his *indigenismo* . . . was animated by a modernising nationalism, which promoted the incorporation and assimilation of Indian communities into the urban Hispanic population. The ultimate and paradoxical aim of official *indigenismo* in Mexico was thus to liberate the country from the dead weight of a native past, or, to put the case more clearly, finally to destroy the native culture which had emerged during the colonial period."[38]

For Gamio, cited by Means, race appreciation would entail the vacating of the heretofore "aggressive" energies of the indigenous peoples of Mexico, "by attracting their individual members toward the other group which they have always regarded as hostile, incorporating them, blending them in with it for the purpose of making the nation coherent and homogeneous and of causing the language to become unified and the culture to tend to one form" (155). The discourse of democracy is linked here, as elsewhere, to incorporation, blending or racial and cultural mixture, and to an idea of wholeness and singularity, the sine qua non of peace. In fact, democracy as a form of rule, and peace as the absence of conflict become inextricably linked in democratic discourse as a symbolic framework. Whether articulated as a national form or as a cosmopolitan form, democracy produces "a coherent whole" through a process of taking in. In this case, "our own" civilization (presumably of the United States, where Means lives and writes) and that of Europe incorporate what is good and beneficial in order to create a beautiful, ethical, and unconflicted whole.[39] In democratic race appreciation, as in more overt allusions to a cannibalistic model, the focus is on what is incorporated. What happens to what is remaindered?

The idea that representation in a democracy would imply leaving one's blackness behind was a concern raised by Du Bois in relation to Brazil and Central America. In a 1924 article published in the *New Republic,* W. E. B. Du Bois described for North American readers the outcome of the Third Pan-African Congress that had been held two months earlier in London. He reported that the Executive Committee had approved a "Charter of Rights," which identified eight "irreducible" points that "embody the legitimate and immediate needs of people of African descent." These general points, having to do with self-determination, applicable to all people of African descent throughout the world, were followed by a list that detailed a number of specific cases in Africa and the Americas deemed worthy of special attention. Among these demands was one of particular interest for my study: "We urge in Brazil and Central America that the people of African descent no longer be satisfied with a solution to the Negro problem which involves their absorption into another race, without allowing Negroes *as such* full recognition of their manhood and their right to be."[40] Du Bois does not say what prompted him and the other attendees at the conference to include the demand described above. Contributors to the black press in Brazil, however, also had articulated in the same year the concern that: "his [the Negro's] value is challenged at every step in the desire to make him disappear (extingui-lo)."[41]

I emphasized "as such" in the quotation from "The Charter of Rights" because this phrase recalls a question formulated by Du Bois in his earliest writings, a question that provides the foundation for his conception of double consciousness. He had wondered in the *Conservation of Races* whether it would be possible to be a Negro, meaning a Negro *as such,* and an American at the same time.[42] As I will show in detail in chapter 3, Du Bois uses a metaphor of cannibalism to suggest that the answer is no, because becoming American requires a choice that remainders blackness. Through Du Bois, it is possible to see how this persistent and seemingly North American question resonates in and in relation to a South American context.

I want to offer one more example before I summarize how the questions of consent, assimilation understood as an act of incorporation or cannibalism, and democracy are connected. This story is taken from an account of a community of Confederates, known as *Confederados* in Portuguese, who went to Brazil after the Civil War:

> To the absolute horror of the first-generation Confederados (many of whom had fought furiously at Manassas, Gettyburg, and Chickamunga for states' rights, including the right to own black slaves), some of their children began marrying Brazilians, some of whom obviously had Negro blood. They imposed a strong taboo on marriages with Brazilians, insisting that their children marry Americans, preferably from within the Confederado community. A dilemma of sorts was introduced in 1920, when a daughter of one of the most prominent Confederado families, true to the Confederado code, married an American, a black American, who had his own sugarcane plantation in the Santa Barbara area. The act of this young lady seemed to throw a short circuit into the complex cultural bias of the American colonists. There was no outcry — none. The man, after all, was an American, and the couple was welcomed warmly into the colony, now dominated by second and third-generation Confederados. The Americans, like their Brazilian neighbors, had learned how to change a person from black to white.[43]

This story clarifies that the presence of the husband met the requirement that he become white, fulfilling the terms of a "racial contract," which Charles Mills defines as a "set of formal or informal agreements or meta-agreements" that undergirds a racial state that benefits whites. "It will be obvious," according to Mills, "that the Racial Contract is not a contract to which a nonwhite subset of humans can be a genuinely consenting party (though, depending again on the circumstances, it may sometimes be politic to pretend that this is the case)."[44] I would like to expand Mills's formulation to include the possibility that representation within the (white) racial state means accepting the terms of the racial contract as a condition for entering into it.

From the perspective of the Confederado community, which simultaneously stands in for Brazil and the United States, theirs is still a white community, consolidated by the husband who has been transformed into a white man. The story highlights that the husband cannot be in the community unless he is white. The issue is not that the husband is black and in the community. The existence of the white racial state that this community exemplifies makes this a logical impossibility, as impossible as being Black, *as such,* and American at the same time. No longer black, he has become American. The Brazilian example, rather than solving the "race problem" or the color line by creating a space for mixture or amalgamation, reconstructs whiteness and reasserts white supremacy. The husband's presence, therefore, because, rather than in spite of, the color of his skin has the effect of making the community more rather than less white, leaving its sense of white privilege and the desirability of whiteness intact as blackness is remaindered. In a revealing footnote to their own study of Southern emigration to Brazil, Cyrus B. Dawsey and James M. Dawsey observe that in 1987, a Museum of Immigration was built in the town in which Harter's story takes place. The permanent exhibition, the only one inside the building, is titled, "Americans in Brazil," while a temporary exhibit on the "Negro" heritage was mounted outside of the building in an unprotected setting.[45]

The issue then isn't that "Brazil has not been and never will be a racial democracy," as Howard Winant has suggested,[46] but rather that it precisely has been a very effective one. This is a point made so powerfully by the preceding anecdote. Like the census, it shows that what is important is not so much the actual becoming white as manifesting at least the appearance of the desire as a condition for joining the racial contract and achieving representation. This observation may contribute to an understanding of what exactly in the ideology of whitening as it is expressed through racial democracy has had such an impact on organizing around issues of racial justice.[47] Howard Winant asks if black Brazilians have not been duped into participating in racial democracy, which he says is very unlikely, then why is there not a greater mobilization in favor of democracy? I would suggest that the category of democracy needs to be rethought if by democracy we think only in terms of inclusion. As I will show, the solution to exclusion may not be more inclusion or a different form of inclusion. The works I examine in *Cannibal Democracy* suggest a reconsideration of inclusion, especially since, as the logic of the remainder makes clear, black Americans were never really outside to begin with.

The trope for the process of inclusion is cannibalism. The weightiness of this metaphor, overdetermined by its associations with violence, the primitive, taboo, and the sacred, reveals the generalized ambivalence about the assimilation of formerly enslaved Africans. Brazil is often held up — in contrast to the segregationist United States — as a model for multiracial democracy founded on an ideal of racial mixture. It makes all the difference to the notion of mixture who is eating whom and that miscegenation has been seen historically as a (hierarchical) process of whitening. People of African descent are thus understood to disappear into the mixture, so that actually existing Blacks occupy the condition of remainders. Even into the present, Blacks are submitted to a kind of official disappearance in Brazilian democracy and are required on the level of representation, as exemplified by the census, to leave their blackness behind as a remainder. Attention to metaphors of incorporation can spur a reconsideration of the seemingly benign goals of integration and racial democracy and offer access to how liberal understandings of democratic harmony are based on the elimination of the reminders of the violence on which this unrealized harmony rests.

The metaphor of cannibalism and the remainder, which recurs in the discussions of race and democracy for which the question of assimilation was and continues to be central, was both crucial and upsetting in many ways for black writers, as well, preventing any lasting sense of having satisfactorily resolved the problem of democratic inclusion for themselves. As I will demonstrate, although the United States and Brazil participate in different discourses of racialization, following the path of the remainder shows the work that each does for the other in revealing the internal or national contradictions of democratic inclusion and in negotiating the troubling tensions and incongruities intrinsic to the very ideal of democracy.

The writers that I examine in this study give a sense of ambivalent attitudes toward inclusion based on incorporation. Some will advocate inclusion; but this inclusion can do no more than continuously reincorporate the remainders. There is another possibility — that of the resistant remainder, the remainder that resists reincorporation, and, therefore abjection, even as the incorporating body resists it as a reminder. This resisting remainder, modeled in my book through wide-ranging examples, including Charles Chesnutt's 1901 novel, *The Marrow of Tradition*, at the opening of the twentieth century and the artwork of María Magdalena Campos-Pons at its close, suggests a way out of the binaries — inclusion or exclusion, assimilation or separatism — that have so dominated the way we have thought about Americanness.

United by Anthropophagism

Antropofagia é o principio da nacionalização intellectual e moral da nossa tribu.

Anthropophagy is the foundation [and point of departure] of the intellectual and moral nationalization of our tribe.

— Oswald de Andrade, "De Anthropophagia"

La conception d'une culture fondée sur ce qu'on appellerait l'anthropophagie métaphorique nous paraît guidée par le projet d'une assimilation parfaite de la totalité à l'être, avec abolition de tout conflit.

The conception of a culture founded on what one might call a metaphoric anthropophagism seems to be guided by the goal of a complete assimilation of the totality [of the world] into the self, thereby doing away with all conflict.

— P. F. de Queiroz-Siqueira, "Un singulier manifeste"

ACCORDING TO CONVENTIONAL READINGS, the Semana de Arte Moderna (Week of Modern Art) inaugurated Brazil's modernist movement. It was an event that one of the organizers called "o primeiro sintoma espiritual da transmutação de nossa consciência" (the first intellectual symptom of the transformation of our consciousness).[1] From 11 to the 18 February 1922, the Municipal Theatre in São Paulo was the site of art exhibitions, dance and music performances, lectures and readings that were met with more derision than applause. Mário de Andrade's older brother recalls being taken aback at the reception to his brother's speech at the theater. The shocked audience, according to his description conservative followers of classicist models in art and music, booed Mário, as they did other participants, and pelted him with eggs and tomatoes.[2]

The year 1922, however, represented a culmination, rather than the beginning, of the discussions and debates that had been taking place among

Brazilians for many years. Wilson Martins states: "It was the modernists who created the Week of Modern Art and not the Week of Modern Art that created Modernism."[3] In fact, Mário de Andrade insisted that the Brazilian modernist movement, conscious of itself as such, had begun years earlier with the return of Anita Malfatti to São Paulo.[4]

In 1917, Anita Malfatti, a painter born in São Paulo in 1889 to an Italian father and a North American mother of German birth, showed her work in a solo exhibition titled, "Exposição de Pintura Moderna Anita Malfatti." This exhibit included the paintings she had completed in New York after a five-year tour of Europe and the United States, during which she had developed a style characterized by a jolting use of color (including the bright yellow and green of the Brazilian flag) and discontinuity of shape and perspective. These paintings, among them: *O japonês* (The Japanese Man), *O homem amarelo* (The Yellow Man), *A boba* (The Stupid Woman), *A estudante russa* (The Russian Student), *A mulher de cabelos verdes,* (The Woman with Green Hair), created a sensation in São Paulo and initiated a polemical debate.

In October 1917, Monteiro Lobato[5] sponsored a contest for artistic representations of Saci, an entity from Brazilian indigenous mythology who is both good and evil. In Brazilian popular iconography, Saci is represented as a black man with one leg who wears a red hood and smokes a pipe. A trickster figure, Saci is said to whistle mysteriously to frighten travelers and cattle in the night when, because of his color, it is nearly impossible to find him.[6] The contest based on this popular figure, which would later appear in *Macunaíma,* marked modernism's break with the subject matter of conservative, academic painting oriented toward Europe, in favor of the exploration of national themes. Malfatti's entry was shown along with those of other finalists and attracted the attention of various influential journalists who encouraged her to mount an exhibition of her own work. The exhibit opened on 12 December 1917. At first, the exhibit attracted much positive attention and several of the paintings were sold. On 20 December, however, Monteiro Lobato published a scathing critique of the exhibit and of Anita Malfatti, a critique that was amplified in an article titled "Paranoia ou mistificação" (Paranoia or Mystification?).[7] Lobato's diatribe prompted other articles critical of the artist and her work, and many of the paintings that had been sold were returned to the artist. In response, Oswald de Andrade published an article in January 1918 defending Anita Malfatti and thus began a friendship, which would expand by 1922 into the "grupo dos cinco" (the gang of five), composed of Mário de Andrade, Oswald de Andrade (who had met each other in 1917),[8] the widely known novelist and journalist Menotti del Picchia, Anita Malfatti, and Társila de Amaral, another artist who had recently returned from Paris and who would eventually marry Oswald. The energies of the group would be directed toward promoting "liberdade formal e ideias nacionalistas" (formal liberty and nationalist ideas).[9]

The date of the Semana de Arte Moderna coincided with national celebrations commemorating the centennial anniversary of the independence of Brazil from Portugal. Many of the organizers used the stage to continue the examination of Brazil's national character undertaken in their earlier works, including Menotti del Picchia's *Juca Mulato* (1917) and Monteiro Lobato's *Urupês* (1918). Graça Aranha, a member of the Academia Brasileira das Letras (Brazilian Academy of Letters) who had returned in October 1921 from Europe and immediately joined the modernists in their battle for the modernization of form and language, gave the opening speech of the Semana de Arte Moderna. This speech, titled "O espirito moderna" (The Modern Spirit), proposed the publication of a Brazilian dictionary of the Portuguese language, the rejection of academic literary forms, and support only for literature that drew on Brazilian folklore treated in the modern style.[10] Moreover, his speech included the themes he explored more systematically in an essay on Brazil's national character titled, "Metafísica Brasileira" (Brazilian Metaphysics).

For Graça Aranha, the defining Brazilian characteristic was an imagination that grew out of the magical beliefs and environment of the "primitive" Indians and Blacks in concert with the saudade (melancholic nostalgia) of the Portuguese settler. In this characterization, Graça Aranha repeated the conventions of the nineteenth century, most famously expressed in Olavo Bilac's poetic rendering of Brazil's "três raças tristes" (three sad races). According to Graça Aranha, Brazilians could not overcome the degenerative effects of their environment. Their future would not be secured through antitropicalism, or the absolute rejection of all things tropical. Triumph would only come through the conscious and active incorporation of the primitive forces that, according to white intellectuals and those who identified with them, had overwhelmed the nation.[11]

The issues of race and national identity that had preoccupied intellectuals and statesmen since the nineteenth century also preoccupied the modernists. Oswald de Andrade stated in an article published in May 1921:

> A questão racial entre nós é uma questão paulista. O resto do país, se continuar connosco, mover-se-á, como o *corpo* que obedece, empós do nosso caminho, da nossa vontade. . . . E a questão paulista é uma questão futurista. Nunca nenhuma aglomeração humana estêve tão fatalizada a futurismos de atividades, de indústria, de história e de arte como a aglomeraçao paulista. Que somos nós, forçadamente, iniludivelmente, se não futuristas . . .[12]

> Our [Brazil's] racial question is a *paulista* [native to São Paulo] matter. The rest of the country, if it sticks with us, will move, like a *body* that obeys, possessed by our way, by our will. . . . And this *paulista* question is a futurist question. No human agglomeration was ever so destined for futurism in activity, in industry, in history, in art, as the paulista agglomeration. What are we if not necessarily, unmistakably futurists?

The urban cosmopolitanism and modernity of São Paulo offered, therefore, an optimistic alternative to that "velha lenda da trinidade racial formadora" (old fable of a formative racial trinity).[13] The solution the modernists foresaw was not tied to the past in a mythical joining of three races, but in the future dictated by São Paulo's present with its telegraphs, airplanes, automobiles, factories and, especially, its white immigrants. Menotti del Picchia writes:

> . . . as levas imigratórias para aqui vindas modificaram visceralmente nossa ambiência étnica. E o país com êsses contingentes variados e fortes, começou a representar no mundo um papel mais vasto, num crescendo de atuaçao e prestígio, até chegar aos nossos dias como um das naçoes de maiores possibilidades de todo o universo."[14]

> . . . the immigrant contingents that have come here viscerally modified our ethnic atmosphere. And the country, as a result of these strong and varied contingents, in a crescendo of increasing activity and prestige, began to play a more important role in the world, eventually attaining its current position, and so arriving today as one of the nations with the greatest potential in all of the universe.

Menotti del Picchia claimed that the new immigrants had vanquished the three sad races. The Indian "nao ficou mais que uma vaga memória nos compêndios de história do Brasil e nos museus . . . [e] o negro ficou também ilhado dentro da raça caucasiana" (was naught but a vague memory in the historical compendium of Brazil and its museums . . . [and] the Black was also marooned within the white race).[15] Menotti del Picchia subscribed, as did the modernists in general, to the belief that the Brazilian "race" was in the process of formation and would be realized in the future due to the beneficial effect of:

> . . . tôdas as universais virtudes positivas dos povos imigrados — força de adaptaçao, ânsia de inédito, instinto de conquista. Essa, sim, será a raça brasileira. . . . O Brasil está ainda nesse período em que todos os contingentes étnicos são absorvidos.[16]

> . . . all of the generally positive virtues of the immigrant peoples — the ability to adapt, the thirst for the new, the instinct for conquest. This, indeed, will be the Brazilian race. . . . Brazil is still in the period in which all of the ethnic contingents are being absorbed.

The manner in which the modernists negotiated the apparently contradictory desire for, on the one hand, the specificity of a Brazilian national identity, and on the other hand, a universality which would link Brazil to Europe on the basis of equality rather than colonial dependence would set the terms in which or against which Brazilian artists, writers, musicians, and critics would define their work and continue to do so to this day. According to Roberto Reis, scholars have approached the modernist period in a way that reflects an institutionalized view of the movement as providing a radical break from the past as marked by the value Brazilian modernists placed on a national culture. He observes that this attachment to the idea of rupture masks the continuities that account for the many contradictory elements within the movement.[17] In his call for a reassessment of the period, the critic Silviano Santiago argues that: "I think the unsparing nature of the reevaluation will be in showing that all the modernists were more or less committed to the project of modernizing Brazil, all had developmentalist mentality, in all the need for being up-to-date was of capital importance, and all wanted to make Brazil enter History, a History that would be pure industrialization" (cited in Reis, 24). In fact, according to Celia de Azevedo, from the time of Abolition, the transition from an economy based on slave labor to an incipient economy based on wage labor was displaced and obscured by the emphasis on industrialization, development, urbanization, and class formation. In the process of this displacement, Blacks suddenly disappeared from the stage.[18]

In the spirit of this reevaluation, I undertake to examine in this chapter, primarily through the work of Mário de Andrade, one ambivalent relationship of the modernists to their project, as described above by Silviano Santiago. As my argument unfolds, I will address the disappearance of Blacks from the perspective of the cannibalistic model so prominent in the work of the Brazilian modernists in its first phase (1922–30). It is important to keep in sight that Brazilian modernism and anthropophagism cannot be mapped neatly onto one another; anthropophagism is only one of the many articulations of Brazilian modernism. The points where they do meet, however, have a particular significance for my discussion.

Furthermore, this reassessment will take Mário de Andrade's biography into account. While clearly a leader in the movement, he differed substantially from his elite cohort. While often referred to as the "Papa" or Pope of Modernism, Mário's relationship to the privilege taken for granted by many of his intimates was quite precarious, and he never experienced the financial and social security shared by the rest of his cohort. Mário de Andrade was born in the city of São Paulo on 9 October 1893. His mother's father, Joaquim Leite Moraes, had married under unusual circumstances for the time. While at law school in São Paulo, he had fallen in love with Ana Francisca Gomes da Silva, described as a mulatta, poor, and slightly older than he. When she became pregnant, they turned against custom, which required the son of a wealthy white family to abandon the mother and the child. Despite the scandal and the resulting family breach, they married, and their second child, Maria Luísa, would be Mário's mother. Joaquim Leite Moraes had a schoolmate who became involved with one of Ana Francisca's relatives, also a mulatta and also poor. When she became pregnant, the father of her children, following societal expectations, abandoned them. The eldest son, Carlos Augusto de Andrade, born in 1855, would marry Maria Luísa and become Mário's father. According to Mário, Carlos Augusto began to work at the age of twelve as a typesetter in order to support his mother and his sister, and prided himself on being a "self-made man." Despite a lack of formal schooling, Carlos Augusto learned Italian and French, wrote Portuguese flawlessly, was very knowledgeable in mathematics and accounting, and loved Italian classical music and the French realist novel. "Mário herdou de ambos os lados, pelos duas avós, seus traços de mestiço, diferente dos pais e dos irmãos que tinham branqueado" (Mário inherited from

both sides [of the family], from both grandmothers, his racially mixed features, distinguishing him from his parents and his siblings who had been
whitened).[19]

Moacir Werneck de Castro, a friend of Mário de Andrade, recalls that the
writer was more likely to address issues of racial discrimination with foreign
visitors than with Brazilians. He points out that in her memoir, the Argentinian journalist María Rosa Oliver recollects that Mário insisted that he had
refused invitations to visit the United States, "simplesmente por ser mulatto"
(simply because [I am] mulatto) and because "tenho sangre negro" (I have
black blood in me). He said to her that he did not so much fear that he would
be personally discriminated against because his identity card listed him as
white, "mas outros iguais a mim sofrem, e isso não poderia tolerar" (but others just like me suffer [from discrimination] and I could not bear that) (64).

Werneck de Castro implies that this discussion could not have taken place
in their Brazilian circle because good taste and fear of offense would have
prevented it. He suggests, moreover, that Mário's awareness of the power
of categories finds its most concrete expression in his refusal to categorize
himself publicly, especially in terms of his race and sexuality. "Improviso do
mal da América" (Improvisation on America's Ills), a poem written in 1928,
is often read as an example of this refusal of categories:

> Mas eu não posso me sentir negro nem vermelho!
> De certo que essas côres também tecem minha roupa arlequinal.
> Mas eu não me sinto negro, mas eu não sinto vermelho,
> Me sinto só branco, relumeando caridade e acolhamento,
> Purificado na revolta contra os brancos, as pátrias, as guerras,
> As posses, as preguiças e ignorâncais!
> Me sinto só branco, só branco em minha vida crivada de raças.

> But I can feel neither black nor red!
> Certainly these colors are also woven into my harlequin's clothes.
> But I don't feel black, but I don't feel red,
> I feel only white, radiating benevolence and welcome,
> Purified in the revolt against the whites, the nations, the wars,
> The wealth, the laziness, and ignorance.
> I feel white, only white in my life riddled with races.[20]

According to a leading scholar of Mário de Andrade's work, Telê Porto Ancona
Lopez, the racial category "white" provides a synthesis of the racial categories

that precede the final verse, a synthesis that reflects the prevailing racial ideologies. She suggests that the poem is an allegory for Brazil and its identity.[21]

In 1928, the same year he wrote this poem, Mário de Andrade published a novel that similarly addressed his nation's sense of racial and cultural formlessness. *Macunaíma: O herói sem nenhum caráter* (*Macunaíma: The Hero without Any Character*) is a work widely regarded as a masterpiece of Brazilian literature. The "mal" of the poem's title "Improviso do mal da América," (Improvisation on America's Ills) recalls the "mal" of the couplet repeated throughout the novel: "Pouca saúde e muita saúva, os males do Brasil são" (Poor health and many ants / These are the ills that plague Brazil). As I will demonstrate, the novel shares several important words with the poem: prequiça (sloth), mal (ills), and also the fact that the hero Macunaíma becomes white. *Macunaíma* reached bookstores soon after the publication of Oswald's *Manifesto Antropófago* (Anthropophagist Manifesto). Irritated at the idea that the public would think that he merely copied the theme of cannibalism from Oswald, Mário tried to distance his work from the *Manifesto* and claimed the priority of his novel.[22] The cannibalism of the novel and the cannibalism of the *Manifesto,* nevertheless, can be fruitfully read together.

As I stated in the introduction, the modernists' project as outlined by Oswald de Andrade in the "Manifesto Antropófago" involves swallowing and absorbing what is useful in a culture. The cannibalism attributed to the indigenous population of Brazil served as a model for a redefined cultural relationship between Brazil and the outside world (defined largely as Europe)—a relationship in which foreign influences would not be copied but digested and absorbed as a precondition to the creation of a new, more independent national civilization.

The focus on cannibalism as a model for national identity formation invites many questions: What are the implications of defining a national identity according to a concept of mixture? Is this necessarily a subversive position? Does it imply a radical posture in relation to binary structures? Does it offer an alternative to essentialist identities? What are the implications of insisting on an identity acknowledged as fictional, divided and contaminated in a philosophical and political context that valorizes identity as unitary, stable, and coherent? What is the relation of the internal to the external or the incorporated to the inassimilable or indigestible—or in other words—the remainder or excrement?

Incorporation and Cordiality

The modernists' description of Brazilian identity formation shares much with psychoanalytic accounts of individual identity formation. Mário de Andrade and Oswald de Andrade were avid, if idiosyncratic, readers of Freud. The "Manifesto Antropófago" makes overt references to *Totem and Taboo*. Mário de Andrade's library contains a collection of Freud's works that he read in the original German and in French and English translations. Among the texts is *Trois essais sur la théorie de la sexualité* (*Three Essays on the Theory of Sexuality*), heavily annotated with Mário's marginal comments revealing his particular interest in repression and sublimation.

According to Sigmund Freud, the tendency toward unity is the particular characteristic of the ego. For Freud, orality provides the basic paradigm for the psychic processes—introjection, incorporation, identification and internalization—that define the ego and contribute to the first stages of libidinal development. Through these processes the ego protects itself against loss or destruction by assimilating the lost or threatening object. In psychoanalytic theory the limits of the body provide a prototype for all separations between inside and outside. Incorporation literally depends on a notion of the bounded body. Freud compares these above-named processes (or aspects of these processes) to cannibalism.

In the 1915 edition of the *Three Essays on the Theory of Sexuality*, Freud introduces the idea of an oral organization of the psyche, an idea that will be important for the development of his theories of the ego. According to Freud, self-fashioning involves "the assimilation of one ego to another, as a result of which the first ego behaves like the second in certain respects, imitates it and in a sense takes it into itself. Identification has not been unsuitably compared with oral, cannibalistic incorporation of the other person."[23]

The oral encounter with the world is, for Freud, the most fundamental encounter in the sense that it is linked with what is most infantile and primitive in the development of human beings individually or collectively. The activity of nutrition provides the model or prototype for understanding and organizing the subject's relation to the world. A somatic feature, the mouth, determines the mode of the relationship to an object, incorporation. Emphasis should be placed on the relational aspect of this prototype since it allows for transposition onto other forms such as incorporation through the skin, breathing, sight, hearing, etc. Incorporation is the process whereby the subject, more or less on the level of phantasy, has an object penetrate his body and keeps it "inside" his body. Incorporation constitutes an instinctual aim[24] and a mode of object-relationship which are characteristic of the oral stage; although it has a special relationship with the mouth and with the ingestion of food, it may also be lived out in relationship to other erotogenic zones and other functions. Incorporation provides the corporal model for introjection and identification.[25]

According to Freudian definitions, incorporation can signify: 1) the taking in (in the sense of penetration) of an object for pleasure; 2) the taking in of an object in order to appropriate its qualities, properties or attributes; 3) the saving and/or destruction of an object.

This first aspect of incorporation links eating to sex. In Brazilian Portuguese this link is very clearly made in that *comer* (to eat) is also *comer* (to have sexual intercourse with). But who is eating? And since this is a discussion of cannibalism: Who is eating whom? The consuming body, as we will see demonstrated repeatedly, is not only racially marked as white, but also gendered as male. It is important to note that the *mulata* plays a very significant role in the linking of race and nation, for it is through her body that *embranquecimento* (whitening) takes place. That it is "whitening" that is taking place and not "blackening" is reinforced by the example of a classic, ever-popular samba from the late 1920s. The singer, positioned as white by the lyrics, pursues the *mulata,* who, despite the contrary evidence of her hair, is identifiable as a *mulata* by the color of her skin. The singer joyfully declares that "como a cor não pega" (since color is not catching/contagious), he can safely court her.[26]

The second aspect of incorporation (the assimilation of the qualities of the eaten), in which identification is experienced and symbolized in a bodily fashion, is developed in Freud's *Totem and Taboo.*[27] Freud reviewed literature on cannibalism as well as the anthropological interpretations of this material by J. G. Frazer, A. Lang, Franz Boas, J. J. Atkinson, and others, in developing his psychoanalytic interpretation of Darwin's theories of the primal horde, by which he intended to explain the advent of social organization, moral restrictions, and religion. Freud's point of departure is Darwin's description of the primal horde dominated by the violent and jealous father who, in order to keep the women to himself, drove away his sons as they grew old enough to represent competition. According to Freud's scenario, the day came when the brothers who had been driven out of the horde banded together, killed and, because they were cannibals, devoured the father. In accordance with the logic of cannibalism conveyed by ethnographic reports, the brothers who both feared and envied the father, accomplished their identification with him in the act of devouring him, thereby acquiring a portion of his strength:

> They hated their father, who presented such a formidable obstacle to their craving for power and their sexual desires: but they loved and admired him too. After they got rid of him, they had satisfied their hatred and put into effect their wish to identify with him, the affection they felt for him was bound to make itself felt. . . . A sense of guilt made its appearance. The dead father became stronger than the living one had been.

The brothers addressed their guilt by forbidding the killing of the totem animal, which was a substitute for the father (143), and the totemic meal would be a "repetition and commemoration of this memorable and criminal deed" (142). The elimination of the primal father was repressed as an active memory but left indelible traces in the history of humanity (155).

Using Freud's description of the totemic meal as a guide, Oswald de Andrade developed a theory of Brazilian national identity that took as its inaugural moment the cannibalization of the father, a reference to Bishop Sardinha who had been sent from Portugal and purportedly cannibalized by the Tupinamba Indians. Oswald dates the manifesto as having been written in the 374th year, in a calendar that reinforces the act as the beginning of specifically Brazilian time. The Tupinamba to whom Oswald refers were synonymous with cannibalism in the European imagination, although it was in fact the Caribs who gave their name to the act of anthropophagy.[28] One of the earliest, if not the first, representations of Native Americans dates from 1505 and shows a Tupinamba chewing an arm while the rest of the body roasts in the fire. This vision of the Tupinamba was reinforced by the widely read sixteenth century narratives by the German sailor Hans Staden (voyage in 1554), the French travelers André Thevet (1555)[29] and Jean de Léry as well as the writings of the Jesuit missionaries José de Anchieta, Manuel da Nóbrega, Juan Navarro, Fernão Cardim, and Francisco Soares,[30] among others.

In his "Manifesto Antropófago" (Anthropophagist Manifesto), Oswald de Andrade calls for the return of the repressed that is cannibalism. He advocates a return to the time before the power of the father was strengthened through internalization and before institutions were constructed to enforce respect for the taboo: "Antropofagia. A transformação permanente do Tabu em totem" (Anthropophagy. The permanent transformation of the Taboo into the totem).[31] Many critics see the "Manifesto Antropófago" as a rejection of the internalized law of the father and, therefore, as an anticolonialist gesture and a cry of protest against Portuguese influence. They point out that the long history of colonization and oppression by the Portuguese includes the collusion of the Church and Crown in eradicating the supposed cannibalism of the indigenous people of Brazil in order to impose colonial rule.[32] This is a valid interpretation insofar as it addresses the relationship of Brazil to Portugal and to the colonial past. It does not, however, address the question of the construction of Brazil's identity, especially in regard to race and issues of progress and development, alluded to by Silviano Santiago at the beginning of this chapter.

When Paris embraced primitivism, moreover, Brazilian modernists could turn more confidently to the "primitive" black and indigenous populations of Brazil without the insecurity expressed by the earlier generation. In the "Manifesto Antropófago," Oswald de Andrade uses the cult of the primitive among European artists to make Brazil a point of reference for Europe. In a neat rewriting of the usual schemes of progress and development which persist in discussions of "First World" and "Third World," Oswald has Brazil precede Europe, making America the source of democracy and, therefore, more and sooner "civilized" than Europe:

> Queremos a revolução Caraíba. Maior que a Revolução Francesa. A unificação de todas as revoltas eficazes na direção do homem. Sem nós a Europa não teria nem sequer sua pobre declaração dos direitos do homem. (354)

> We want the Carib Revolution. Greater than the French Revolution. The unification of all productive revolts for the progress of humanity. Without us, Europe wouldn't even have its paltry declaration of the rights of man. (39)

Brazilian modernism may have been chronologically late, but its model, cannibalism, marked, in fact, the real beginning of the modern world.

The modernist relationship to the "primitive" remains, nevertheless, ambivalent, as manifested in one of the hallmarks of the "Manifesto Antropófago," the desire to reconcile perceived opposites (the primitive and the civilized, the body and the mind, black and white). In the following passage, Oswald registers the anxiety of his generation of white elites about the role of Blacks in the nation seeking an advanced place in the technological future (represented as a train in the following passage):

> Uma sugestão de Blaise Cendrars: — Tendes as locomotivas cheias, ides partir. Um negro gira a manivela do desvio rototivo em que estais. O menor descuido vos fará partir na direção oposta ao vosso destino.

> A suggestion of Blaise Cendrars: — You have the trains loaded, you are ready to leave. A negro turns the crank of the turn-table beneath you. The slightest mistake will make you leave in the direction opposite to your destination.[33]

The old fear that Blacks (who are clearly not among the "you") will derail Brazil's march toward progress is reiterated here in Oswald's "Manifesto da Poesia Pau-Brasil," albeit in the words of the French poet and friend of the modernists. In the "Manifesto Antropófago," the coming together of what might be described as diverse elements is expressed hierarchically through the metaphor of cannibalism (one eats and the other is eaten) and, as in all metaphors, one term is sublimated into the other to establish identity.

The third aspect of incorporation, which involves the destruction of the consumed object, is developed further by Freud in *Beyond the Pleasure Principle:* "During the oral stage the organization of the libido, the act of obtaining erotic mastery over an object coincides with that object's destruction."[34] Karl Abraham[35] and Melanie Klein[36] built on this idea, calling attention to the ambivalent nature and the sadistic aspect of the oral stage, which associates the activity of biting with destruction. Implied in all the meanings of incorporation is the desirability (for reasons of health or pleasure) of maintaining the good within the body and the bad outside the body: "The original pleasure-ego wants to introject into itself everything that is good and to eject from itself everything that is 'bad.'"[37] In *The Shell and the Kernel,* Nicholas Abraham and Maria Torok argue against the conflation of introjection and incorporation. They distinguish between introjection as a good/ healthy responses to the loss of a love object and incorporation as a bad/ pathological one. Incorporation is a failed introjection.[38] Introjection names and recognizes the loss, allowing the ego to reorganize itself to accommodate that loss. Incorporation is oriented toward preserving the integrity of the ego. It silences and encrypts the loss, enabling the ego to act as if the loss had never taken place. Cannibalism depends on incorporation.

Eating, however, does have its risks. It is not always possible to keep what is perceived to be harmful outside of the body. There is always the danger of an inadvertent taking into the body — through contagion, for example — that could lead to the destruction of the body. For my discussion of the idea of the remainder as it relates to issues of race and democracy, a productive approach would be via Jacques Derrida's elaboration of the *pharmakon,* that which upon ingestion can function as both the remedy and the poison.[39] In discussing the logical underpinnings of the *pharmakon,* Derrida highlights the fact that the blend or mixture is perceived as an impurity. The pharmakon penetrates the limits of the body, introducing a foreign element.

In his 1857 play, *O Demonio Familiar* (The Devil You Know, or The Family Devil), José de Alencar expresses the elite's anxiety that animated discussions of black citizenship around the time of Abolition. Alencar portrays the slave, Pedro, as the source of all the intrigue and confusion that threatens the moral, physical, and emotional security of a Rio de Janeiro family. In order to reestablish the well-being of his family, the master liberates the slave and expels him from their midst, thereby removing the danger he represents.[40] In the play, enslaved Africans are portrayed as aggressors and housebreakers who threaten the internal purity and security of the Brazilian nation and who, therefore, must be expelled from the body politic. This nineteenth-century narrative is displaced in the early twentieth century by the postslavery narrative of assimilation implied in cannibalism. Blacks are to be incorporated as a "good remedy" — as a vaccine against the debilitating effects of the tropical environment — and the integrity of the white national body is aggressively reconstituted through an ideology of *embranquecimento.* After the invasion of the *pharmakon,* the *inside* has to be reestablished as the *inside* and the *outside* as the *outside,* and the limits of the body reasserted.

In Brazil, the desire for a fixed identity was threatened by the reality of miscegenation. Faced with the impossibility, as a result of widespread miscegenation, of maintaining the binary racial oppositions that were reinforced in the postbellum United States and in Europe, the elite was forced to find another mechanism to form a national identity that would suit them. Both its deep anxiety that Brazil had failed to produce a homogeneous nation (or at least one rooted in the division between black and white) and its fear that racial degeneracy menaced the nation were mitigated by the possibility that racial mixture could be seen in a positive rather than a negative light.[41] This reinterpretation gave rise to a model of identity formation that resolved the question of difference through the incorporation and assimilation of that difference, thereby ensuring the identity of the dominant (socially, economically, politically) white. It is this last point that we must keep in mind while reading the first lines of the "Manifesto Antropófago": "Só a antropófagia nos une. Socialmente. Economicamente. Filosoficamente" (Only anthropophagy unites us. Socially. Economically. Philosophically).

The possibility of *constructing* whiteness became an attractive possibility for an elite worried for its existence. Moreover, the very high rate of white immigration to Brazil during the first two decades of the twentieth century played an important role in assuring the elite that blackness could and would be transformed into whiteness. This assurance was strengthened by the high mortality rate that "consumed" a large percentage of the black and mulatto population.[42] Unable to overcome a sense of a threat to the nation through a separation of races, the white Brazilian elite had recourse to another type of defense: the assimilation of the foreign element into the body, an assimilation that retained the integrity of the eater at the expense of the eaten and preserved an advantageous power relationship for the eater. Yet, the logic of incorporation based on the model of nutrition is that the incorporation cannot be total; there must be a remainder, an excretion. This remainder can be seen as something that has been rejected from the body, but it can also be seen as something that refuses to be incorporated, as sign of resistance.

Attention to the remainder allows us to reflect back on various theorizations of a constitutive outside. These theorizations explain the visibility of identity as a definition of what it, the identity, *is not*. The constitutive outside (whether described as an "other" or whether described as expelled in order to maintain the purity of identity) is often linked to the "foreign." As I will discuss in detail in chapter 3, black activism for full citizenship and representation in Brazil and the United States revolve around a refusal of "foreignness." In other words, Africans are produced as black at precisely the moment they cease to be foreign through the experience of slavery.[43] The experience of slavery has incorporated Africans and made something new that cannot be properly understood according to any paradigm of foreignness. The foreign is a relation; the remainder, however, is disavowed.

Anthropophagism/Cannibalism

The relation of the Brazilian modernists to the European avant-garde is most complex at the point where they both take up cannibalism as a metaphor. For the Brazilian modernists, the roots of their appropriation of anthropophagism lie in the futurism, surrealism, and Dadaism to which Oswald de Andrade had been exposed during his stays in Paris, where he frequented the same artists' studios as Fernand Léger, Pablo Picasso, and Jean Cocteau. It was through the intervention of his friend Blaise Cendrars, the French poet and author of the influential *Anthologie Nègre,* that Oswald de Andrade's "Manifesto da Poesia Pau-Brasil" was published in Paris in 1924. It was during these trips that Oswald became familiar with the avant-garde journals *Le Coq, Cannibale, Le Coeur à Barbe, Proverbe, 391,* and *Littérature.* He would also meet Francis Picabia, author of the "Manifeste Cannibale" that was published in *Dadaphone* of March 1920 and served as an inspiration for Oswald de Andrade's manifesto. It was, in fact, Paris that made Oswald and the other modernists consider the possibilities for a Brazilian national identity of linking their notion of the primitive to what would be most modern: "Nunca se pode sentir tão bem, na ambiencia de Paris, o encontro sugestivo do tambor negro e do canto indigena. Essas forças étnicas estão em plena modernidade"[44] (Nowhere would one experience so truly, [as] in the atmosphere of Paris, the suggestive encounter with the black drum and the Indian song). When Blaise Cendrars came to Brazil in 1924 as a guest of Oswald de Andrade, he accompanied Oswald de Andrade, Mário de Andrade, Társila de Amaral, and D. Olivia Guedes Penteado (a wealthy patron of the modernists) on a trip to the state of Minas Gerais in search of the artwork of Aleijadinho (a mulatto artist who sculpted the statuary for the churches of the interior of Minas Gerais during the eighteenth century). For Mário de Andrade, this trip was the first to the interior of Brazil; it would leave a lasting impression that would mark his work by reviving his interest in ethnography and folklore.

Oswald de Andrade was in Paris during the vogue for ethnographic exoticism that was everywhere to be seen in museums such as the Musée de l'Homme; artists' studios such as those of Léger and Picasso; and galleries such as the Galérie Devambez, which had mounted the First Exhibition of African and Asiatic Art in 1919.[45] While the figure of the cannibal was embraced as part of the vogue, it already had a long-established pedigree in Europe. The cannibal had been an emblem of Montaigne's sixteenth-century humanism, was included in Voltaire's *Dictionnaire philosophique* (1764), and had appeared in Rousseau's *Discours sur l'origine et les fondements de l'inegalité parmi les hommes* (1754). Having been located by anthropologists in a remote prehistoric past, the cannibal took on a strong symbolic value. According to Benedito Nunes: "Abriu-se, de Nietzsche a Freud, o caminho que

fez do canibalismo o signo de um sindrome ancestral, ou para usarmos a linguagem de Oswald, uma semáfora da condição humana."[46] (From Nietzsche
to Freud, exists a path that made of cannibalism a sign of an ancestral syn-
drome, or if we use Oswald's terms, a semaphore for the human condition.)

Although the European avant-garde had already made good use of the
metaphor of cannibalism by the time that Oswald de Andrade wrote his
manifesto, its Brazilian incarnation is not reducible to European cannibalism. For the European avant-garde, cannibalism was associated with psychological and social motivations and was expressed through violent images
and metaphors that contributed to Dada's and surrealism's aesthetic of shock
and aggression. Mário de Andrade's *Macunaíma*,[47] is, however, emblematic
of Brazilian anthropophagism in that it is a practice of cannibalism on many
levels. The novel enacts cannibalism on: 1) a textual level by incorporating other texts through plagiarism; 2) a linguistic level by incorporating
other languages into Portuguese; 3) a thematic level through the cannibalistic activities of its characters; and 4) on a formal level my incorporating
various genres into the novel, producing what Mário called a "rapsódia"
(rhapsody), an improvisational composition having no fixed form.[48] These
acts of cannibalism work together to produce the ideal Brazilian, even as
they attest to the impossibility of this project.

Plagiarism, or Textual Cannibalism

In an unpublished preface to *Macunaíma*, Mário de Andrade states that
his goal in writing the novel was to explore the issue of Brazilian national
identity:

> O que me interessou por *Macunaíma* foi incontestavelmente a preocupação em
> que vivo de trabalhar e descobrir o mais que possa a entidade nacional dos brasil-
> eiros. Ora depois de pelejar muito verifiqei uma coisa que parece certa: o brasileiro
> não tem nenhum caráter."[49]

> What interested me in *Macunaíma* was undeniably my preoccupation with shap-
> ing and discovering as much as I can [about] the Brazilian national being. But after
> struggling a great deal I realized something that seems to be true: the Brazilian is
> without any character.

This realization provides the full title of Mário's novel, *Macunaíma: O
herói sem nenhum caráter* (*Macunaíma: The Hero without Any Character*). For Mário, it is appropriate that the Brazilian hero have no character,

"além do incaracterístico de uma raça ainda em formação"[50] (beyond the lack of characteristic associated with a race still in formation). This lack of character[istics] as it relates to a race and to a nationality still in formation is reflected in Macunaíma's birth as a black man to an indigenous woman, and in his miraculous transformation from a black man to a white man.

Among the many responses to the publication of *Macunaíma* in July 1928 was an entry by Raimundo Moraes in the *Dicionário de Cousas da Amazónia* (The Dictionary of Amazonian Things). Moraes defends Mário de Andrade against the suggestion that he plagiarized his tale from a book by Teodor Koch-Grünberg:

> Os maldizentes afirmam que o livro *Macunaíma* do festejado escritor, Mário de Andrade, é todo inspirado no *Vom [sic] Roraima zum Orinoco* do sábio (Koch-Grünberg). Desconhecendo eu o livro do naturalista germânico, não creio nesse boato, pois o romancista patrício, com quem privei em Manaus, possui talento e imaginação que dispensam inspirações estranha.

> Slanderers assert that the book *Macunaíma* by the celebrated author Mário de Andrade, is wholly inspired [influenced] by *Von Roraima zum Orinoco* by the German scholar Koch-Grünberg. Although I am not familiar with the German naturalist's book, I do not believe these rumors since the novelist, my countryman, with whom I lived on intimate terms in the Amazons, possesses the talent and imagination that does without foreign inspiration [influence].[51]

Mário rejects his defense and responds by admitting not only to the plagiarism of Koch-Grünberg but also of many other authors:

> Copiei, sim, meu querido defensor. O que me espanta e acho sublime de bondade, é os maldizentes se esquecerem de tudo quanto sabem, restringindo a minha cópia a Koch-Grünberg, quando copiei tudos. E até o sr., na cena da Bioúna. Confesso que copiei, copiei as vezes textualmente.[52]

> I copied, yes, my dear defender. What surprises me and what I think too, too sublime is that my detractors forget what they know by restricting my copying to Koch-Grünberg, when I copied everyone. And even you, sir, in the Bioúna scene. I confess that I copied, I copied sometimes word for word.

The risks of incorporation imagined by Moraes in his defense of Mário de Andrade suggest worry about the real possibility of overcoming the foreign influences and using them to the incorporator's advantage. In the case of *Macunaíma*, these fears, on a first approach, appear groundless in that the incorporated texts cannot overcome the prevailing attitudes toward race.

The cannibals are male and white, and the narrative preserves a hierarchical structure in which it is better to eat than to be eaten.

Although Mário de Andrade endorses copying—or what he calls plagiarism—he does so in a nuanced manner. On one occasion he wrote a strongly worded letter to his student and assistant, Oneyda de Alvarenga, in which he accused her of using his work without giving proper attribution, an accusation that almost ended their friendship:

> Não sou de forma alguma contra o plágio em trabalhos de qualquer natureza. . . . O plágio tem qualidades ótimas: enriquece a gente, disentorpece uma explicação intelectual do excesso de citações, permite a gente milhorar idéias alheias boa, mas mal expressas incidentalmente, etc. etc. Porém o plágio tem de ser consciente, porque só a consciência do roubo permite atinger a milhoria da coisa roubada . . .

> I am in no way against plagiarism in works of no matter what type. Plagiarism has excellent qualities. It enriches us, it relieves an intellectual explication of excessive footnotes, it allows us to improve another's ideas that might be good but otherwise poorly expressed, etc., etc. However, plagiarism has to be conscious because only the consciousness of stealing allows for the improvement of the stolen thing.[53]

He continues, in the letter, to explain that although he substitutes the word "steal" for the word "plagiarize," "steal" is not quite accurate because of its negative connotation. According to Mário, to plagiarize is simply to appropriate what is in the public domain and, therefore, belongs to everyone. "Bad" plagiarism involves a taking in which is unconscious and passive. This plagiarism could be associated with contagion. "Good" plagiarism involves an active, conscious taking in which appropriates the strength of the incorporated for the incorporator's benefit. "Good" plagiarism assumes the structure of cannibalism, a cannibalism that actively takes in material which can be digested and turned into the material of the eater's body and, in this case, his body of work. In this way Mário de Andrade anticipates Cocteau's observation: "Notre esprit digère bien. L'objet profondement assimilé . . . provoque un réalisme superieur à la simple copie infidèle"[54] (Our minds digest well. The well-assimilated object . . . produces a realism, which is superior to [that of] the common unfaithful copy). The implication is that Mário uses a cannibalistic model to create a more authentic identity. Incorporation takes place in Mário's texts not to produce a mixture that would be an end in and of itself, but as a process of assimilation that will produce the Brazilian.

The novel, or "rapsódia," to use Mário de Andrade's term, traces

Macunaíma's origins in the Amazonian forest, his trip to São Paulo, and his return to the forest before ascending into the heavens to become the Big Dipper. In the "Epilogue" we learn how Macunaíma's story comes to be told:

> Então o homem descobriu na ramaria um papagaio verde de bico dourado espiando pra ele. Falou: Da o pé, papagaio. O papagaio veio a pousar na cabeça do homem e os dois se acompanheiraram. Então o pássaro principiou falando numa fala mansa, muito nova, muito! que era canto e que era cachiri, com mel de pau, que era boa e possuía a traição das frutas desconhecidas do mato. O tribo se acabara, a família virara sombras, a maloca ruíra minada pelas saúvas e Macunaíma subira pro céu, porém ficara o aruaí do séquito daqueles tempos de dantes em que o herói fora o grande Macunaíma imperador. E só o papagaio no silêncio do Uraricoera preservava do esquecimento os casos e a fala desaparecida. Só o papagaio conservava no silêncio as frases e feitos do herói. Tudo ele contou pro homem e depois abriu asa rumo de Lisboa. E o homem sou eu, minha gente, e eu fiquei pra vos contar a história. (168)

> There in the foliage, the man discovered a green parrot with a golden beak looking at him. He said, "Come down, parrot, come down!" The parrot came down and perched on the man's head, and the two went along together. The parrot started to talk in a gentle tongue, something new, completely new! Some of it was song, some like cassiri sweetened with honey, some of it had the lovely fickle flavor of unknown forest fruits. The vanished tribe, the family turned into ghosts, the tumbledown hut undermined by termites, Macunaíma's ascent to heaven, how the parrots and macaws formed a canopy in the far-off times when the hero was the Great Emperor, Macunaíma: in the silence of Uraricoera only the parrot had rescued from oblivion those happenings and the language which had disappeared. Only the parrot had preserved in that vast silence the words and deeds of the hero. All this he related to the man, then spread his wings and set his course for Lisbon. And that man, dear reader, was myself, and I stayed on to tell you this story. (168)

Ironically, this parrot is not a Brazilian parrot but a German one. Mário de Andrade came to his story of "Brazil's Indigenous past" and Brazil's hero via Europe in the form of legends collected by the German ethnographer Teodor Koch-Grünberg. Mário made no secret of his debt to Koch-Grünberg, who had traveled throughout Brazil between 1911 and 1913. Mário relied particularly on volume 2 of *Von Roroima zum Orinoco*, which contained the myths and legends of the Taulipang and Arekuna people. The texts that were incorporated into *Macunaíma*, however, were not simply and entirely incorporated but selectively and according to a certain pattern. The name Macunaíma (Makunaíma) was taken from Koch-Grünberg.[55] In the collection of myths and legends related to Koch-Grünberg, Makunaíma is the hero of the tribe and the creator of the Taulipang people. According to Koch-Grünberg, Makunaíma's name is made up of two words which join to mean the "Great Evil" (maku = evil, ima = great).[56] Koch-Grünberg's Makunaíma is the youngest of five brothers, two of whom, Ma'nape and Zigue, appear most often with Makunaíma. These two brothers, with their names also spelled differently, are retained in Mário's novel. An examination of the source material retained shows a pattern of manipulation in relation to race. The birth of Makunaíma is not described in Koch-Grünberg's collection. In Mário de Andrade's narrative, Macunaíma is born in the middle of the forest to an old woman of the Tapanhuma tribe. In the novel, it is claimed that the name of the tribe signifies "black." It is significant that Mário did not take the name of Makunaíma's people offered by Koch-Grünberg, preferring instead to find the name of another tribe that, correctly or incorrectly, signifies black. Macunaíma, unlike Koch-Grünberg's Makunaíma, is "preto retinto" (dark black) and a "crianca feia" (ugly child). As a result of an encounter with an animal/spirit in the forest, Macunaíma grows a man's body but keeps the head of a child. The important manipulations of Koch-Grünberg's account are, therefore, that Makunaíma becomes black, ugly, lazy, and an adult with a child's head. After the death of their mother, the three brothers travel through the forest. They meet Ci, Mãe do Mato (the mother/empress of the Forest), whom Macunaíma rapes with the help of his brothers. Macunaima, who at this point is still black, and Ci have a child, the only child of the many interracial relations in the narrative. Ci has one shriveled breast, a sign, according to the text, that she belongs to the tribe of the mulheres sozinhas (solitary women), otherwise known as Amazons. A Cobra Preta (Black Snake) bites Ci's other breast, and her child is poisoned while nursing. In a letter to Manuel Bandeira, Mário stresses that he chose the color black for the snake by chance as he very easily could have chosen the color green. The choice hardly seems a coincidence given that Mário adheres closely to superstitions associated with the color black, a subject that he had studied.[57] Maanape and Jiguê, for example, become sick with leprosy and die. Under their contagious influence, Macunaíma, having become a white man, gets sick but overcomes the disease. By the last third of the book, every character marked visually as black or of mixed race or indigenous has become sick and/or died. Their illnesses must be seen in the context of the couplet that Macunaíma repeats throughout the book:

"Pouca saúde e muita saúva, os males do Brazil são" (Poor health and many ants, these are the ills that plague Brazil).

Throughout the novel, Macunaíma has fought for the possession of *muiraquitã*, an amulet representative of national identity.[58] As soon as he captures the *muiraquitã*, he loses it again and succumbs to the forces that threaten Brazilian identity:

> A Ursa Maior é Macunaíma. É mesmo o herói capenga que de tanto penar na terra sem saúde e com muita saúva, se aborreceu de tudo, foi-se embora e banza solitário no campo vasto do céu. (166)

> The Great Bear is Macunaíma. And the hero himself, crippled with so much suffering on earth, lacking health and plagued with too many ants, abominating everything, has gone far away, and broods alone in the vast expanse of heaven. (165)

Miscegenated Language

Incorporation takes place on a linguistic level as well on the textual and formal levels described above. The modernists were interested in discovering Brazilian language that would convey (if not create) the specificity of Brazilian identity. In the chapter of *Macunaíma*, titled "Pauí-Pódole" (Pauí-Pódole, the Father of the Crested Curassows), Mário makes use of one of the legends from Koch-Grünberg's collection. The story taken from Koch-Grünberg describes how human beings and animals came to have anuses. Once upon a time, human beings and animals didn't have anuses and defecated through their mouths. At this time there existed an animal, "anus," known as Puíto, who, for his amusement, would break wind in the faces of the other animals and then run away. One day the very annoyed animals got together and resolved to catch Puíto and make him pay for his fun. They chased him and chased him all over the forest but were unable to catch him until two parrots, flying on ahead almost at the border of Guyana and Brazil, caught Puíto, tied him down, and waited for the other animals to catch up to them. All the animals of the forest cut up Puíto, who was very large, and claimed their pieces. The tapir in his haste took a big piece without waiting for it to be divided, and the parrot, deer, and doves took more befitting small pieces. The toad had to beg for his bit, so the parrots threw him his piece, which landed on his back. This, according to the tale, is how every living being came to have an anus. Otherwise, we would have to evacuate through our mouths or explode.[59]

In *Macuaíma*, the story from Koch-Grünberg is reduced to one word, *puíto.* In Mário's version, Macunaíma, now in São Paulo, decides to increase his understanding of spoken Brazilian and written Portuguese, a distinction also satirized in Macunaíma's letter to the Amazonians: "Macunaíma aproveitava a espera se aperfeiçoando nas duas línguas da terra, o brasileiro falado e o português escrito"(87) (Macunaíma took advantage of the wait to perfect himself in the two languages of the land, spoken Brazilian and written Portuguese). As he wanders about the city on the Day of Flowers, a young woman approaches, puts a flower in his boutonniere and asks for a dime. Macunaíma is embarrassed because he doesn't know the word for boutonniere. He considers orifice and rejects it because it belongs to written Portuguese. He considers hole but rejects this word for being too vague. He settles on *puíto:* "A senhora me arrumou com um dia-de-judeu! Nunca mais me bote flor neste . . . neste puíto, dona!" (88) (You've gone and utterly ruined this day for me, miss. Never put a flower in this . . . in this . . . arse-hole again!) (81).

Goodland's translation is misleading because in the Portuguese original the word, *puíto,* is left as a foreign word, not understood by its readers of Portuguese, in the same way that it is not understood by the flower girl. In other words, the translation highlights a point that the Brazilian text obscures, which is that this word, *puíto,* is a *palavrão,* a "dirty" word, and that it enters the Brazilian spoken language as well as written Portuguese without anyone (meaning the Brazilians) understanding its resistant "dirty" meaning. On one level this could be seen as an example of a "miscegenated" language, or in Bakhtinian terms, heteroglossia,[60] but in this case the linguistic "miscegenation" (in which a word from an indigenous language is mixed into the Brazilian language) produces an excremental remainder that resists not only assimilation but also being known.

It is not coincidental in a text that makes use of a metaphorics of the body that this particular word incorporated into the Brazilian language has to do with the body. By reducing the tale in which people were forced to evacuate through the mouth to one word *puíto,* Mário makes Macunaíma utter "dirty" words, makes him literally talk shit. In this way, according to Eneide Maria de Souza, the organ, in the indigenous text, and the word, in *Macunaíma,* are incorporated into human beings and into Brazilian language.[61] Like Freud's famous assertion that civilization began when human beings stood up, thereby leading to a separation between the nose (and mouth) and the anus, so too the incorporation of the tale which marks the separation of the mouth (with its eating function) from the anus (with its defecating function) can be seen as a move toward civilization, a move reinforced not only by the removal of the word's dirty meaning once it has been incorporated into Portuguese, but also by the respectable etymology that Mário gives it by providing puíto with a (false) Latin ancestor: ". . . a palavra 'botoeira' viera a dar em 'puíto,' por meio de uma palavra inter-mediária, a voz latina 'rabanitius' (botoeira-rabanitius-puíto), sendo que rabanitius embora não encontrada nos documentos medievais, afirmaram os doutos que na certa existira e fora corrente no sermo vulgaris" (89) (. . . the word "buttonhole" had become transmuted into the word "arsehole" via an intermediate Greek [sic] word, "bumphole" [buttonhole-bumphole-arsehole]. But although the word "bumphole" had never been found in any medieval documents, the highbrows swore it has existed and had been cur-rent in vulgar speech) (83).

Macunaíma, the Cannibal

The cannibalism that takes place at the thematic level also produces resistant remainders. In *Macunaíma: Ruptura e Tradiçao*, Suzana Camargo main-tains that Rabelais' *Gargantua* is an intertext of *Macunaíma*. Using Bakhtin as a theoretical base, she analyzes the relationship of *Gargantua* and *Macu-naíma* to each other and to the body. One aspect that *Macunaíma* and *Gar-gantua* share is that the grotesque body and eating are inscribed in both narratives. According to Bakhtin:

> The most distinctive character of the [grotesque] body is its open, unfinished nature, most fully revealed in the act of eating where the body transgresses its lim-its. The encounter of the man with the world, which takes place inside the open, biting, rending, chewing mouth, is one of the most ancient, and most important objects of human thought and imagery. Here man tastes world, introduces it into his own body, makes it part of himself. . . . Man's encounter with the world in the act of eating is joyful, triumphant; he triumphs over the world, devours it with-out being devoured himself. The limits between man and the world are erased, to man's advantage.[62]

If this incorporation works to man's advantage, it does not work to the advantage of all "men" — or women.

What is seen as subversive in Bakhtin, however, becomes suspect when race or indeed gender are factored in. If we keep in mind that *comer* means both to eat and to have sexual intercourse, the ways in which the scatalogical, alimentary, and sexual registers are associated warrant our attention. In the novel, nearly all of the sexual scenes are overtly linked to cannibalism and/or the incorporation of food. In the beginning of the novel, Macunaíma tricks his brother Jiguê's wife, Sofará, into taking him into the forest, where he is transformed into Prince Charming. Their sexual acts involve consumption of the hero's extremities by Sofará. In São Paulo, Susi, Jiguê's lover with whom Macumaíma has an affair, pulls manioc out of her vagina for Macunaíma to eat. No sooner does Vei, the sun, offer her daughter to Macunaíma along with a dowry consisting of "Europa, France and Bahia," under the condition that he remain faithful to the girl, than he immediately takes up with the white women of the city, including a Portuguese fishwife: "Logo topou com uma que fora varina lá na terrinha do compadre chegadinho-chegadinho e inda cheirava no-mais! um fartum de peixe" (69) (Within moments he spotted a fishwife hawking her wares on a plot of land belonging to her godfather, a recently arrived Portuguese immigrant. Her skin was white and she was heavily perfumed; she reeked to high heaven of stale fish) (64).

The fishwife's association with fish and her earlier experiences with Vei link her to another scene that repeats these two elements, a scene that is an allegory of the Brazilian consumed by European culture. At the end of the novel, Vei, disgusted with Macunaíma for not having married her daughter, thereby linking himself to the civilization of the tropics, punishes him. She makes the hero jump into the cold waters of the Uraricoera (the temperature representing European civilization) to chase the unattainable image of a white woman (evocative of the Portuguese fishwife that he choose when he rejected the indigenous daughter) undulating in the water. He is attacked, mangled, and destroyed and, in the process, he loses the *muiraquitã,* the amulet given to him by Ci, the Mother of the Forest. The quest to find and keep a national identity (represented by the *muiraquitã*) fails in relation to Europe, which overcomes Macunaíma, but not in relation to the Blacks and indigenous people who have been effectively overcome by the (white) cannibals of the novel, including Macunaíma. In order to appreciate the complexity of this relationship to the outside of Brazil and to the inside of Brazil, the implications of Macunaíma's racial transformation must be kept in mind. In the European/American discourse of racialization (rehearsed with despair by the Brazilian elite), Macunaíma is racially mixed, a mulatto (if not Black) according to law and tradition. In the discourse of *embranquecimento,*

Macunaíma has become white, and it is only when he is white that he is a cannibal.

Mário de Andrade dedicates *Macunaíma* to Paulo Prado, a member of a wealthy, traditional São Paulo family who was a financial and intellectual supporter of the modernists. Published in the same year as Mário's *Macunaíma*, Prado's *Retrato do Brasil* is a meditation on the history of what he calls Brazil's characteristic sadness and melancholy, which he (like many historians before him) links to a history of laziness and sensuality resulting from the influences of the climate, the land, and of the indigenous and African women. The expression that Macunaíma utters throughout the novel "Ai que preguiça" links the indigenous name for an animal, *Aig*, whose name in Portuguese is preguiça (laziness)[63] with the attribute, laziness, most characteristic, according to Prado, of the Brazilian.[64] The very title of Prado's work, *Retrato do Brasil* (Portrait of Brazil), as well as its content place this work squarely within the tradition of late nineteenth- and early twentieth-century Brazilian writers who sought to determine Brazil's national character. The writers and statesmen whom I discussed in the introduction were pessimistic about Brazil's ability to form a stable national identity in the face of miscegenation. Like Euclides de Cunha, Prado discusses the impact of miscegenation on the formation of a national type in negative terms:

> O mestiço brasileiro tem fornecido indubitavelmente à communidade exemplares notaveis de intelligencia, de cultura, de valor moral. Por outro lado, as populaçoes offerecem tal fraqueza physica, organismos tao indefesos contra a doença e os vicios, que é uma interrogaçao natural indagar si esse estado de coisas nao provem do intenso cruzamento das raças e sub-raças. . . . No Brasil, si ha mal, elle está feito, irremediavelmente: esperemos, na lentidão do processo cosmico, a decifração do enigma com a serenidade dos experimentadores de laboratório.

> The Brazilian mulatto has undoubtedly furnished notable examples of intelligence, breeding and moral value to the community. On the other hand, this population shows such physical weakness, their organisms completely defenseless against disease and vices, that it is natural to ask if this state of things isn't the result of the intense crossing of races and sub-races. . . . In Brazil, if there is harm in this, it has been done, irremediably. We wait in the slowness of the cosmic process for the uncoding of this enigma with the patience of laboratory researchers.[65]

This association of Brazil with a laboratory will be carried over into *Macunaíma* in the form of a couplet repeated throughout the novel: "Pouca saúde e muita saúva, os males do Brasil são" (Poor health and many ants / These are the ills of Brazil).[66] This couplet brings together the celebrated phrase by the Brazilian doctor, Miguel Pereira: "O Brasil é um vasto hospital" (Brazil is an enormous hospital), and the phrase by the French traveler, August de Saint-Hilaire: "Ou o Brasil acaba com a saúva, ou a saúva acaba com o Brasil" (Either Brazil finishes off the ants or the ants will finish off Brazil).[67] Both phrases make reference to prevailing notions of the ill-health of the body politic[68] and are linked to *Retrato do Brasil* by a popular rhyme cited by Paulo Prado: "São desgraças do Brasil . . . preguiça, / Ferrugem, formiga e mofo" (154) (The misfortunes of Brazil are . . . laziness, rust, ants and mildew). Prado's work provides an important intertext for Mário's novel, especially in relation to questions of race and how race is tied to the health and stability of the body politic, a tie reinforced by the reiterative nature of the refrain.

As I noted before, the miscegenated body is seen to carry the threatening mark of a racial instability, a racial fluidity that can move "forward" in the "proper" direction toward whiteness or "backward" toward blackness. In *Macunaíma* racial instability remains in the realm of the primitive, of the jungle. Is it a coincidence that the races of the three brothers become fixed at the moment that they pass from the jungle to the city? Is an apparently fixed race a requirement for crossing the border into the city and into modernity? Mário de Andrade suggests that modernity itself fixes rather than dispels race.

Uma feita a Sol cobrira os três manos duma escaminha de suor e Macunaíma se lembrou de tomar banho. . . . Entao Macunaíma enxergou numa lapa bem no meio do rio uma cova cheia d'água. E a cova era que nem a marca dum pé gigante. Abicaram. O herói depois de muitos gritos por causa do frio da água entrou na cova e se lavou inteirinho. Mas a água era encantada porque aquele buraco na lapa era marca do pezão do Sumé, do tempo em que andava pregando o evangelho de Jesus pra indiada brasileira. Quando o herói saiu do banho estava branco louro e de olhos azuizinhos, água lavara o pretume dele. E ninguém não seria capaz mais de indicar nele um filho da tribo retinto dos Tapanhumas.

Nem bem Jiguê percebeu o milagre, se atirou na marca do pezão do Sumé. Porém a água já estava muito suja da negrura do herói e por mais que Jiguê esfregasse feito maluco atirando água pra todos os lados só conseguiu ficar da cor do bronze novo. Macunaíma teve dó e consolou: Olhe, mano Jiguê, branco você ficou não, porém pretume foi-se e antes fanhoso que sem nariz.

Maanape então é que foi se lavar, mas Jiquê esborifara toda a água encantada pra fora da cova. Tinha só um bocado lá no fundo e Maanape conseguiu molhar só a palma dos pés e das mãos. Por isso ficou negro bem filho da tribo dos Tapanhu-mas. Só que as palmas das mãos e dos pés dele são vermelhas por terem se limpado na água santa. Macunaíma teve dó e consolou: Não se avexe, mano Maanape, não se avexe não, mais sofreu o nosso tio Judas!

E estava lindíssima na Sol da lapa os três manos um louro um vermelho outro negro. (37–38)

The heat of the Sun had covered the three brothers with a scum of sweat, and Macunaíma was thinking of taking a bath. . . . Just then Macunaíma caught sight of an islet right in the middle of the stream in which there was a hollow the shape of a giant's footprint, full of water. They landed there. The hero, squealing because the water was so cold, washed himself all over. But this water was magic water, for the hollow was St. Thomas's footprint, a relic from the time when he went around preaching and bringing the teachings of Jesus to the Indians of Brazil. When the hero had finished his bath he was white-skinned, blue-eyed and fair-haired; the holy water had washed away all his blackness; there was nothing left to show in any way that he was a son of the black tribe of Tapanhumas. As soon as Jiguê saw this miracle he sprang into St. Thomas' footprint. But by this time the water was very dirty from the hero's ivory blackness, so although Jiguê mopped himself like mad, splashing the water in all directions, he was left the color of freshly minted bronze. Macunaíma was bothered by this and to comfort him said, "Look, brother Jiguê, you didn't become white, but at least the blackness has gone away. Half a loaf is better than no bread!"

Then Manaape went to wash, but Jiguê had splashed all the water out of the pool. There was only a cupful left at the bottom, so that Maanape could wet only the palms of his hands and the soles of his feet. That's why he remained Black like a good son of the Tapanhuma tribe with only the palms of his hands and the soles of his feet pink after their washing in holy water. This grieved Macunaíma, who consoled him by saying, "Don't be vexed, brother Manaape, don't let it get you down! Worse things happen at sea!" The three brothers made a superb picture standing erect and naked on the rock in the sun; one fair, one red-skinned, one black. (31–32)

In his collection of Taulipang legends, Koch-Grünberg recounts how Maku-naíma created human beings but makes no allusion to race. Boddam-Whetham writing in 1879, however, records, in his ethnographic collection from the same region, the following origin of races myth:

The Caribs in their account of creation say that the Great Spirit sat on a mora tree, and picking off pieces of the bark threw them in a stream and they became different animals. Then the Great Spirit—Makanaima [sic]—made a large mold and out of this fresh clean clay, the white man stepped. After it got a little dirty the

Indian was formed, and the Spirit being called away on business for a long period the mold became black and unclean, and out of it walked the negro.[69]

J. R. Swanton also records a story that follows the same pattern (white, Indian, black). He records, however, a variant where the hierarchy is Indian, white, black.[70] All of the indigenous tales begin with white people who are transformed into people of other races. In Mário's version, however, all the brothers are black before the bath. This account is consistent with the Brazilian elites' attitudes toward race and *embranquecimento*.

When we recall Celia Maria Marinho de Azevedo's observation that with the advent of urban industrialization Blacks (seen as incapable of dealing with technology) disappeared from the economic stage, it is notable that Macunaíma turns white before entering the city of São Paulo, where he participates in the technologically advanced civilization. In the city, Macunaíma's enemy is the giant cannibal Piamã, an Italian immigrant. During the period in which *Macunaíma* was written, the Brazilian government had a policy of encouraging immigration from European countries in order to speed up the process of *embranquecimento*. In 1921, the statesmen Fidelis Reis and Cincinato Braga drafted legislation to halt the immigration of non-whites in order to protect the ethnic (read racial) formation of a nation which had already suffered from the introduction of Blacks. This project had the support of the National Academy of Medicine.[71] Significantly, the novel's temporal present of São Paulo does not include the black people who lived there. As we will see in chapters 3 and 4, the 1920s and 1930s saw a marked increase in the number of black political, cultural, and social organizations. Despite social and economic pressures, organizations grew and expanded during this period. In the novel, however, the past is the time of Blacks and indigenous people, the past not of slavery, but of a "primitive" precolonial past. The separation between the two times is marked spatially by the fact that Macunaíma's entourage of animals accompanies him only to the edge of the forest, leaving him (newly white) to enter the city accompanied by his brothers to serve as his helpers.

Mário de Andrade stated in an unpublished preface to *Macunaíma* that he wished to "conceber literariamente o Brasil como entidade homogênea" (conceive Brazil literarily as a homogeneous entity).[72] This homogeneity would be the equivalent of establishing one single national ethnic type.[73] The novel fails miserably in this regard—perhaps a reflection of Mário's ambivalence toward this goal. One is tempted to see the author's unwillingness to publish any of the several prefaces as symptomatic of this ambivalence. The novel does not succeed in maintaining a focus on the interior of an ingesting body; it overflows with the remainders of incorporation.

In the first phase of Brazilian modernism, the idea of a rupture with the past was tied to a vision of the future national cohesion. As Marilene Chauí explains in the following quotation, the seeds for an authoritarian movement that would mark the end of modernism had been sown much earlier.

> In general terms, from 1920 until 1937 [the date of the establishment of the authoritarian, highly centralized, corporate *Estado Novo* government] intellectuals were concerned with two major problems which constitute elements for their nationalism: Brazilians' lack of knowledge of Brazilian reality and the need to free themselves from imported political, theoretical and cultural models. On both the left and the right, intellectuals assign themselves the task of creating or awakening a national consciousness, of demonstrating the disjunction between institutions and reality, of producing a scientific and rational policy, and of undertaking a social and political and cultural *revolution*. The theme of revolution is constant, but its meaning, obviously, is not always the same, depending on the way the "Brazilian crisis" is diagnosed, the way "national salvation" is conceived, and the agents designated to undertake the task. At any rate, one thing is common to all: the presupposition that the understanding and the overcoming of the crisis, and the revolution itself, depend exclusively on an intellectual elite or a political vanguard. The progressives speak of the need to "civilize Brazil," conservatives of the need to reestablish traditions, order, and the discipline that liberal modernity had destroyed. Both cases, however, have one point in common: both "civilization" and tradition demand an organic conception of society and politics, an organicity that depends on the re-creation of the Nation and the installation of a centralized state, even at the expense of having an authoritarian government.[74]

The revolution, however conceived, promised a utopian future. The vision of the future in *Macunaíma* is, however, decidedly dystopic.

After recounting his story to the parrot in a language that, after him, will have no more human speakers, Macunaíma finds himself wounded and alone. To take her revenge on Macunaíma for refusing to marry one of her daughters, Vei, the Sun, forces him to jump in a lake by burning him with her heat. When he returns to shore, he is bloody and missing his nose, ears, testicles, a leg and the *muiraquitã*. He gathers up his body parts and sews them back on, and deciding that he cannot live in this world without the *muiraquitã*, he climbs to the sky where, transformed, he will sparkle "uselessly" in the sky as Ursa Major, the Great Bear. On his journey between earth and sky, he suffers further rejections. Those whom he meets and asks for shelter turn him away because they remember the occasion of their last meeting, when Macunaíma had been covered with excrement as a punishment for one of his adventures. In fact, the novel revels in excrement. In addition to the scatological story of Puíto, the novel describes how the first fire came from the anus of an old woman. Macunaíma urinates and is urinated on. The characters vomit and defecate. Black ants, distinct from the biting red *saúva* of the couplet, appear regularly and seemingly without reason, whenever and wherever there is waste. Mário de Andrade's novel overflows with prominent attention to the remainders of incorporation unacknowledged in other practices of literary anthropophagism during the modernist period. His work implicitly undermines any attempt to apprehend Brazil as a peaceful whole.

Excremental Medicine

Mário de Andrade's fascination with excrement did not exhaust itself with *Macunaíma*. In 1937, he published *Namoros com a medicina* (Flirtations with Medicine), the result of decades of research. This slim volume contains two essays. The first essay addresses the therapeutic effects of music and was published in a medical journal to which Mário de Andrade was a regular contributor. Mário laughingly assures the reader that the second essay, "A medicina dos excretos" (Excremental Medicine), has never appeared anywhere. The essay brings together material that the author had recorded on note cards over his career and saved in the extensive files for which he was notorious. The essay catalogues cures from Brazil as well as other areas of the world that make use of excrement for their effect. Much of the scatological material that finds its way into *Macunaíma*, including the Puíto story that I analyzed above, is found here in greater detail. The essay also introduces a way of reading what could be called the excremental logic of the poem "Improviso do mal da América," which I discussed earlier in this chapter.

At several points in "A medicina dos excretos," Mário refers to the practice of using cow dung to purify sugar: "Com o excremento o açúcar *se purifica* e aperfeiçoa. *O açúcar se limpa.* O excremento adquire assim um conceito de elemento lustral, purificador" (The sugar is purified and perfected with the excrement. *The sugar becomes clean.* Excrement, in this way becomes known as a clarifying, purifying element).[75] A few pages later Mário returns to the topic:

> Aludindo ao costume de refinarem o açúcar com bosta de vaca, lembrei que muito provàvelmente êsse poder purificador do excremento teria contribuido, por associação de imagens, para a persistência de uso de excretos, na cura das moléstias que de alguma forma se manifestam na pele. Com efeito são bem numerosos os exemplos que posso produzir, provando que os excretos são sistemàticamente empregados em variadissimos casos de alteração epidérmica. (74)

> Thinking back to the practice of refining sugar with cow dung, I realized that very probably excrement's purifying power could have contributed, through an association of images, to the persistent use of excretions in the treatment of problems that manifest themselves on the skin. In fact many are the examples that I can give proving that excretions are systematically used in all kinds of cases of alterations to the skin.

These treatments include the use of urine to "'branquear a tez' (que é exatamente o caso da refinação da açúcar) ("whiten the face" [which is exactly the case with the refinement of sugar]); the use of feces to lighten the skin; the application of dung to diminish the hips of black women (82). This purifying action of excrement, its power to whiten, derives from the complex relation to the outside and inside. Mário concludes his essay by observing that excrement is associated with what is sacrificed in order to obtain health. In "Improviso do mal da América," the red and the black ("I can feel neither black nor red! . . . / I feel white, only white, in my life riddled with races"), colors popularly used to designate racial groups, are sacrificed and mourned. In a fashion similar to the census campaign that I analyzed in the introduction, this poem (and *Macunaíma* in its failure to find a place in this world for its black and indigenous characters) suggests that representation within an ideal of racial democracy requires a choice that would remainder blackness[76] as a viable marker of a social and political position, resulting (on the level of representation) in the impossibility of being at one and the same time, black and Brazilian. Mário's refusal to embrace the illusion of a peaceful whole without remainders is also a refusal to embrace the logic that would see the remainder as abject, as that which has been rejected and a source of shame. His work models a more complex view of the remainder that would see it as the result of resistance.

TWO

Bringing in the Dead

Nostalgia and the Refusal of Loss in Gilberto Freyre's
Casa Grande e Senzala

*A ama negra fez muitas vezes com as palavras o mesmo que com a comida:
machucou-as, tirou-lhes as espinhas, os ossos, as durezas, só deixando para
a boca do menino branco as sílabas moles.*

*The Negro nurse did very often with words what she did with food: she
mashed them, removed the bones, took away their hardness, and left them
as soft and pleasing syllables in the mouth of the white child.*

—Gilberto Freyre, *Casa Grande e Senzala*

"Colour Line Land": Brazilian Modernism and the United States

IN THE EARLY 1940s, Carleton Sprague Smith, the archivist for the music
section of New York Public Library, visited Brazil. His stay coincided with
a public-relations initiative on the part of a group of Brazilian intellectuals and business leaders and the U.S. government—represented by Nelson
Rockefeller, then coordinator of Interamerican Affairs—to counter Nazi
Germany's influence on Brazil's *Estado Novo* government during the Second World War. The group promoted its goals through a series of lectures,
titled, "Lessons from an American Way of Life," on literature, film, education, agriculture, medicine, and business delivered by well-known Brazilian
public figures. Mário de Andrade delivered a successful speech on North
American music, in which he argued for the recognition of the contributions
of African Americans to the national aesthetic and a new conception of art.
While Mário had found it strategic to avoid a critique of segregation in a talk
calculated to make of the United States a model of democracy—in contrast
to Brazil's authoritarian *Estado Novo* government—he was well aware of
the contradictions in the "American way of life." In fact, soon after he gave
the speech, he asked his friend Paulo Duarte, the exiled anthropologist then
living in New York, to circulate a copy among his "Yankee friends" just to

"tick them off." Duarte replied that Mário's speech probably wouldn't make much of an impression. He believed that the current North American fascination with all things Brazilian was not sincere but a cover for the desire for Brazilian resources.[1]

For all of its silence on the topic of segregation, the speech can be seen as a response to a disagreement that Mário had had with the visiting Sprague Smith. According to Mário, who insisted on referring to the United States as "Colour Line Land" in his report of the event, the library official had tried to convince Mário that "em Colour Line Land existe liberdade e o exercício verdadeiro de democracia" (liberty and the true expression of democracy exist in Color Line Land). Mário rejected this assertion by reminding Sprague Smith of the case of the Scottsboro boys, a case in which nine young black men were unjustly convicted of raping two white women, which had received extensive coverage in the Brazilian black press. So marked was Mário de Andrade by the visitor's assertions that in 1944 he published the poem "Cançao de Dixie" (Dixieland Song) in which he declared:

Mas por que tanto esquivança!
Lá tem boa vizinhança,
Com prisões de ouro maciço
Lá te darão bem bom lanche
E também muito bom linche,
Mas se você não e negro,
O que você tem com isso!

No, I'll never be
In Colour Line Land

É a terra maravilhosa
Chamada pelo Amigo Urso,
Lá ninguem não cobra entrada
Se a pessoa é convidada
Depois lhe dão com discurso,
Abraço tão apertado
Que você morre asfixiado,
Feliz de ser estimado.

No, I'll never be
In Colour Line Land.

But why such contempt!
[When] over there you'll find nice neighborhoods,
With prisons made of solid gold.

[When] over there, they'll give you such yummy snacks
Then treat you to a really good lynching.
But if you are not a Negro
What's that got to do with you!

No, I'll never be
In Colour Line Land

It's the land of enchantment
So says a two-faced friend
Over there no one'll charge admission
As long as you've been invited
In that case, they'll hit you with a speech,
[and] a hug so tight
That you'll die suffocated,
Happy to be so loved.

No, I'll never be
In Colour Line Land[2]

Since the 1920s, Mário de Andrade had repeatedly declined invitations
to visit "Colour Line Land." Regardless of his ambivalence about publicly
addressing his racial background, he was capable of viewing himself through
the eyes of another, through the eyes of the United States, and of recognizing and taking seriously the implications of this view for himself and, as I
noted in the last chapter, for others like him who, in the United States, suffer
discrimination and violence because of their color. For Mário de Andrade's
fellow Brazilian, the sociologist Gilberto Freyre, however, the experience
of seeing himself through the eyes of the United States would produce an
unanticipated anxiety that would run through his most famous work. The
disgust and shame at seeing what, in the United States, passed for the representative Brazilian motivated him formally to study questions of race.[3]
This desire to rehabilitate the image of the representative Brazilian in the
eyes of those looking at Brazil from the outside would mark Freyre's work
on Brazilian history in the form of an implied and extended comparison of
Brazilian slavery and its legacy to that of the United States. Gilberto Freyre
published *Casa Grande e Senzala* (*The Masters and the Slaves*), which has
had thirty-four editions in Portuguese, as well as numerous editions in more
than twelve languages, in 1933, five years after Mário de Andrade had published *Macunaíma*.[4]

In the late 1980s the Brazilian filmmaker, Joaquim Pedro de Andrade,
who had directed the film version of Mário de Andrade's *Macunaíma*,

accepted a commission to film Gilberto Freyre's *Casa Grande e Senzala*. An eclectic and idiosyncratic sociological study of Brazil's history, Freyre's work was not an obvious choice for a feature film. Joaquim Pedro de Andrade's untimely death prevented the completion of the film. His screenplay of *Casa Grande e Senzala,*[5] however, reflects a reading that destabilizes Freyre's prioritization of the master/slave hierarchy (from the master's point of view) represented by the architectural organization of the plantation's Big House and slave quarters. In an interview appended to the published screenplay, Andrade says that he changed the title to *Casa Grande e cia* (Casa Grande and Company) to convey the inclusion of the perspectives of women, Blacks, and indigenous people. The finale of the proposed film, "was to consist in a polyphonic series of rival celebrations — the *quilombolas*[6] would celebrate the founding of a maroon community, the Portuguese would celebrate their victories over the Indians, and so forth, while the final intertitle was to link indigenous resistance (in the form of cannibalism) to the Africanized spirituality of the *orixás* (spirits) . . ."[7]

Joaquim Pedro de Andrade's plan for the film of *Casa Grande e Senzala* corresponds to my linking of Mário de Andrade's and Gilberto Freyre's work and to my analysis of the structures of incorporation shared by Mário's elaboration of anthropophagism and Freyre's elaboration of miscegenation as a route to racial democracy. As I pointed out in the previous chapter, Mário de Andrade's parodic appropriation of the fantasy of a cannibalistic indigenous population to recast Brazil's past and present required formal innovations. Gilberto Freyre similarly found that the conventions of academic sociological writing were inadequate for the story he wanted to tell. Freyre claims that *Casa Grande e Senzala* sought to analyze and interpret relations between the European and what he calls "two primitive cultures" in tropical Brazil. For a model of his attempt to express through writing an integration that would resolve contradictions, he looked to Pablo Picasso, who, he argues, had achieved this in his art — an art that unified ("primitive") anthropological material with European aesthetic theory and methods (xxi). Like the modernists, Freyre saw his work as marking a break with the past, especially with past interpretations of the role of Blacks and indigenous people in Brazilian society. He especially sought to redeem Blacks and mulattoes and to express optimism for Brazil's future. His theories and interpretations, however, undermine this claim to rupture with the past in that they retain many of the ideas of his nineteenth-century predecessors. Despite his assertions to the contrary, Freyre neither describes nor prescribes a union or mixture of "contradictory elements," or of different races equally apprehended. In *Casa Grande e Senzala*, he resolves differences by sublimating what he calls "primitive cultures," through a process of assimilation, into a Brazilian national identity. Racial democracy—an influential yet contested idea associated with the work of Gilberto Freyre—strives to foreclose racism through the promotion of racial mixture, a mixture that would result from the incorporation of black and indigenous people into the white race.

Foreign Bodies, Foreign Lands

Casa Grande e Senzala was based on the thesis that Freyre had written while a graduate student at Columbia University during the 1920s. In order to address what he considered the most pressing problems of his day, Freyre produced a work that was both a diagnosis of and a prescription for the treatment of Brazil's "ills." According to Freyre, the most important "problem" facing Brazil was miscegenation. In the introduction he states that:

> Era como se tudo dependesse de mim e dos de minha geração; da nossa maneira de resolver questões seculares. E dos problemas brasileiros, nenhum que me inquietasse tanto como o da miscigenação.[8]

> It was as if everything was dependent upon me and those of my generation, upon the manner in which we succeeded in solving age old questions. And of all the problems confronting Brazil, there was none that gave me so much anxiety as that of miscegenation.[9]

He continues:

> Vi uma vez, depois de mais de três anos maciços de ausência do Brasil, um bando de marinheiros nacionais—mulatos e cafuzos—descendo não me lembro se de *São Paulo* ou do *Minas* pela neve mole de Brooklyn. Deram-me a impressão de caricaturas de homens. E veio-me à lembrança a frase de um livro de viajante americano que acabara de ler sobre o Brasil: "The fearfully mongrel aspect of most of the population." A miscigenação resultava naquilo. Faltou-me quem me dissesse então, como em 1929 Roquette-Pinto aos arianistas do Congresso Brasileiro de Eugenia, que não eram simplesmente mulatos ou cafuzos os indivíduos que eu julgava representarem o Brasil, mas cafuzos e mulatos *doentes*. (lvii)

> Once upon a time, after three straight years of absence from my country, I caught sight of a group of Brazilian seamen—mulattoes and *cafuzos*—crossing the

Brooklyn Bridge. I no longer remember whether they were from São Paulo or from Minas, but they impressed me as being caricatures of men, and there came to mind a phrase from a book on Brazil by an American traveler: "The fearful mongrel aspect of the population." That was the sort of thing to which miscegenation led. I ought to have had someone to tell me then what Roquette Pinto had told the Aryanizers of the Brazilian Eugenics Congress in 1929: that these individuals whom I looked upon as representative of Brazil were not simply mulattoes or *cafusos* but *sickly* ones. (xxvii)

Freyre's language of pathology in this passage is firmly in line with turn-of-the-century discussions that biologized the terms of social, economic, and political crisis that followed in the wake of the abolition of slavery in 1888 and the establishment of the Republic in 1889. According to Jurandir Freire Costa, the white elite and those who identified with it believed that the crises were not precipitated by historical or political factors but by the tropical environment of the country and the physical and racial constitution of its people. Their view was that the Brazilian state was not able to promote the harmonious development of the nation because heat and mixture with "inferior races" had rendered the population lazy, undisciplined, and unintelligent. The nonwhite population was seen as biologically inferior and, therefore, incapable of adapting to democratic society. They were deemed responsible for the social upheaval that undermined the smooth functioning of the regime. While nothing could be done about the climate, the racial "problem" could still be resolved. Costa maintains that turn-of-the-century Brazilian intellectuals deemed it impossible that democracy could be instituted in Brazil the way it had been in the United States and in Europe because of Brazil's racial particularities. The republican order could not and would not, even under the guise of respecting the democratic social contract, accept the presence of Blacks and mulattoes in a society of free men. Consequently, if the republic wanted to save democracy, the first step would be to manage the "health" of people of color, until, through miscegenation, they would be made worthy of integration into society.

En síntese, o raciocínio destes intellectuais resumia-se em um postulado: enquanto o brasileiro não fosse branco, não teria direito à democracia. Este advertência, entre outras consqüências, deveria induzir os negros e mestiços a procurarem embranquecer a pele e aos brancos, pobres e ricos, a execer a opresão sob o pretexto de defender a democracia.

Finally, the reasoning of these intellectuals could be summed up in the following postulate: until the Brazilian is white, he will not have any right to democracy. This warning had, among other consequences, the effect of inducing blacks to try to whiten their skins and whites, both poor and rich, to oppress [them] under the guise of defending democracy.[10]

According to Lévi-Strauss, societies are organized according to two models. One type of societal organization shares a structure with cannibalism. These societies "regard the absorption of certain individuals possessing dangerous powers as the only means of neutralizing those powers and even of turning them to advantage." These societies, in other words, are formed according to a model of incorporation. The second type of societal organization shares a structure with anthropemy, a word that is linked etymologically to the Greek *émein* — to vomit. This type of society ejects dangerous individuals from the social body and/or separates them through temporary or permanent exile or incarceration, reinforced by the existence of a police force and jails.[11]

Although Lévi-Strauss sets up these two societies in opposition to each other, both structurally and temporally (anthropophagist societies are associated with primitive social formations and anthropemic societies with more advanced societies) they are not as opposed as he makes them appear. The two formations share a vision of a society whose integrity and unity must be performed and protected at all costs. "Unity is always effected by means of brutality."[12] This brutality can take the form of repression (understood in all its senses, including forgetting) or of exclusion as presented in Lévi-Strauss's description of the anthropemic society. The logic of incorporation underlying the anthropophagist society, however, is that there must be an excremental remainder. This remainder could be thought of as that which the body rejects as inassimilable. It differs from *émein* (vomit) in that it is not rejected whole, but broken down in order to remove what is useful. Another way to understand the remainder is to see it as a resistance, as that which refuses to be incorporated. The remainder is no longer what it was, but it resists assimilation into the body on the body's terms. It is this resistance that the social body represses since it recalls not only the porous nature of the body (that things can come in and out without the body's control), but is also a reminder of the body's ultimate failure as a totalizing structure.

Participation in the elites' definition of democracy and notions of citizenship[13] certainly was not the only option for Blacks who insisted on their civil rights as Brazilians, although myths of racial democracy obscure this fact. The discourse of racial democracy disavowed those that it produced as "black," even as these Blacks claimed for themselves, precisely in the name of democracy, a position as a resistant remainder. The 1904 Revolt of the Vaccine provides an example of this. It was one of the first tests of the democracy that was established with the republic in 1889. In the interest of making the capital city, Rio de Janeiro, equal to the cities of Europe, the government of President Rodrigo Alves, advised by the minister of the interior, social Darwinist Joaquim Murtinho, began, in 1903, a public works project funded through foreign loans. The director of the Department of Public Health, Oswaldo Cruz, set about the construction of wide boulevards modeled after those of Paris by contracting 1,800 workers to tear down the homes of the poor Blacks and mulattoes who occupied the center of the city. In addition, Cruz used this opportunity to put into place a sanitation project with the goal of wiping out yellow fever and bubonic plague. His method made use of 2,500 sanitation workers who, accompanied by the police, would enter homes, clean them, isolate and quarantine those who were ill, and condemn or destroy homes as they deemed necessary. This state of affairs provided the backdrop for the institution of a mandatory vaccine. An immediate outcry followed on the part of residents who saw this law as an unconstitutional assault on their civil right to privacy. They took to the streets and met government troops gathered from around the nation. Rio's chief of police insisted that the rebellion was the work "das fezes sociais" (the dregs of society; literally, the social feces) made up of petty thieves, criminals, Blacks and mulattoes who were merely observed by the honest working class that, he claimed, remained on the margin of the activity. Yet the ranks of the rebels clearly included a large, racially diverse group of unionists and artisans protesting the invasion of their private lives by the state. For the many Blacks, however, who participated in and led the revolt, there was an additional aspect to the rebellion that related to their specificity as black citizens. For one of the black participants interviewed by a journalist whom he insisted on addressing colloquially as "cidadão" (citizen), the protest against the government program for vaccination was secondary to the need "mostrar ao governo que ele não põe o pé no pescoço do povo" (to show the government that it cannot walk all over the people).

The revolt was justified in that "não andarem dizendo que o povo é carneiro. De vez em quando é bom a negrada mostrar que sabe morrer como homem!" (they no longer can say that we are sheep. Every once in a while it's good for black folk to show that we know how to die like men!).[14]

This declaration challenges attempts to write organized black resistance out of the social contract, a resistance that led establishment figures to complain that Blacks no longer knew their place. A journalist from the 1930s, responding to increasing black activism during that period, complained that Blacks:

> ... perderam hoje todo o senso de hierarquia. . . . Uma coisa é perfeitamente nítida: o Brasil quer ser um país branco. É o branco que vai absorver o negro e não o negro que, no futuro, vai prevalecer sobre o branco. Ora, o lirismo sociológico, de Gilberto Freyre, aliado à perda de toda disciplina, permitiu a confusão que hoje se nota e que levou o negro à conviccão de que o brasileiro legítimo é ele.[15]

> ... today have lost all respect for hierarchy. . . . One thing is perfectly clear: Brazil wants to be a white nation. It is the white who will absorb the black and not the black who, in the future, will prevail over the white. So, Gilberto Freyre's sociological lyricism, in combination with a total loss of discipline, has given rise to the confusion that we note these days and which has led the black to think that he is the legitimate Brazilian.

Freyre's work, however, both prompted and ultimately resolved the concerns articulated by this journalist. From Freyre's perspective, the body politic has a sickness that it must rid itself of. The "problem" with miscegenation is not miscegenation in and of itself, but miscegenation as the perpetuation of a sickness. In this assessment, Blacks maintain the status of a contagious foreign body, described much as a *pharmakon*. A healthy body is one that overcomes the weakening effects of an offending organism and retains its good qualities.

> Considerados esse pontos, que nos parecem de importância fundamental para o estudo da influência africana sobre a cultura, o caráter e a eugenia do brasileiro, sentimo-nos agora mais à vontade para o esforço de procurar surpreender aspectos mais íntimos dessa influência e desse contágio. (314)

> Having considered these points [the ethnic groups to which Africans belong, physical characteristics, relative intelligence, etc.], which appear to me to be of basic importance in studying the African influence on Brazilian culture, character and eugenics, I now feel more inclined to undertake the task of discovering the more intimate aspects of this contagious influence. (321)

Faced with miscegenation as a threat to the superiority of whites, Freyre transforms miscegenation into a narrative of assimilation — a narrative that has a homological similarity to cannibalism. Miscegenation as a process, however, introduces an element of instability into the process of reproducing the ideal Brazilian as Brazilian. For Euclides da Cunha, these are the risks involved in miscegenation. Early in *Os Sertões* (1902), a work that chronicles an epic battle between government troops and followers of a charismatic leader in the interior of the northeast of Brazil, da Cunha inserts a chapter titled "Um parêntesis irritante" (An irritating parenthesis). The mixture of races is harmful, he claims, because the resulting individual existence, brief as it is, undermines centuries of natural selection and consolidation of a race. Mestizos and mulattoes are by nature unstable, incapable of reproducing themselves as they are but only as approximations of one or the other of the component races. In da Cunha's conception, Brazil cannot claim a unity of race and, therefore, violates what he calls natural laws — instead of the nation originating from a race (as in the guiding myths of Europe) the nation must be constructed in order to form the race.[16] This being the case, da Cunha worries that one could never be certain that the Brazilian race would move in the right direction. Since hereditary theory provides the

> mecanismo contraditório que reproduz o idêntico e ao mesmo tempo produz diferenças. A degeneração aparece como peturbação na reprodução, que pode se restringir à esfera do individuo, ou se estender a um grupo étnico ou social, como uma verdadeira patologia[17]

> contradictory mechanism which reproduces the identical at the same time that it produces differences. Degeneration appears as a truly pathological disturbance within reproduction, which might be limited to the sphere of the individual, or expanded to include an entire ethnic or social group.

In order to make his argument for miscegenation, Freyre had: 1) to show that miscegenation was a eugenic activity, making of the European with a negligible amount of black "blood" the ideal man for the tropics and establishing that this blood could act as an inoculation rather than a poison; 2) to remove any agency on the part of Africans and their descendents, making them willing participants in the process of *embranquecimento,* thereby ensuring that the process would continue in the right direction; and 3) to demonstrate that miscegenation would be a process rather than an end in and of itself. This process would take place within the architecture of the Big House and slave quarters, an architecture that increases the force of the "blood-stream," which would leave "identical traces generation after generation."[18]

> Esta força, na formação brasileira, agiu do alto das casas-grandes, que foram centros de coesão patriarchal e religiosa; os pontos de apoio para a organização nacional. (lxiii)

> This force [which binds those who live in close proximity to one another] in the formation of Brazilian life was exerted from above downward, emanating from the Big Houses that were the center of the patriarchal and religious cohesion, the point of support for the organized society of the nation. (xxxiii)

The architecture of the Big House and the slave quarters stands in for Brazil. That the "support for the organized structure of the nation" is threatened by miscegenation is made clear by the manner in which Freyre renders this threat to Brazil in an anecdote concerning a slave owner who, inspired by a legend, literally mixes the blood of enslaved Africans into the foundations of the Big House in order to ensure the continuity of his domain.

> [The] houses were the expressions of enormous feudal might. "Ugly and Strong." Thick walls. Deep foundations, anointed with whale oil. There is a legend in the Northeast to the effect that a certain plantation owner, more anxious than usual to assure the perpetuity of his dwelling, was not content until he had had a couple of slaves killed and buried beneath the foundation stones. The sweat and at times the blood of Negroes was the oil, rather than that of the whale, that helped give the Big House foundations their fortress-like consistency.

> The ironical part of it is, however, that owing to a failure of the human potential all this arrogant solidity of form and material was very frequently wasted, and in the third or fourth generation enormous houses built to last for centuries would crumble, . . . the great-grandsons and even the grandsons being unable to preserve the ancestral heritage. (xxxv)

If the architecture of the plantation stands in for Brazil, this anecdote serves as an allegory for the degeneration associated with miscegenation. Freyre takes upon himself the task of diagnosing this decay — and correcting it — by reinterpreting miscegenation as a path to preserving the health of the nation: "Tornou-se, assim, o africano um decidido agente patogênico no seio da sociedade brasileira. . . . O negro foi patogênico, mas a serviço do branco; como parte irresponsável de um sistema articulado por outros" (321) (Thus it was that the African became, decidedly, a pathogenic agent in the bosom [literally *breast*] of Brazilian society. . . . The negro *was* pathogenic, but by way of serving the whites as the irresponsible part of a system that had been put together by whites)(330).

Freyre claims that he makes a distinction between *race* and *culture* in a manner consistent with the teachings of Franz Boas with whom he had studied and who had influenced Freyre's thinking on miscegenation. Boas insisted upon distinguishing between factors that are biologically or racially determined and those that are socially or culturally determined. This distinction was significant because it allowed Boas to maintain that environmental factors rather than biological determinism led to the "degeneration" of Blacks that was so much discussed by social scientists of this period. Freyre's practice contradicts this effort. Whether for racial or environmental factors, Blacks, in Freyre's neo-Lamarckian schema, are still permanently inferior to whites. His interpretation of Brazilian national identity depends on a belief in the opposition between civilization and primitivism: "One is justified in associating anthropology with history, folklore with literature, when one has to deal, as in the case of Brazil, with a human development in which "rational" and "irrational," "civilized" and "primitive" elements have mingled intimately, all contributing to the process of adaptation to life in a tropical and quasi-tropical area of a new type of society and a new harmony among otherwise antagonistic men — white and black, European and brown, civilized and primitive (xxii).[19] Moreover, this opposition is based on a strict hierarchy. Recalling the Great Chain of Being, Freyre cites Adolph d'Assier's observation that on Brazilian plantations, monkeys received their blessing from the slave boys, who were blessed by the aged Blacks, who, in turn, were blessed by their white masters (lxxiii, Portuguese; xlii, English).

Freyre's narrative of assimilation depended upon heterosexual reproduction, leading to his emphasis throughout *Casa Grande e Senzala* on sex and sexuality. In his description of the characteristics that distinguished Portugal as a colonizer from England and France, Freyre draws attention to Portugal's geographic location and history of sustained invasions. Unlike the French and English who, according to Freyre, insisted on separating themselves in the colonies, Portugal, throughout its history, had incorporated its invaders. Because Portugal had no geographical barrier to provide a defense against the Goths, Celts, Arabs, Spanish, Jews, and others who penetrated its territory, the Portuguese availed themselves of a "wall of flesh" (195) that "digested" (201) all aggressors. Freyre demonstrates some ambivalence in resorting to this explanation of the Portuguese colonizers' predisposition to miscegenation in his identification of the precariousness and instability of Portugal's situation:

> A singular predisposição do português para a colonização híbrida e escravocrata dos trópicos, explica-a em grande parte o seu passado étnico, ou antes, cultural, de povo indefinido entre Europa e a África. Nem intransigentemente de uma nem de outra, mas das duas. (5)

> The singular predisposition of the Portuguese to the hybrid, slave-exploiting colonization of the tropics is to be explained in large part by the ethnic or, better, the cultural past of a people existing indeterminately between Europe and Africa and belonging uncompromisingly to neither one or the other of the two continents. (7)

In addition, he associates this unstable geographical situation with bisexuality: "Espécie de bicontinentalidade que correspondesse na população assim vaga e incerta à bissexualidade no indivíduo" (6) ("this species of bi-continentalism that, in a population so vague and ill-defined, corresponds to bisexuality in the individual") (7). This dangerous vagueness, in Freyre's view, can be turned to advantage when it characterizes the flexibility of the Portuguese, who, unlike the Spanish, for example, do not fear mixture and recognize its capacity for creating unities. The centralized, patriarchal order of the Big House and slave quarters—like a strong, centralized oligarchic state—would ensure that the mixture (and *embranquecimento*) could proceed in the correct order and that the Portuguese and their descendants would be the cannibalizers rather than the cannibalized.

The process of *embranquecimento* depends on reproduction by a heterosexual couple, specifically a white man and a (progressively lighter) Black or Indigenous woman.

> A índia e a negra-mina a princípio, depois a mulata, a cabrocha, quadrona, a oitava, tornando-se caseiras, concubinas, e até esposas legítimas dos senhores brancos, agiram poderosamente no sentido de democratização social no Brasil. (lx)

> The Indian woman and the "*mina*," or the negro woman, in the beginning, and later the mulatto, the cabrocha, the quadroon, and the octoroon, becoming domestics, concubines, and even the lawful wives of their white masters exerted a powerful influence for social democracy in Brazil. (xxx)

The women are described in a movement toward whiteness. As the women become apparently whiter, they achieve greater social status: first as servants, then as mistresses and finally as wives to the white men.[20] Miscegenation aided the Portuguese by turning them into "o tipo ideal do homem ideal para os trópicos, europeu com sangue negro ou índio a avivar-lhe a energia" (47) (the ideal type of [ideal] man for the tropics, a European with Negro or Indian blood to revive his energy) (71). Miscegenation could thus be turned into a positive force and a eugenic activity.

Freyre asserts that in the territory that would become Brazil the first contact was—literally and metaphorically—between Portuguese men and Indian women who were both "highly sexed," (94) a description he also uses for black women. According to Freyre, this feminine characteristic, in addition to their greater strength and stability relative to the men, made these women the allies of the Portuguese colonizers:

> A toda contribuição que se exigiu dela na formação social do Brasil—a do corpo que foi a primeira a oferecer ao branco, a do trabalho doméstico e mesmo agrícola, a de estabilidade . . . a cunhã correspondeu vantajosamente. (116)

> Whatever the demands that were made of her in connection with the formation of the Brazilian society—that of her body, which she was the first to offer to the white man; that of her domestic and even her agricultural labor; that of stability . . . whatever the demands, the *cunhã* [indigenous woman] gave an excellent account of herself. (118)

Freyre compares the women favorably with the men, who are seen as without utility in the formation of Brazil. In his description of black and indigenous men, Freyre goes to great length to prove their disinterest in women and their inability to be productive as fathers or, in the case of indigenous men, in the extraction of wealth. For Freyre, if men prefer a home life to one of movement and warfare, they must be weak and effeminate, bisexual when they are not homosexual. This presentation of the men has a strategic significance in that it appears to disqualify them as potential fathers:

> Passa por ser defeito da raça, comunicado ao brasileiro, o erotismo, a luxúria, a depravação sexual. Mas o que se tem apurado entre os povos negros da África, como entre os entre os primitivos em geral—já o salientamos em capítulo anterior é maior moderação do apetite sexual que entre os europeus. É uma sexualidade, a dos negros africanos, que para excitar-se necessita de estímulos picantes. Danças afrodisíacas. Culto fálico. Orgias. (315–16)

> Eroticism, lust, sexual depravity have come to be looked upon as a defect in the African race; but what has been found to be the case among primitive peoples in general, as I have pointed out in a previous chapter, is a greater moderation of the

sexual appetite than exists among Europeans. African sexuality is one that stands in need of constant excitation and sharp stimuli. Aphrodisiac dances. A phallic cult. Orgies. (323; see also 335)

By undermining the sexuality of Blacks, Freyre makes clear that reproduction is a project by and for white men. The initiative for sexual activity and sexual activity itself come from white males who will carry out the reproduction of the nation through white women and through the mulatta. Black men are so desexualized in Freyre's work as to be barely capable of engendering children. According to Freyre the reproductive power is augmented in "civilized man" because, like domesticated animals, civilized men have more developed reproductive systems; because his reproductive glands receive the nutrition that might otherwise go to fueling the hunting and working capacity in the primitive man; and because civilized men have the leisure to act on their sexual urges (329). More importantly for Freyre, however, the white masters have bodies that are small relative to the *"membrum virile,"* in contrast to the bodies of the black slaves, which are large with childish sexual organs, reinforcing their positions as "poor reproducers" (429). The father of the nation is thus the white man, the only appropriate sexual partner for both white women and women of color, who, according to the quotation cited above, undergo their own process of *embranquecimento* from *mina* to mulatta to quadroon to octoroon.

Freyre focuses so fixedly on the partnering of black and indigenous women with white men in the formation of Brazil that he barely takes the time to raise and then dismiss a report of sexual activity between black men and white women published in Manoel Bomfim's *América Latina*. Throughout *Casa Grande e Senzala*, Freyre drew indiscriminately from academic sources, observation, anecdote, and gossip to make his argument. The idea that white women could bear miscegenated children is so threatening, however, that he rejects it as preposterous, as so much unfounded and malicious gossip, and criticizes Bomfim for repeating it (353).

Freyre seeks to demonstrate that "a cultura de que se contagiou e enriqueceu a brasileira" (309) ("the culture which contaminated and enriched the Brazilian one") (312) would not be a poison but a cure. He traces over many pages the various ethnic groups from which the Africans were brought by force to Brazil. He shows that these Africans were the most intelligent, the strongest, "the most comely of body," the lightest in skin color with features most approximating the European (295–316), so as to demonstrate that the material in the vaccine was a very mild form of the disease and acted as an inoculation against the illness affecting the body politic: "A formação brasileira foi beneficiada pelo melhor da cultura negra da África, absorvendo elementos por assim dizer de elite que faltaram na mesma proporção no Sul dos Estados Unidos" (299–300) ("Brazilian society in its formative stage benefited from the best that African Negro culture had to offer; it absorbed those elite elements, if one may put it that way, which were lacking in the same proportion in the southern United States") (299). According to Freyre, Brazilian Blacks were so pliant and easily assimilated into "whiteness" that so far as the *caboclos* (a mestizo of Indian and white parents) were concerned, the Blacks were a *Europeanizing* force (311, my emphasis).

The history of resistance on the part of Africans and their descendants — which could be seen as a resistance to a project of *embranquecimento* — is erased in Gilberto Freyre's account of assimilation through miscegenation into a national identity founded on a white body, save for one important instance. In a brief section meant to show that miscegenation was not limited to the coast of the country, Freyre acknowledges that the Blacks who were in the interior of the country during the time of slavery were there because they had escaped from the plantations and set up their communities known as *quilombos*. He cites Roquette Pinto: "'Muitos escravos fugiam para aquilombar nas matas, nas vizinhanças de tribos índias. A fuga das mulheres era mais difícil; de sorte que o rapto das índias foi largamente praticado pelos pretos quilombados'" (45) ("Many slaves fled to the *quilombos* in the forests, in the vicinity of the Indian tribes. Inasmuch as it was difficult for their own women to flee, the rape of Indian women was widely practiced by the Black *quilombolas*") (69, 86). It had been important throughout *Casa Grande e Senzala* to demonstrate that all involved willingly undertook the miscegenation that would lead to the construction of a stable, homogeneous identity for the nation. No mention of rape by the colonizers or slave owners is ever made.[21] In a work in which his strategy is to show the utility and inevitability of his narrative of assimilation, Freyre has removed any agency from black and indigenous men. It is therefore not surprising that an instance of their resistance to slavery should be linked to rape. In the course of *Casa Grande e Senzala*, Gilberto Freyre desexualizes and disempowers black and indigenous peoples in order to make them "safe" for incorporation into the body politic and represses particularly the history of the quilombos.

The most famous quilombo, the República de Palmares, existed in the interior of what is now the state of Alagoas, Brazil. It began with a group of about forty enslaved people from Guinea, who took advantage of the thick forest and fertile soil to begin a community. This community attracted many other men and women who had escaped from plantations. It attracted, in addition, indigenous people and others oppressed by slavery as well as some white women and fugitives from the law. The population soon grew to between 20 and 30 thousand inhabitants and its territory extended over 27,000 kilometers divided into many cities, each specializing in a product or activity (agriculture, textile production, hunting, pottery making). According to a seventeenth-century observer,[22] the main activity of the quilombo was agricultural, but the quilombolas repudiated the plantation system, opting instead for the cultivation of small plots of diversified crops. The excess production was turned over to the government for its maintenance. By 1697, three generations had been born and raised in this system. The government consisted of a king elected by the people and a council made up of chiefs from each city. Diplomatic relations were established in order to sign peace treaties with colonial representatives. According to an article in one of the black newspapers of the 1920s, Zumbi, one of the most important rulers of Palmares, "com o perpassar dos annos será glorificado como o sustentaculo da liberdade de sua raça, e de seus descendentes que somos nós"[23] (with the passage of time, [Zumbi] will be glorified as the champion for the liberty of his race, and of his descendants, who we are). For this writer, Palmares is the home of ancestors and provides a foundational story for Afro-Brazilians. Palmares is also a monument to the desire to be both Black and Brazilian.

Once the quilombo had established itself as a stable entity, Palmares was perceived by the colonial power to be a significant threat to their control of the country. The quilombo had to be destroyed since it posed a threat to "nossa unidade nacional" (our national unity).[24] This was so not only because the quilombo, for these authorities, functioned as a foreign body, but also because it presented a model of national cohesion far more efficient than that of the slavery-based imperial government. "Palmares era uma negação, pelo seu exemplo econômico, politico e social da estrutura escravagista-colonialista. O seu exemplo era um desafio permanente e um incentivo às lutas contra o sistema colonial no seu conjunto" (119) (Palmares, because of its economic, political, and social example, was a negation of the colonial-slavery system. The example [of Palmares] was a permanent provocation and an incentive to battles against the entire colonial system).

Freyre retold the story of Brazil's racial formation as one of cooperative incorporation and through this process, Blacks were turned into a "Europeanizing influence" (285). This served to reinforce the sense of the process of *embranquecimento* as inevitable, coherent, and no longer susceptible to the risks of "backward" movement expressed by Euclides da Cunha, among others. Black and indigenous women were recruited to this process; black and indigenous men were excluded from it (in Freyre's refusal to represent their ability or desire to reproduce). In a section of *Casa Grande e Senzala* in which he has discussed the tendency toward bisexuality and homosexuality in the indigenous male, preparing, in this way, his argument for his substitution by the white male, Freyre describes another cooperative relationship—this one between the *culumim* (young Indian boy) and the missionary priest.

> No Brasil o padre serviu-se principalmente do culumim, para recolher de sua boca o material que formou a língua tupi-guarani—o instrumento mais poderoso de intercomunicação entre a duas culturas: a do invasor e a da raça conquistada. . . . Língua que seria, com toda sua artificialidade, uma das bases mais sólidas da unidade do Brasil. (148)

> In Brazil the missionary priest made use, chiefly, of the Indian lad in gathering from the latter's mouth the material out of which he formed the Tupí-Guaraní tongue, the most potent instrument of intercommunication between the two cultures, that of the invader and that of the conquered race. . . . A tongue which, with all its artificiality was to become one of the most solid bases of Brazilian national unity. (166)

In this homoerotic partnership of "intellectual intercourse" (168), the *culumim,* who is associated by description to black and indigenous women, plays a crucial role in Brazil's formation:

> O culumim tornou-se o cúmplice do invasor na obra de tirar à cultura osso por osso, para melhor assimilação da parte mole aos padrões de moral católica e de vida européia. (147)

> The *culumim,* or Indian lad, becomes the accomplice of the invader in *drawing the bones,* one after another, from the native culture, in order that the soft portion

might be the more readily assimilated to the patterns of Catholic morality and European life. (164, my emphasis)

This role involves preparing indigenous culture, like food for a child (I will return to this image shortly) rendering it suitable for easy incorporation. The *culumim,* significantly, does not eat but prepares what the white priest will ingest.

Throughout *Casa Grande e Senzala,* Freyre has made a case for the racial formation of the Brazilian through the body of the ever-lighter mulatta. In this she is supported by the labor of the darker-skinned women:

> Não só para fins amorosos, como em torno ao recém-nascido, reunirem-se, no Brasil, as duas correntes místicas: a portuguesa, de um lado; a africana ou a ameríndia, do outro. Aquela representada pelo pai ou pelo pai e mãe brancos; esta pela mãe índia ou negra, pela ama-de-leite, pela mãe de criação, pela mãe preta, pela escrava africana. (327)

> It was not merely for amorous purposes, but for those having to do with the new born as well, that the two mystic currents, the Portuguese on the one hand and the African or the Amerindian on the other, were united in Brazil. In the one case the representative is the white father, or [white] father and mother; in the other it is the Indian or Negro mother, the wet nurse, the foster mother, the "black mammy" the African female slave. (337)

The maternal breast (of a white or racially mixed mother) in Gilberto Freyre's history of Brazil is substituted by the breast of the enslaved black woman. The wet nurse nourishes the child, providing him—the child is always male in *Casa Grande e Senzala*—with the nutrition he needs to survive, although, as Freyre is quick to point out, she may also pass on the "germs of diseases and superstitions" that could kill the child (372).

In 1832, Brazil's first college of medicine was established in Salvador de Bahia. Between the late 1860s and 1880s, as discussions of the effects of slavery on the general health and hygiene of the Brazilian (slave-owning) family gained importance, increasing numbers of medical students wrote theses on this subject. Among the topics to receive the most attention was that of breast-feeding. Because scientists believed at that time that physical and emotional experiences resulted in permanent invisible changes to the organism, changes which, in conjunction with "hereditary characteristics" could be transmitted to offspring in childbirth or through breast-feeding, medical doctors warned families that their reliance on the *apparent* good health and beauty of the wet-nurses presented a danger to children.[25] Implicit in this warning is the idea that, in a context of racial miscegenation, appearance and visual evidence, for those who did not know how really to read the body, was radically insufficient.[26] This warning also testifies to the difficulty of reasserting the inside as inside and the outside as outside after an act of incorporation, a difficulty that the discourse of racial democracy minimizes.

For Freyre the risks of taking in unhealthy elements were more than outweighed by the beneficial ones ingested along with the milk: i.e., the kindliness and enriched imagination as well as a predilection for the *mulata* that would serve a eugenic function for the Brazilian nation. Freyre quotes an eighteenth-century French traveler on this point: "Les portugais naturels du Brésil préfèrent la possession d'une femme noire ou mulâtre à la plus belle femme. . . . Pour moi je crois qu'élevés & nourris par ces Esclaves, ils en prennent l'inclination avec le lait" (The Portuguese born in Brazil prefer to have a black or mulatto woman rather than the most beautiful woman. . . . I think that, raised and nursed by the slaves, they take in this inclination with their milk) (445). Interestingly, the word *femme* (woman), without a modifier, describes only white women as women. Because of this predilection for women of color: "O intercurso sexual de brancos dos melhores estoques—inclusive eclesiásticos,[27] sem dúvida nenhuma, dos elementos mais seletos e eugênicos na formação brasileira—com escravas negras e mulatas foi formidável" (442) ("The sexual intercourse of whites of the best stocks—including clergy—is undoubtedly one of the most select and eugenic elements in the formation of Brazilian society") (446).

When the child is no longer breast-fed, he, in Freyre's chronology, learns from the nurse the language of Brazil. This language is wholly appropriate to the new nation of the tropics. Like the "ideal man for the tropics white with a little black or Indian blood to liven him up," the new language is strengthened and enlivened by the incorporation of African words and pronunciation.

Language develops as a result of a good response to the loss of the breast, a response that fills the mouth with words, which, like milk, emanate from the black wet nurse:

A ama negra fez muitas vezes com as palavras o mesmos que com a comida: machucou-as, tirou-lhes as espinhas, os ossos, as durezas, só deixando para a boca do menino branco as sílabas moles. (331)

The negro nurse did very often with words what she did with food: she mashed them, removed the bones, took away their hardness, and left them as soft and pleasing syllables in the mouth of the white child. (343)

Having provided soft food as a substitution for the loss of her breast, she then provides a soft language, appropriate for assimilation. This language of Brazil was often criticized for carrying the marks of its miscegenation.[28] The creation of the new national language is created through the incorporation of the "foreign element," which has been regarded as a threat to the body politic and which repeats the construction of the ideal Brazilian in Freyre's narrative of assimilation:

> No ambiente relasso da escravidão brasileira, as linguas africanas, *sem motivos para se sustituirem à parte, em oposição à dos brancos,* dissolveram-se nela, enriquecendo-a de expressivos modos de dizer, de toda uma série de palavras deliciosas de pitoresco; agrestes e novas no seu sabor; muitas vezes substituindo com vantagem vocábulos portugueses, como que gastos e puídos pelo uso. (333, my emphasis)

> In the relaxed atmosphere of Brazilian slavery the African tongues, *without any motive for continuing a separate existence in opposition to the language of the whites,* became dissolved in the latter, enriching it with expressive modes of speech and a whole set of delightfully picturesque terms that were new and untamed in flavor and that, many times advantageously, replaced Portuguese words that were worn and spoiled with usage. (345, my emphasis)

Freyre's argument for dialogism cannot mask the inherent power relations or its political and social agenda. It is always the Black and indigenous that will dissolve, willingly, into white, and the white that will incorporate them.

Introjection/Incorporation

Freyre's elaboration of the acquisition of language corresponds so closely to Nicholas Abraham and Maria Torok's description of introjection that it is worth pausing to explore the connection.

In *The Shell and the Kernel,*[29] Abraham and Torok note that in a Freudian framework the trauma of loss leads the subject to incorporate the lost object into the ego. This procedure is a way of bringing in the dead in order to buy the time necessary to "readjust the internal economy and to redistribute one's investments" (111). In Freud's schema of managing loss, they argue, the ego, temporarily in the case of mourning or permanently in the case of melancholia, becomes what it cannot give up and denies, by silencing the encrypted object, the very loss of that object. Abraham and Torok call attention to the conflation of the terms *incorporation* and *introjection* in Freud's overall work, a conflation that does not give enough credit to the complexity of the relationship to the lost object. They, however, distinguish between incorporation as a bad/pathological response to the loss of a love object and introjection as a good/healthy one that acknowledges and accounts for the loss through the acquisition of symbolic and metaphoric language capable of representing the loss (110–15).

For Abraham and Torok the initial situation of the withdrawal of the mother's breast provides a first opportunity for introjection. The child misses the mother's breast, explores anxiously the empty interior of the mouth, fills it with cries and then, through the mediation of the mother, with words:

> Learning to fill the emptiness of the mouth with words is the initial model for introjection. . . . Introjecting a desire, a pain, a situation means channeling them through language into a communion of empty mouths. This is how the literal ingestion of food becomes introjection when viewed figuratively. The passage from food to language in the mouth presupposes the successful replacement of the object's presence with the self's cognizance of its absence. Since language acts and makes up for absence by representing, by *giving figurative shape* to presence, it can only be *comprehended* or *shared* in a "community of empty mouths. (128)

According to Abraham and Torok, incorporation, however, is a "failed introjection." Incorporation is conservative and turns to fantasy, which operates to preserve the status quo, in order to permit the ego to act as if the loss had not taken place. Introjection involves the readjustment of the ego. Incorporation works to preserve the static integrity of the ego:

> Such is the fantasy of *incorporation*. Introducing all or part of a love object or a thing into one's own body, possessing, expelling or alternately acquiring, keeping, losing it—here are the varieties of fantasy indicating, in the typical forms of possession or feigned dispossession, a basic intrapsychic situation: the situation created by the reality of a loss sustained by the psyche. If accepted and worked through, the loss would require major readjustment. But the fantasy of incorporation merely simulates profound psychic transformation through magic; it does so by implementing literally something that has only figurative meaning. So in order not to have to "swallow" a loss, we fantasize swallowing (or having swallowed) that which has been lost, as if it were some kind of thing. Two interrelated proce-

dures constitute the magic of incorporation: *demetaphorization* (taking literally what is meant figuratively) and *objectification* (pretending that the suffering is not an injury to the subject but instead a loss sustained by the love object). The magical "cure" by incorporation exempts the subject from the painful process of reorganization. When in the form of imaginary or real nourishment, we ingest the live object we miss, this means that *we refuse to mourn* and that we shun the consequences of mourning even though our psyche is fully bereaved. Incorporation is the refusal to reclaim as our own the part of ourselves that we placed in what we lost: incorporation is the refusal to acknowledge the full import of the loss, a loss that, if recognized as such, would effectively transform us. In fine, incorporation is the refusal to introject loss. The fantasy of incorporation reveals a gap within the psyche: it points to something that is missing just where introjection should have occurred. (126–27)

It seems that what distinguishes introjection from incorporation[30] is the relationship to remainders. In their refinement of Sandor Ferenzci's earlier adoption of the term to describe the inverse process to projection, Abraham and Torok point out that "introjection is not compensation but growth" (113). A healthy ego, then, has the capacity through adjustment of taking in any desire, loss, pain, or situation without coming undone. This inexorable movement of growth distinguishes the "healthy" ego from the "unhealthy" one and implies that health requires the absence of acknowledged remainders. Like capitalism, described by Baudrillard and discussed in chapter 5 of this book, as a remainderless system, introjection similarly brooks no remainders. In the case of introjection, as described by Abraham and Torok, everything can be, indeed must be, invested and reinvested in the growth and expansion of the ego — in the interest of health. If introjection gives language to what has been lost, it does so by naming what will be overcome. If the work of introjection is to ensure the health of the ego through growth, remainders cannot be permanently tolerated. Furthermore, if introjection denies remainders and acknowledges loss, incorporation denies loss and produces remainders:

> . . . every time an incorporation is uncovered, it can be attributed to an undisclosable grief that befalls an ego already partitioned on account of a previous objectal experience tainted with shame. The crypt perpetuates the dividing walls by its very nature. No crypt arises without the shared secrets having already split the subject's topography. In the realm of shame and secrecy, however, we need to determine *who* it is that ought to blush, *who* is to hide. Is it the subject for having been guilty of crimes, of shameful or unseemly acts? That supposition will not help lay

the foundation for a single crypt. Crypts are constructed only when the shameful secret is the love object's doing and when the subject functions as an ego ideal. It is therefore the *object's* secret that needs to be kept, *his* shame covered up. . . . The debased object will be "fecalized," that is, actually rendered excremental. (131)[31]

The Secret of the Past

Most readers of Freyre's work have remarked on his nostalgia for the patriarchal past. This nostalgic quality, however, is not peculiar to Freyre's work. Scholar after scholar has noted the persistent theme of sadness, melancholy, nostalgia resumed in the Portuguese word *saudade*.[32] Variously ascribed to one or all of the "component races" of the Brazilian racial mixture, *saudade* is said to contribute to the chronic sadness of the Brazilian people, a sadness that is perpetuated through miscegenation. Antônio Sérgio Bueno cites a 1929 article published in a modernist literary supplement titled *Leite Crioulo*[33] (Creole/Mulatto Milk):

Eugenia. Galton teve idea *[sic]*. Aí está uma cousa boa para corrigir a incuria da nacionalidade. . . . É tempo da gente fazer como a barata. Mudar de casca. Ficar limpo de todo . . .
Presentemente o que nos interessa é entrar em confito com a nostalgia. Eugenia para a alma brasileira. Eugenizar. Não o negro. Esse, por si mesmo, se anula pela mestiçagem. Todo o Brasil, sim. Fezê-lo feliz. Obter seletivamente tipos que melhorem a nossa raça. Como Blackwell, criador inglês de gado. Mas ao invés de obtermos, como ele, mas carne que osso, vamos conseguir mais alegria que nostalgia . . . (120)

Eugenics. Galton had an idea. That [idea] would good way to solve the chronic illness of nationality. . . . It is about time that we make like cockroaches. Change our shells. Become nice and clean . . .
At this time, we are interested in doing battle with nostalgia. Eugenics for the Brazilian soul. To eugenicize. Not the black. This one will be done away with through miscegenation. But all of Brazil, yes. Make it happy. To select the types that will improve our race. Like Blackwell, the English cattle breeder. But rather than obtaining, like him, more flesh (meat) than bone, we'll get more happiness than nostalgia . . .

According to Bueno, this passage associates Galton's eugenics to Blackwell's breeding and adapts it to the Brazilian environment. The parallelism in the article links whites and flesh and happiness as contrasted to sadness and bones and Blacks. Bueno provides this equation to illustrate the relationship:

Alegria:carne:branco :: tristeza:osso:negro

Happiness:flesh:white :: sadness:bone:black

The racial miscegenation that will lead to the *embranquecimento*/whitening fails in that something remains. The bones represent this remainder. The bones that are drawn out of the language by the *culumim* and by the Negro nurse are reserved as an act of resistance to the process of incorporation because, as I will elaborate in the final chapter of this study, bones demand an act of compensation.

In *Casa Grande e Senzala,* Freyre devotes a great deal of attention to describing food preparation. He discusses it in relation to the production of aphrodisiacs, as well as to the maintenance of health, hygiene, and the disposal of waste in the Big House. "Um traço importante de infiltração de cultura negra na economia e na vida doméstica do brasileiro resta-nos a acentuar: a culinária" (453) (There is one important aspect of the infiltration of Negro culture into the domestic life and the economy of the Brazilian that remains to be stressed, and that is the culinary aspect) (459). He reinforces, through the focus on the verb *comer,* a complex sense of incorporation as the important theme of his "narrative of assimilation."[34]

Freyre defended food prepared by Africans and their descendants against the charge that it contributes to intestinal disorders such as "indigestões, diarréas, disenterias, hemorróidas e todas as moléstias das vias digestivas" (458) (indigestion, diarrhea, dysentery, hemorrhoids and all diseases of the digestive tract) (467). Although he admitted that eating too much of this food will certainly cause indigestion (in the sense that the food cannot or will not be incorporated into the body and will be expelled from the body), a small amount in combination with the proper counterbalancing ingredients could strengthen the body of the whites who eat this type of food (470).

After the discussion of the preparation of food and the maintenance of cleanliness in the household, *Casa Grande e Senzala* ends abruptly with a discussion of the diseases that affect Blacks in Brazil: "Doenças africanas seguiram-nos até o Brasil, devastando-os nas senzalas. . . . E comunicando-se às vezes aos brancos das casas-grandes. A África também se tomou vingança dos maus tratos recibido da Europa" (464) (African diseases also followed them to Brazil, wreaking havoc in the slave huts. . . . The diseases at times were communicated to the whites of the Big Houses; in this manner did Africa take vengeance for the ill treatment she had received from Europe) (475). Having introduced the idea of black resentment and agency, Freyre immediately undermines it. The sentences that follow exhaustively catalogue the diseases contracted from whites that have contributed to very high rates of black mortality. The last sentence of the work cites the pervasiveness of tapeworm in Blacks: "Os vermes e particularmente a toenia . . . abundão muito" (464) (Worms, especially the tapeworm, . . . are to be found in great abundance) (475). Freyre's work ends with the image of the tapeworm, a parasite that, living inside the body, drains the host of all its food, force, and energy, causing it to eventually "crumble" and die. This observation recalls the anecdote that Freyre repeated in the introduction to *Casa Grande e Senzala,* in which the foundation of the nation, represented by the Casa Grande, crumbles when the blood of Blacks is literally mixed in (miscegenated). Throughout this work, Blacks appear as threats to the body politic, when they make themselves difficult to digest, thereby resisting assimilation to the body.

Earlier in *Casa Grande e Senzala,* Freyre had described an optimistic view of complete assimilation:

A verdade é que no Brasil, ao contrario do que se observa noutros paises da América e da África de recente colonização européia, a cultura primitiva—tanto a ameríndia como a africana—não se vem isolando em bolões duros, secos e indigestos, inassimiláveis ao sistema social do europeu. (160)

The truth is that in Brazil, contrary to what is observed in other American countries and in those parts of Africa that have been recently colonized by Europeans, the primitive culture has not been isolated into hard, dry, indigestible lumps incapable of being assimilated by the European social system. (181)

Yet by the end of his book and despite his assertions to the contrary, these indigestible lumps or residue do exist and prevent the sense of happiness that should accompany the process that has produced the ideal Brazilian:

Todo brasileiro, mesmo o alvo, de cabelo louro, traz na alma, quando não na alma e no corpo—há muita gente de jenipapo ou mancha mongólica pelo Brasil— a sombra, ou pelo menos a pinta, do indígena ou do negro. (283)

Every Brazilian, even the light-skinned fair-haired one carries about with him in his soul, when not in soul and body alike—for there are many in Brazil with the mongrel mark of the genipap—the shadow, or at least the birthmark of the aborigine or the Negro. (278)

This mark, a metaphor for the remainder, disrupts finally Gilberto Freyre's narrative of assimilation. The vision of peace, cordiality and wholeness that characterized Freyre's vision is not brought to fruition; *Casa Grande e Senzala* ends abruptly without a formal conclusion or concluding remarks. This vision, nevertheless, would be a shared and cherished part of U.S. African American characterizations of Brazil and influence discussions of black citizenship in the United States, the subject of the next chapter.

THREE

The Foreigner and the Remainder

Of them I am singularly clairvoyant. I see in and through them. I view them from unusual points of vantage. Not as a foreigner do I come, for I am native, not foreign, bone of their thought and flesh of their language. Mine is not the knowledge of the traveler or the colonial composite of dear memories, words and wonder. Nor yet is my knowledge that which servants have of their masters, or mass of class, or capitalist of artisan. Rather I see these souls undressed and from the back and side. I see the workings of their entrails. I know their thoughts and they know that I know. This knowledge makes them now embarrassed, now furious. They deny my right to live and be and call me misbirth!

—W. E. B. Du Bois, *Darkwater*

IN THE PRECEDING TWO CHAPTERS, I developed a theoretical framework based on a model of cannibalism and explored the significance of the metaphor of cannibalism to the concept of racial democracy in relation to the Brazilian context most immediately associated with these ideas. In the next two chapters, I will shift my focus from Brazilian writers I have discussed to the real and imagined exchanges between writers in the United States and Brazil. I will demonstrate how the metaphor of cannibalism circulated between Brazil and the United States. The ubiquity of the metaphor of cannibalism in the discussions about race and democracy that were so pressing at the turn of the last century—Brazil abolished slavery in 1888 and declared the republic in 1889; *Plessy v. Ferguson* formalized the "separate but equal" doctrine in the United States in 1896—is not only an effect of mutual influence but also an indication of the metaphor's appropriateness for describing identity formation.

The metaphor of cannibalism and its logical remainder was consciously and unconsciously embraced to address issues of exclusion and inclusion in multiracial societies resulting from a history of slavery and immigration, since rhetoric that privileged complete assimilation or exclusion was inadequate to account for the situation of black Americans. In his 1897 essay, "The Conservation of Races," W. E. B. Du Bois describes this situation as a:

> dilemma, and it is a puzzling one, I admit. No Negro who has given earnest thought to the situation of his people in America has failed, at some time in his life, to find himself at these cross-roads; has failed to ask himself at some time: What, after all, am I? Am I an American or am I a Negro? Can I be both? Or is it my duty to cease to be a Negro as soon as possible and be an American? If I strive as a Negro, am I not perpetuating the very cleft that threatens and separates black and white America? Is not my only possible practical aim the subduction of all that is Negro in me to the American? Does my black blood place upon me any more obligation to assert my nationality than German, or Irish or Italian blood would?[1]

This passage, indeed the essay as a whole, is suggestive not only for its staging of the tension between blackness and Americanness, but also for the way that it distinguishes between race, which, as I will demonstrate, is necessarily transnational, and ethnicity, which is national, showing that each category functions differently. Their conflation imposes an impossible choice on black people who want to be represented as black people and as Americans. Taking Du Bois's distinction as a point of departure, I will argue for the difference between the foreign (linked to the ethnic and national) and the remainder to show how the remainder is ultimately the more productive way to conceive of the relationship between race and democracy.

As I noted in the introduction to this study, my focus on the process of remaindering and on the figure of the remainder derived from cannibalism could seem to be a subtle change in emphasis. I insist on the remainder because, as I will demonstrate in what follows, it permits a more complex and potentially useful way of describing how exclusion works in a multiracial democratic society. Exclusion is generally understood as incompatible with democratic formations; yet, as Carl Schmitt asserts in a quotation I cited in the introduction, democracy can exclude a segment of the governed without ceasing to be a democracy. In response to Schmitt's observation, Chantal Mouffe points out that democracy, in fact, depends on exclusion because it provides the opportunity to trace a dividing line between those who belong to the demos and can claim representation and equal rights and those who cannot. Schmitt's contention that there must be an outside of the demos in order to establish its integrity and visibility depends on the idea of the foreigner.

The writers that I address in the following two chapters suggest in various ways that the pursuit of new modalities of inclusion is doomed to repeat the very exclusions they argue against, suggesting instead models for a relationship to the remainder as such. In this chapter, I will focus on selected writings from the extensive works of W. E. B. Du Bois and Charles Chesnutt to propose that it is more fruitful to think about blackness as what is left over or remaindered rather than what is left out or foreign to the process of creating the American.

"Not as a foreigner do I come . . ."

As the epigraph to this chapter makes clear, if the recourse to the metaphor of cannibalism and its remainders to describe the process by which an American identity is formed was not peculiar to Brazilian writers, neither was the idea of racial democracy. The idea of racial democracy, if not the term itself, appeared in the works of African American writers from the United States long before it was articulated in Gilberto Freyre's works. Before Gilberto Freyre presented the master's thesis that would form the foundation of *Casa Grande e Senzala* to the political science department at Columbia University in 1922, a full decade before its publication in Brazil and long before the English translation was available in the United States, many of the ideas familiar from his work had already appeared in various books and articles addressed to a black audience. Works like *South America: Observations and Impression* by the British historian James Bryce (1914) and Harry Johnston's *The Negro in the New World* (1910), as well as NAACP Secretary Roy Nash's article in *The Crisis*, "The Origin of Negro Slavery in Brazil" and his book *The Conquest of Brazil* (1926), among others, all argued that the quality of slavery in Brazil created the conditions for the cordial relations between the races that obviated the color line. Bryce, for example, writes that:

> It [the black population in Brazil] is well treated — slavery was seldom harsh among the kindly natured, easy-going Portuguese — and bears no ill-will to its former masters. Neither do they feel towards it that repulsion which marks the attitude of the whites to the negroes in North America. . . . [This] shows that race repugnance is no such constant and permanent factor in human affairs as members of the Teutonic people are apt to assume. (479–82)[2]

These studies were read and cited by W. E. B. Du Bois, Booker T. Washington, and even by Gilberto Freyre himself.[3]

In his article "Brazilian Racial Democracy, 1900–90: An American Counterpoint," historian George Reid Andrews surveys how Brazil was characterized as a racial democracy in a conversation about race that took place as a "counterpoint" between the United States and Brazil over the twentieth century. He observes, however, that "[g]iven the disparities in power and influence between them, up until now the impact of that conversation has been greater in Brazil than in the United States."[4] The disparity that he calls attention to has had the additional effect of obscuring the extent to which the image of Brazil as a racial democracy, arguably invented as much in the United States as in Brazil, not only predates Freyre's work but also has had a significant and underappreciated role in discussions of race and democracy in the United States. If Brazilian intellectuals at the end of the nineteenth and beginning of the twentieth centuries used the United States as an example, a point of reference, or a cautionary tale, so did black writers from the United States similarly use the example of Brazil in their works.

In 1919, José Clarana, the anomalous writer I introduced in my preface, published in Rio de Janeiro, Brazil, *Os estados unidos pela civilisação e a civilisação dos Estados Unidos*[5] (The States United by Civilization and the Civilization of the United States). The title of this collection of essays plays on the homology between the official names of the two nations that he examined in this work. When the republic was declared in 1889, Brazil's name was changed to the United States of Brazil and its constitution and government were modeled on those of the United States of America. For Clarana, this homology reinforces their shared history, which includes the intertwined legacy of slavery. The second part of the title, which initially seems to refer to the United States of America but over the course of the essays will come to denote Brazil as well, confounds the two nations and introduces the overall concern of the work: Can a nation that practices racism be considered civilized and democratic, and can a nation that tolerates racism in another be considered any less racist and any more civilized and democratic? The urgency of this question was prompted by an increase in lynchings during this period, which Clarana discusses at length in his essays.

According to Clarana, Brazil owes a debt to the United States. If Brazil does not experience the racial violence that prevails in the United States and can claim not to have a color line, it is because the Civil War had provided an example of a costly confrontation to be avoided. He maintains that this moral debt requires that Brazilians protest the situation of black people in the United States:

> Mas é do lado moral que se impõe a nossa intervenção nos negocios negros dos Estados Unidos. Se não temos um problema de côr, é porque foi quasi totalmente resolvido para nós pela Guerra Civil naquelle país. Desde que o governo daquella Republica, a qual tem prestado grande serviços á civilização, se confessa incapaz de combater a praga que vae assolando, cumpre-nos, como simples dever de gratidão, chamar aquelle povo á razão, afim de dar coragem e segurança ás mãos que lá não falatariam para extirpar o monstruoso cancro que consume a alma daquella gente.

> It is, however, a moral imperative that requires our intervention in negro affairs in the United States. If we don't have a problem with color, it is because it was almost totally resolved for us by that country's Civil War. Since the government of that Republic, which has rendered great service to civilization, admits that it is incapable of combating the scourge that is attacking it, it is up to us, as a simple debt of gratitude, to call that population to reason, in order to give courage and support to the many hands that would yank out the monstrous cancer that consumes the soul of that populous. (39–40)

For Clarana, this moral debt extends beyond the one owed to the United States government to encompass one owed to black Americans. Noting that Brazil is referred to in the United States as a "país de negros" (a black country), Clarana criticizes Brazilian attempts to deny this designation by only seeking alliances with "nações onde não haja negros" (nations where there are no Blacks) (16).

> Eu creio que, nos Estados Unidos, o negro está demonstrando a sua virilidade em fórma tal que, se o Brazil fôr, de facto, "um país de negros," seria mais respeitado, actualmente, do que antes naquella Republica. O negro americano que, sózinho, se defende contra a oppressão, nos está fazendo, e a toda a humanidade, um serviço de inestimável valor para o futuro, pois não ha duvida que um povo que seja obrigado a fazer justiça aos que são estimados os infimos dos homens, a farão mais facilmente aos que julgam dos melhores. Julgam-se, mas não são julgados assim. O europeu meridional, o africano, o asiatico e o americano indigena são degráus transferiveis duma mesma escada fragil com que se tem edificado a civilisação dominante de hoje. O brasileiro, que proclama a sua brancura igual á do argentino e do chileno, terá talvez, como estes, uma divida para com o negro americano, a qual não possam pagar. (17–18)

I believe that, in the United States, the Negro is showing his power in such a way that, if Brazil were, in fact, a "black country," it would find itself more respected now than it had been in that country [the United States]. The black American who, alone, defends himself against oppression, is doing us, and all of humanity, a favor of inestimable value for the future, because without a doubt a people obliged to dispense justice to those they deem the most inferior of men will be more likely to give it to those judged to be superior. These may judge themselves superior, but they are not judged [by others] this way. The southern European, the African, the Asian, the indigenous American are all mutually substitutable steps in a fragile ladder with which has been built today's dominant civilization. The Brazilian, who proclaims his whiteness equal to that of the Argentinian and the Chilean, perhaps like them, owes a debt toward the black American, whom he can never repay.

Clarana suggests that the whiteness of Brazil, Chile, and Argentina, tenuous as it is, particularly from the perspective of the United States, benefits in two ways from the activism of black Americans. First, the fight for the rights of black people translates into gains for all countries judged inferior due to their situation in what would later be called the Third World, dependent or developing nations, thereby holding forth a promise of what could be called a cosmopolitan democracy. Second, the very whiteness of these nations is tied to the othering of blackness on an international level, an othering that is disavowed on the level of the nation.

The historical context of the essays in *Os estados unidos pela civilisação e a civilisação dos Estados Unidos* is the First World War, and the inspiration for them comes from the author's dismay at reports of lynchings in the United States that pass without comment in Brazil. Clarana finds this lack of interest especially distressing when compared with attention-getting protests against the massacres of Jews in the Ukraine, Poland, Galicia, and Romania in which leading Brazilian and Argentinian political, church, and cultural leaders took part. Clarana singles out a mulatto bishop, who refused to answer Clarana's demand for an explanation for the contrasting response to each event, agreeing to say mass for the Europeans but not for black Americans. He sees the bishop's attitude a one of many examples of the racial logic that motivates international relations and permits the spread of "American negrophobia." Clarana suggests, as Du Bois and Alain Locke do, that the color line is international, and that embracing it may be the passkey into the condition of modernity and cosmopolitanism.

Clarana argues, furthermore, that if the recognition of a moral debt or a feeling of gratitude does not spur all Brazilians to action against the color line and the violence required to maintain it, a sense of self-preservation should. Given what defines a person as black in the United States, he asks, could the safety of any Brazilian in that country be assured? Referring to a recent lynching described in a recent newspaper report, Clarana notes that the lynched chauffeur of a restaurant patron in Chicago could easily be Brazilian and wonders if a riotous racist mob ever stopped to establish the victim's nationality, social status, or even if the color of his skin does in fact make him black. Clarana concludes that only luck has saved the increasing numbers of Brazilians in the United States from racially motivated violence (39–40).

Implicit in Clarana's argument is the idea that foreignness is not a protection for black people. This seems a surprising assertion given that passing narratives consistently figure the passer who has passed from the condition of being black as foreign, represented as a more desirable and safer state: Paul (Jean Toomer, "Bona and Paul," *Cane*); Helga and Audrey Denney (Nella Larsen, *Quicksand*); Irene and Clare (Larsen, *Passing*); Narrator (James Weldon Johnson, *Autobiography of an Ex-Coloured Man*); Angela/Angèle and Tony Cross (Jessie Redmon Fauset, *Plum Bun*). While many readers have interpreted this condition of foreignness as highlighting the outsider status of black people, I would argue that a process more complex is being suggested. If black people can become American only by becoming foreign — either by passing racially or by leaving the United States as migrants (here I am referring to the colonization projects I will discuss in more detail that would resettle black people from the United States in Africa, the Caribbean, Europe, or South America), then black people can no more be foreign and black than they can be American and black. Clarana, fifteen years after Du Bois described this dilemma in *The Conservation of Races*, remarks on "a public which understands that an American may be anything but a Negro; the descendants of African Blacks being always the *denationalized* Negro even if he is a white man."[6] In what follows I will argue that the turn to the foreign — to South America and particularly to Brazil — provides an opportunity for writers to explore Du Bois's rejected option of "the subduction of all that is Negro" in the quest for full participation in the American democracy. I will focus on Chesnutt's work via Du Bois's in order to suggest how their discussions of foreignness highlight the peculiar condition of those whom a racial logic has constituted as neither inside nor outside but as a remainder.

In *The Souls of Black Folk,* W. E. B. Du Bois defined double consciousness as "the sense of always looking at oneself through the eyes of another, of measuring one's soul by the tape of a world that looks on in contempt and pity."[7] This experience would, at first, seem to derive from a process of estrangement, of making the self foreign to the self in order to create a sense of, and more importantly, a *sensing* of the sense of the self's racialized identity.[8] Yet, as the title of this section, "Not as a foreigner do I come . . . ,"[9] attests, the vocabulary of foreignness, so important to discussions of ethnicity and Americanization at the turn of the last century, could not so easily be applied to the descendants of Africans in the United States: "which yields him [the Negro] no true self-consciousness but only lets him see himself through the revelation of the other world." In her discussion of double consciousness, Priscilla Wald calls attention to the status of self-consciousness in the following elucidation of Du Bois's concept:

> Self-consciousness was a pervasive term at the turn of the century. . . . In that context, "self-consciousness" increasingly measured the successful education of "people into homogeneity of social desire" in the interest of "national unity and strength". . . . But the African American, as Du Bois notes, is excluded from that self consciousness and experiences a discrepancy between the consciousness of a black self and of an American self. From that discrepancy, Du Bois generates an analysis in which consciousness reproduces a particular (homogenized) self—a self that experiences *difference* as *inferiority.* In Du Bois' reformulation the comfortable correspondence, the wholeness, creates rather than reflects the self. (187)

It is not coincidental that the exemplary scenes of coming into racial awareness take place in a school setting.[10] This setting only serves to reinforce that one is educated into identifying with a point of view and with seeing that position (white American) as comfortable and whole.[11] The school setting, furthermore, marks the move from familial identifications to identifications mediated by the state. What does not correspond to the point of view deriving from, if not producing, that position is remaindered as blackness. The denial of a sense of wholeness that will come to exist only in whiteness can be experienced, as in the case of the "ex-coloured man," as a loss marked by shame. If there is grief associated with the moment of the establishment of double consciousness, for Du Bois, that grief is repaired by a "gift of second sight," which is attained through the process of incorporation, a gift that is the property of the remainder:

Of them I am singularly clairvoyant. I see in and through them. I view them from unusual points of vantage. Not as a foreigner do I come, for I am native, not foreign, bone of their thought and flesh of their language. Mine is not the knowledge of the traveler or the colonial composite of dear memories, words and wonder. Nor yet is my knowledge that which servants have of their masters, or mass of class, or capitalist of artisan. Rather I see these souls undressed and from the back and side. I see the workings of their entrails. I know their thoughts and they know that I know. This knowledge makes them now embarrassed, now furious. They deny my right to live and be and call me misbirth!

The remainder is what has passed through the "entrails" and gained a privileged knowledge that defies any attempt to reduce it, the remainder, to categorization as abject. "I see the workings of their entrails. I know their thoughts and they know I know. This knowledge makes them now embarrassed, now furious" (17). The embarrassment and fury of whites point to their desire to erase the remainder that sees and resists, thereby short-circuiting the establishment of the double consciousness that marks the Negro as black and the absence of which marks the white as white.

For Du Bois, the gift of second sight permits the remainder to sense (as in double consciousness) the process of its becoming, as well as to record and be a record of that process. In *The Souls of Black Folk,* Du Bois says that he is "bone of the bone and flesh of the flesh of them that live within the Veil" (viii). This biblical allusion corresponds to the story of Eve's creation from Adam's rib in Genesis 2:21: "This is now bone of my bones, and flesh of my flesh. She will be called 'woman,' because she was taken out of Man." In "The Souls of White Folk" Du Bois says he is "bone of their thought and flesh of their language" (17). This revision of the biblical quotation highlights the constructed nature of racial categories. The biblical allusion to the word made flesh indicates both the performative incarnation of a racializing discourse and the resistance to that discourse by materializing its effects. The bone of their thought suggests the indigestible residue — the resisting remainder. In this light, the idea of the Negro as the remainder is more troubling to the idea of Americanness than would be the idea of Negro as foreigner.

The foreigner, historically (in terms of turn-of-the-century immigration policy based on assimilation) and theoretically can always be (re)incorporated in a way that the remainder cannot. The remainder is not simply outside; it does not arrive or live separately within. The remainder is a reminder that won't keep the peace. Similarly to the case of Brazil, the remainder in the context of the United States reveals the mechanism of representation through which the American is discursively produced. Blackness (like whiteness) is produced through this process of remaindering and does not precede it. The remainder comes not from outside or from an act of repression; it comes from within. The very process that promises the erasure of the (black) race as difference — and blackness as inferiority — maintains race as a problem and produces a resistant remainder that is a constant reminder of its failure. The discourse of democracy to which African American writers appealed in the early decades of the twentieth century valued peace, consensus, identification, and understanding. The works by the African American writers that I address in the rest of this chapter and the next ask, however, at what cost?

As articulated in the articles published in the U.S. black press, the arguments for emigration, on the one hand, and the eradication of the color line through miscegenation as promoted in Brazil,[12] on the other, could relieve double consciousness. During the first decades of the twentieth century, writers ranging from James Weldon Johnson to Nella Larsen, Jessie Redmon Fauset, and Langston Hughes, among others, addressed the relationship between race and citizenship, passing (racially and across national borders) and miscegenation/amalgamation, double consciousness and democracy. Among these writers was Charles Chesnutt, who wrote hundreds of essays over his lifetime on a wide range of literary and social topics. Many of these essays address racial prejudice and the color line. To numerous scholars, including Sallyann H. Ferguson, these essays prove Chesnutt to be "essentially a social and literary accommodationist"[13] who used his writings "as a vehicle for racial propaganda . . . primarily concerned with making a case for racial amalgamation."[14] I will argue in what follows that Chesnutt's fiction, specifically *The Marrow of Tradition*, (1901) engages in an important and revealing dialogue with his essays that calls this assessment into question and provides a caution for those who will follow, proclaiming, over the objections of their brothers (and their sisters) to the south, that the future of democracy, of a racial democracy, lay elsewhere.

"In his place": The Color Line, Emigration, and the Foreign

The Marrow of Tradition explores the roots and effects of the violence that was unleashed against black people at the end of the nineteenth century in response to Reconstruction policies aimed at including the recently emancipated slaves in the political life of the United States. Charles Chesnutt was born in Cleveland, Ohio, in 1858 and raised in North Carolina during the Reconstruction. He witnessed how Reconstruction policies had little effect on the prejudices of Southern whites and decided early on to devote his career as a writer to protesting racism and the establishment of the color line. His appearance would have allowed him to pass, but he preferred to use his experiences to explore the logic of the color line: "My physical makeup was such that I knew the psychology of people of mixed blood in so far as it was different from that of other people, and most of my writings ran along the color line. . . . It has more dramatic possibilities than life within clearly defined and widely differentiated groups."[15]

The *Plessy v. Ferguson* decision (1896) established the separate but equal doctrine that supported the color line. In *The Marrow of Tradition,* Chesnutt provides a reenactment of the events surrounding the *Plessy* case within his novelistic account of the 1898 Wilmington riot. Republican reconstructionists in Wilmington, North Carolina, had joined forces with Blacks and with dissatisfied white Democrats to form a "fusionist" party that had success in elections leading up to city council elections in November 1898. White supremacists, fearing a loss of power to the fusionist coalition, made a priority of winning the city council elections. The weeks leading up to the elections were marked by inflammatory demonstrations against black people. Although the Democrats fraudulently won the elections, they nevertheless organized a violent and retaliatory assault on the town's black citizens.

In 1892, Homer (Homère) Plessy, in concert with several prominent black Louisiana public figures, contested an 1890 state law requiring segregated train cars. The law stated that "all railway companies carrying passengers in their coaches in this state shall provide equal but separate accommodations for the white and colored races, by providing two or more passenger coaches for each passenger train, or by dividing the passenger coaches by a partition so as to secure separate accommodations." The facts of the case are well known: Plessy, who otherwise would have passed unnoticed in a car of white passengers, declared himself black to the train conductor. According to a strategy elaborated by the Citizens' Committee to Test the Constitutionality of the Separate Car Law, a group he belonged to, Plessy subsequently was arrested for refusing to switch to a car for "colored" passengers. Plessy went to court, and his lawyers argued, in *Homer Adolph Plessy v. The State*

of Louisiana, that the Separate Car Act violated the Thirteenth and Fourteenth Amendments to the Constitution. On an earlier occasion the trial
judge, John Howard Ferguson, had declared the Separate Car Act unconstitutional on interstate trains. He decided against Plessy in this case, ruling
that the state could choose to regulate railroad companies that operated only
within the state of Louisiana.[16] On appeal, the Supreme Court of Louisiana
upheld Ferguson's decision. The Louisiana Supreme Court's ruling against
Plessy was grounded in a decades-long erosion of the Fourteenth Amend-
ment to the U.S. Constitution that should have guaranteed the rights and
privileges of national citizenship, due process, and equal protection under
the law to all persons born or naturalized in the United States. The court
based its judgment on a notion of differentiated citizenship for Blacks and
for Whites. The decision gave to individual states the power to undermine
federal protections on the grounds that racialization and racial hierarchy
were rooted in natural law and, therefore, could not be changed by civil law.
The Louisiana Supreme Court justices indicated that constitutional amendments "would not have sought and intended the impossible"[17] that legislat-
ing social equality between the races would have represented.

In 1896, the Supreme Court of the United States heard Plessy's case and
again upheld his conviction. Speaking for a seven-person majority, Justice
Henry Brown wrote:

> That [the Separate Car Act] does not conflict with the Thirteenth Amendment,
> which abolished slavery . . . is too clear for argument. . . . A statute which implies
> merely a legal distinction between the white and colored races — a distinction
> which is founded in the color of the two races, and *which must always exist so
> long as white men are distinguished from the other race by color* — has no ten-
> dency to destroy the legal equality of the two races. . . . The object of the [Four-
> teenth Amendment] was undoubtedly to enforce the absolute equality of the two
> races before the law, but in the nature of things it could not have been intended to
> abolish distinctions based upon color, or to enforce social, as distinguished from
> political equality, or a commingling of the two races upon terms unsatisfactory to
> either."[18] (my emphasis)

The lines that I have emphasized hold out a promise that the judge will not
honor. If the color line ("a distinction which is founded in the color of the
two races") will exist only as long as the body is able to give racial evidence
("so long as white men are distinguished from the other race by color"),
then what of the fact that Plessy had to announce himself as black in order

for the court to police his passing, or rather, his not passing? Is there a commingling of the races from the perspective of the court that would not be unsatisfactory to it? I would argue that in exploring these issues through both a domestic and an international frame, Chesnutt calls attention to the complexity of white attitudes toward amalgamation and ultimately defends legal protections in the law for black people as black people.

Many of the events in *The Marrow of Tradition,* which takes place in the fictional Wellington, are seen through the eyes of Dr. Miller, the town's black doctor. He meets the white Dr. Burns by chance as both travel South on a train from Philadelphia to Wellington shortly before the riot. As a student, Dr. Miller had attended medical lectures delivered by Dr. Burns. Attracted by "his earnestness of purpose, his evident talent, and his excellent manners and fine physique," Burns had taken "an interest in his only colored pupil" and arranged a scholarship for him to study in Europe. Although Miller had returned to Wellington to set up a medical practice and a hospital, "[h]e had been strongly tempted to leave the South, and seek a home for his family and a career for himself in the freer North, where race antagonism was less keen, or at least less oppressive, or in Europe, where he never found his color work to his disadvantage. But his people needed him, and he wished to help them, and had sought by means of this institution to contribute to their uplifting" (51). Burns and Miller converse without incident until the train enters Virginia, at which point the conductor calls attention to the sign designating the "whites only" car. Over Burns's objections and in compliance with the desires of Captain George McBane, a white passenger who later plays a significant role in fomenting the riot, the conductor forces Miller to move to the "colored" car where he contemplates the effects of "the law [that] had been in operation only a few months [which] branded and tagged and set apart [the Negro] from the rest of mankind upon the public highways, like an unclean thing" (57).

The intransigence of the color line is reinforced once Miller arrives in Wellington. Dr. Burns comes to Wellington at the invitation of the local white physician, Dr. Price, to undertake an important operation at the home of Major Carteret, the publisher of a newspaper that later stokes the racist ire of the rioters. On the train, Burns asks Miller to assist him, since the operation lies within Miller's area of expertise. At the door of the Carteret home, however, Dr. Price turns Miller away to protect his host's "sacred principle, lying at the very root of our social order, involving the purity and prestige of our [white] race" (72). Although he had taken upon himself the task of barring Miller's entry to the Carteret house, Price feels uncomfortable about enforcing the decision:

> As a physician his method was to ease pain—he would rather take the risk of losing a patient from the use of an anesthetic than from the shock of an operation. He liked Miller, wished him well, and would not wittingly wound his feelings. He really thought him too much of a gentleman for the town, in view of the restrictions with which he must inevitably be hampered. There was something melancholy, to a cultivated mind, about a sensitive, educated man who happened to be off color. Such a person was a sort of social misfit, an odd quantity, educated out of his own class, with no possible hope of entrance into that above it. He felt quite sure that *if he had been in Miller's place*, he would never had settled in the South—he would have moved to Europe, or to the West Indies, or some Central or South American state where questions of color were not vitally important. (74–75, my emphasis)

In his 1891 essay, "A Multitude of Counselors," Chesnutt rejected the emigration by Blacks, which leaders—black and white—had embraced during the nineteenth century as a response to racial division. Thomas Jefferson, for example, had proposed that the inferiority of Blacks and their resentment of captivity made the formerly enslaved and their free descendants unfit to remain in the United States. He advocated the "repatriation" of Blacks to Africa or to colonies in the West Indies.[19] The American Colonization Society founded in 1816 under the leadership of Henry Clay also sought to move free Blacks to Liberia while maintaining intact the institution of slavery, thereby promoting an increase in the white population of the United States.[20] In an 1853 speech, Frederick Douglass acknowledged that conditions for the formerly enslaved could be made so intolerable as to make emigration seem advantageous, "but to compel us to go to Africa is quite another thing. . . . Other and more desirable lands are open to us. We can plant ourselves at the very portals of slavery. We can hover about the Gulf of Mexico. Nearly all the isles of the Caribbean Seas bid us welcome; while the broad and fertile valleys of British Guiana, under the sway of the emancipating Queen, invite us to their treasures, and to nationality. With the Gulf of Mexico on the South, and Canada on the North, we may still keep within hearing the wails of our enslaved people in the United States."[21] In August of 1862, President Lincoln told an invited delegation

of Blacks that the differences between Blacks and Whites were so enduring that each suffered from interaction with the other. He suggested that
Blacks should emigrate to a proposed Central American settlement (Ferguson, 430). Black leaders, such as Samuel Ward, Henry Bibb, and Martin
Delany, whose plan for a black empire in the West Indies was approved by
the National Emigration Convention in 1854, also advocated emigration.[22]
Chesnutt, however, claimed that the wholesale emigration of the ten million U.S. Blacks to South America, Mexico, or Africa would not be practical. He argued that black emigrants could not be certain of their welcome
abroad (he is prescient, foreseeing the reception that emigrants would have
in the 1910s and 1920s), that the expense of relocation would be prohibi-
tive, and that the loss of black labor would have a devastating impact on
the U.S. economy. In response to proposals of this kind, Chesnutt suggested
that if it were true that the races could never live together, the emigration of
Southern *whites* would be far more practical.

> From one point of view scarcely any of the courses proposed are practicable for the
> ten million colored people in the United States. . . . Take, for instance, a wholesale
> emigration of the colored people to South America, or to Mexico. It is questionable
> whether they would be welcomed in any such mass. The expense of transportation,
> the loss of time, the withdrawal of so many laborers, would cost the country as
> much as the late War. . . . The Negro problem seems to worry the people of Geor-
> gia more than that of any other State; and yet the laws of Georgia, to say nothing
> of public opinion, are such to render it absolutely impossible for any organized
> movement for emigration to be successfully carried out. Cheap, abundant and eas-
> ily managed, white labor is not so easily procured that the Southern white planter
> would take their chances of getting along without colored labor. The Negroes must,
> as a mass, remain in the South. A more practicable emigration, that of the Southern
> whites, who are more able to go, strange to say, does not meet with much favor in
> their eyes, and yet, if, as they are so fond of asserting, it is impossible for the two
> races to live together on terms of equality, this is more likely to be the ultimate
> outcome."[23]

It is not clear from this statement if Chesnutt was aware of attempts by
white confederates to emigrate to other countries. A sense of a kindred culture created through a shared experience of slavery bolstered a set of expectations not only among Blacks but also among whites in the United States
that contributed to the zeal with which emigration schemes to Brazil were
embraced by both. In promoting emigration to Brazil in the 1860s, Southern

Confederates noted that Brazil had been an ally to the Southern states during the Civil War, according these states formal recognition and harboring and provisioning ships.[24] The way for the two to four thousand emigrants who reached Brazil (a number of whom eventually returned) had been prepared by the circulation of compelling first-person accounts published in Southern newspapers and widely read books.[25] These white emigrants did not operate in a social vacuum. "Personal acquaintances, family networks, freemasonry, business contacts, churches, and other associations constituted a dense web of relations among former and current slaveholders that encouraged white emigrants to leave the United States and sustained them in Brazil."[26] An account of colonist Sarah Bellona Smith Ferguson describes the motivation for their journey: "Early in 1865, [leaders] Bowen and Frank McMullen, disappointed and sore over 'the lost cause' and fully resolved never to submit to nigger rulers appointed by the Yanks, struck out to find a home for themselves and their families. After traveling over South America, especially Brazil, they reached the city of Iguape in the province of São Paulo, as the state was then called. From the government [and] especially favored by Dom Pedro II, they secured a grant of land of a size sufficient for a colony on the headwaters of the Juquiá."[27] While the government of Brazil's emperor, Dom Pedro II, was not the only one to extend an invitation to the Confederates — Mexico, Peru, Venezuela, Cuba, Jamaica, Canada, England, and Egypt also offered havens to the Southerners — their colony in Brazil was the most successful and long lasting, with communities of descendants existing to the present day.[28]

Even without the background of this information, the full power of Chesnutt's critique comes to the fore when Dr. Price's claim that in Miller's place he would leave the United States to live abroad is read in relation to "A Multitude of Counselors." The barred identification implied in the "if" ("*if* he had been in Miller's place") also speaks to Price's disavowal (as a representative American) of his own self-division (as a "white" American). In facing Miller, he refuses to turn to face himself. Price refuses double consciousness and reasserts himself as an American. Rather than turning Miller away, he could have, out of shame, turned himself away and been the one to leave. In fact, at the conclusion of the novel, the Carterets (who stand in for the Old South) would have sustained the loss of Price much more easily than the loss of Miller.

What Is a White Man?

The appeal against the color line brought before the U.S. Supreme Court by Plessy's lawyer, Albion Tourgée, had, according to Eric Sundquist, a two-pronged approach:

> In addition to detailing the mechanisms by which Jim Crow reconstituted the essence of slavery—the slave being in "bondage" to the entire white race, not just the property of a single owner—Tourgée turned the property argument on its head (and explicated his choice of a very light mulatto such as Homer Plessy to challenge the law) by insisting that the Louisiana segregation law had deprived Plessy of his property, which in this instance, was vested in his "reputation of being white." "Indeed," Tourgée asked, is whiteness "not the most valuable sort of property, being the master-key that unlocks the golden door of opportunity?" Apparently hoping to fool the property-minded justices into recognizing an element of color that would destroy Jim Crow by rendering it chaotic, Tourgée opened himself to the irony that such an argument would in reality protect only those who could pass—the mulatto elite—and define equal protection just as negatively and restrictively as the Court already had, only locating it at a different mark on the color line. (247)

The irony, recognized by Sundquist, in Tourgée's argument before the Supreme Court provides another key to Chesnutt's critique. Dr. Price, rather than Miller, sees the solution to the problem of the color line as lying elsewhere (outside of the United States). Miller, however, seems to recognize the contradiction implied in Sundquist's reading of Tourgée's argument. When Chesnutt put the thought of leaving the United States into Price's mind rather than in Miller's, he reveals what his essays suggest: the "elsewhere" will return as a reminder that if "amalgamation" addresses "the race problem," it does not do so completely. In other words, this approach leaves state-sanctioned racism in place. "Amalgamation," as Chesnutt presents it in "The Future American," "What Is a White Man?" and "A Solution to the Race Problem," always produces a remainder to which, as I will discuss presently, Chesnutt had an admittedly ambivalent response.

Chesnutt developed his theory of the "Future American" in three essays published in the *Boston Evening Transcript* in 1900. "The Future American: What the Race Is Likely to Become in the Process of Time" appeared on August 18; "The Future American: A Stream of Dark Blood in the Veins of Southern Whites" on August 25; and "The Future American: A Complete

Race Amalgamation Likely to Occur" on September 1.[29] The first article opens with a reference to a popular vision of the future American race as composed of the best elements of European races and "the elimination, by some strange alchemy, of all their undesirable traits." Chesnutt points out that this view of the future American is incomplete because it does not take into account the Indians and Negroes that will contribute to its constitution. "Any dream of a pure white race, of the Anglo-Saxon type, for the United States, may well be abandoned as impossible, even if desirable. That the future race will be predominantly white may well be granted; . . . that it will call itself white is reasonably sure; that it will conform closely to the white type is likely; but that it will have absorbed and assimilated the blood of the other two races is as sure as the operation of any law can be" (123).

Chesnutt suggests a mathematical formula by which to calculate the time it would take to achieve the future American. He speculates that if laws were passed requiring intermarriage, the one-eighth of the population that is Negro would marry white spouses (the remaining whites would presumably marry other whites) and their mulatto children, through marriage with whites, would produce quadroons, who would in turn produce octoroons, "who would probably call themselves white." In three generations "the pure white would be entirely eliminated, and there would be no perceptible trace of the blacks left" (125).[30] Chesnutt acknowledges that this artificially regulated process will never take place. He asserts, however, that time and human conduct will yield the same results. The second article demonstrates the extent of racial amalgamation by accounting for the number of legal whites with black ancestry. Included among this number are the writer/composer Alexander Pushkin as well as the writers Alexandre Dumas and Robert Browning. Lest readers exceptionalize these figures due to their foreign origins, the essay ends with a domestic example that Chesnutt will return to in subsequent articles. He recounts that in South Carolina, people with black ancestry can become legally white. Chesnutt proposes (according to a reasoning that anticipates Gilberto Freyre's elaboration of *embranqueci- mento*) that this flexibility derives from "the large preponderance of colored people in the State, which rendered the whites the more willing to augment their own number" (130). The last article restates the thesis of each of the essays: "[t]here can manifestly be no such thing as a peaceful and progressive civilization in a nation divided by two warring races, and homogeneity of type, at least in externals, is a necessary condition of harmonious social progress." This progress would be assured by the improvement of whites, "and if, in time, the more objectionable Negro traits are eliminated, and his better qualities correspondingly developed, his part in the future American may well be an important and valuable one" (135).

The Marrow of Tradition was published one year after the appearance of the Future American essays. The novel echoes several passages from the articles. Dr. Burns is described as "a fine type of Anglo-Saxon, as the term is used in speaking of our composite white population" (49). After Miller has been removed to the colored car, he takes up a newspaper to read an editorial extolling "the inestimable advantages which would follow to certain recently acquired islands by the introduction of American liberty, when the rear door of the car opened to give entrance to Captain George McBane" (57). In this scene, George McBane stands in for all proponents of the color line. His military title and the mention of the newspaper article recall U.S. imperialism. The critique of American imperialism linked to the white racism embodied in Captain McBane is rendered more biting when one recalls "The Future American." In that essay, Chesnutt had condemned the separate but equal doctrine, stating that "[t]he popular argument that the Negro ought to develop his own civilization, and has no right to share in that of the white race, unless by favor, comes with poor grace from those who are forcing their civilization among others at the cannon's mouth [in the expansionist Spanish American war]." The novel, in turn, reflects back on the essays to reinforce this message: U.S. domestic and international policies collude to strengthen the color line. As I will demonstrate shortly, Chesnutt does not let his future American cross the color line, even where the law allows it. This scene on the train, furthermore, serves as a reenactment of the events surrounding the 1896 Plessy v. Ferguson decision. Chesnutt exploits the irony that this case established the color line ("a distinction which is founded in the color of the two races" to quote one of the decisions). Plessy had to announce himself as black in order for the state to police his passing, or rather, his not passing. Like Plessy, Chesnutt announces his future American and bars him from crossing the color line. In fact, rather than endorsing passing himself, he explores how the courts have endorsed it. This is a point he had already explored in the 1889 essay, "What Is a White Man?" in which he suggests that if the court disingenuously assumes that the body will provide racial evidence ("so long as white men are distinguished from the other race by color," also from the decision). This essay demonstrates that there is a commingling of the races that from the perspective of the court and public opinion would be satisfactory to it.

"What Is a White Man?" is an argument against too quickly reading "The Future American" as an unambivalent endorsement of miscegenation as a solution to the "race problem." This essay's ironic tone invites a careful reading. The essay was written in response to a widely circulated pronouncement that "the all-pervading, all conquering Anglo Saxon race" must have exclusive and continuing control over the government, a control that Chesnutt clarifies later in the paragraph as associated with full citizenship rights. Chesnutt points out that the appellation Anglo Saxon is misleading because it masks the important exclusion — not of non-Anglo Saxon whites, but of nonwhites. He asks, given the high rate of racial intermingling, should not the white man ask himself what, indeed, is a white man? This question is especially important if full citizenship is, in fact, so valued. Reviewing the regulation of official racial identity, Chesnutt reveals that, while the moment of its occurrence may vary (one-fourth or one-eighth Negro blood), there is a point at which one ceases to be black in the eyes of the law and of custom and becomes white, if one so chooses. Chesnutt discusses in a more sustained way the South Carolina case he will mention in "The Future American." He cites a long extract from a State Supreme Court decision that acknowledges the difficulty of drawing a fixed color line:

> The definition of the term mulatto, as understood in this state, seems to be vague, signifying generally a person of mixed white or European and Negro parentage, in whatever proportions the blood of the two races may be mingled in the individual. But it is not invariably applicable to every admixture of African blood with the European, nor is one having all the features of the white to be ranked with the degraded class designated by the laws of this state as persons of color, because of some remote taint of the Negro race. The line of distinction, however, is not ascertained by any rule of law. . . . Juries would probably be justified in holding a person to be white in whom the admixture of blood did not exceed the proportion of one-eighth. But it is in all cases a question for the jury, to be determined by them upon the evidence of features and complexion afforded by inspection, the evidence of the rank and station in society [later clarified in yet another decision of that court to mean "by their exercise of the privileges of the white man"]. The only rule which can be laid down by the courts is that where there is a visible admixture of Negro blood, the individual is to be denominated a mulatto or person of color.[31] (70–71)

The court decision points to the conventionality of the attribution of color. Both whiteness and blackness are produced through a process of incorporation, which defines whiteness while remaindering blackness. What disappears into whiteness, i.e., blackness, is made visible in heightened ways in the remainder. The remainder is disavowed by (white) America in the interest of maintaining the illusion of an untroubled identity. In the second Future American essay, Chesnutt recalls the black ancestors of white citizens. Chesnutt pulls these whites back across the color line, even after they had "legally" crossed it into (white) America, revealing his ambivalence about the institutionalized passing into whiteness that the future American requires. If Chesnutt draws his characters back across the color line in his essays and fiction, it is because he recognizes the remainder of the mathematical process that the court "disappears." Like Plessy, Chesnutt will not allow his characters successfully to cross the color line if it means disavowing the remainder. For this reason his essays end with a call for legal rights specifically for Blacks.

Chesnutt wonders, furthermore, why white public opinion so readily accepts the South Carolina court decision. Clearly the law goes against popular representations of passing in fiction by white and black authors where there is no point beyond which a person with any black ancestry becomes white. He gives an explanation in line with Brazilian elaborations of *embranquecimento*:

> It is an interesting question why there should have been, and should still be, for that matter, the law of South Carolina, and why there should exist in that state a condition of public opinion which would accept such a law. Perhaps it may be attributed to the fact that the colored population of South Carolina always outnumbered the white population, and the eagerness of the latter to recruit to their ranks was sufficient to overcome in some measure their prejudice against Negro blood. (71)

Chesnutt does not take the opportunity to analyze this state of affairs as an argument in favor of miscegenation as a solution to the race problem or as proof that the future American race will settle the "complications which have grown out of the presence of the Negro on the continent" (73). Rather, he makes a moral critique. He points out that, if the color line were really about maintaining the purity of the white race, rather than about maintaining power and full citizenship exclusively for whites, whiteness would be more reliably preserved by virtue on the part of whites than by law.

In his 1916 speech addressing miscegenation, "A Solution for the Race Problem," Chesnutt suggests that the nations of South America, so similar in condition and racial makeup to the United States, provide a model of Blacks and whites living together harmoniously. After reviewing for his audience statistics enumerating the significant populations of people of African descent throughout Central and South America and the Caribbean, he gives particular attention to Brazil. He recalls for the audience Theodore Roosevelt's reflection on his visit to Brazil in 1913 published in *Outlook* magazine. According to Roosevelt, in the words Chesnutt quotes at length:

> This difference between the U.S. and Brazil is the tendency of Brazil to absorb the Negro. My observation leads me to believe that in "absorb" I have used exactly the right expression to describe this process. It is the Negro who is being absorbed and not the Negro who is absorbing the white man. . . . This does not mean that Brazilians are or will be become the "mongrel" people that they have been asserted to be by certain writers. . . . The great majority of the men and women I met, the leaders in the world of political and social effort, showed little if any trace of Negro blood than would be shown by the like number of similar men in a European capital.

Roosevelt cites an unidentified Brazilian of "pure white blood," who assures Roosevelt that, although the presence of the Negro is "the real problem" in both the United States and Brazil, the Brazilian method of absorption will work more effectively than the segregation of the United States. Segregation, according to this source, strengthens the Negro population in number and permanence. The Brazilian method ensures the eventual disappearance of the Negro. "You say that this result will be accomplished only by an adulteration, and therefore a weakening, of the pure white blood. I grant that this will have happened as regards a portion, perhaps a third of our population. I regret this, but it is the least objectionable of the alternatives." Roosevelt's interlocutor makes clear that whitening accompanies and is the condition for social mobility for Blacks, pointing out that there is no intermarriage in the upper classes, but only among the lower classes:

> The pure Negro is constantly growing less and less in numbers, and after two or more crosses of the white blood the Negro blood tends to disappear, as far as any different physical, mental, and moral traits of the race are concerned. When he has disappeared his blood will remain an appreciable, but in no way dominant, element in perhaps a third of our people, while the remaining two thirds will be pure whites. Granted that this strain will represent a slight weakening in one-third of the population, the result will be that in our country two-thirds of the population will have kept its full strength, with one third slightly weakened, while the Negro problem will have entirely disappeared. In your country all the white population will have

kept its full strength, but the Negro will remain in increased numbers and with an increased and bitter sense of isolation, so that the problem of his presence will be all the more menacing than at present. I do not say that ours is a perfect solution, but I regard it as a better solution than yours. (394–95)

Despite the obvious racism of this passage, Chesnutt understands the statement as representing the willingness of Brazilian whites to treat blacks on equal terms "without that shrinking sensitive fear of contamination by his blood which stands in the way of his advancement in this country" (395). For Chesnutt, Roosevelt's report reinforced, by contrast with the United States, Brazil's success in producing a "race at least so homogeneous that there will be no race feeling or friction or animosity" (395).

Roosevelt's report of his visit was republished in the major African American newspapers and journals, and endorsed in articles and editorials published in the *Philadelphia Tribune,* the *Crusader,* the *Baltimore Afro-American,* the *Tulsa Star,* the *Negro World,* and the *Chicago Defender,* among others. W. E. B. Du Bois wrote one of the few editorials critical of Roosevelt's report (although not critical of Brazil).[32] He states that Roosevelt provided "three facts and two falsehoods" in his article. "The facts are: 1. Brazil is absorbing the Negro race. 2. There is no color bar to advancement. 3. There is no social bar to advancement, but the mass of full-blooded Negroes are still in the lower social classes." The falsehoods are that people of color in the United States have equal opportunity and that the Brazilians believe that the "Negro element" represents a "slight weakness" (32). To rebut Roosevelt, Du Bois cites extensively and approvingly the words of João Baptista de Lacerda, director of the National Museum of Rio de Janeiro, whom I quoted in the introduction and who was a delegate to the International Races Conference in 1911 also attended by Du Bois, pointing out that Lacerda's remarks attest to the importance of the *métis* (Du Bois's preferred term for mulatto) in the history and culture of Brazil. Du Bois interprets Roosevelt's failure to present the situation in Brazil without falsehood as deriving from a fear of endorsing miscegenation, a fear that leads Roosevelt to obfuscate the fact that whites prefer to marry whites and people of color to marry other people of color without requiring the enforcement of "poverty, crime, prostitution, ignorance, lynching, mob violence and the ruin of democratic government for the unfortunate victims of their lies" (34).

Despite his own positive summary of Roosevelt's article, Chesnutt acknowledges that because of the preservation of the color line, Brazil's "solution for the race problem" is unlikely in the United States:

> So the settlement of the Race question by the Brazilian method of absorbing the Negro is academic rather than practical, and will have to be left to the future. And we are relegated to other methods of getting together with white people so as to live harmoniously and happily with them. Many of them, in fact I think most of them, are good people, and anxious to do the right thing as they see it. All we can do is make them see it as we do, to maintain the principle of equal rights and equal opportunities to all men, with equal rewards according to their deserts, and to so conduct ourselves and develop and use the power, intellectual, political, industrial and spiritual, that is latent in tens of millions of people that it will be impossible to longer deny them these equal rights and opportunities. (400)

While "race hatred makes a sham of democracy" (399) for Chesnutt, the future of the future American achieved through "amalgamation" is too far off, too riddled with contradictions, and too dearly bought to be embraced by black people as a solution to the race problem.

In *The Marrow of Tradition,* Chesnutt acknowledges the remainder that his essays suggest, yet do not directly address. It is the work of his fiction to attend to the remainder. In addition to recounting the story of the riot, the novel explores the relationship of Olivia (Merkell) Carteret, a Southern aristocrat and Janet Miller, Dr. Miller's black wife. Olivia discovers among her father's papers after his death evidence that he had married his black housekeeper and fathered Janet, a legitimate child.

> A fire was burning in the next room, on account of the baby,—there had been a light frost the night before, and the air was somewhat chilly. For the moment the room was empty. Mrs. Carteret came out from her chamber and threw the offending paper into the fire and watched it slowly burn. *When it had been consumed, the carbon residue of one sheet still retained its form,* and she could read the words on the charred portion. A sentence, which had escaped her eye in her rapid reading, stood out in ghostly black upon the gray background: —
> "All the rest and *residue* of my estate I devise and bequeath to my daughter Olivia Merkell, the child of my beloved first wife." (258, my emphasis)

This passage occurs in the middle of the episode in which Olivia tries to do away with the proof of a legacy from her father to the child he had with his black housekeeper, evidence that would force her to acknowledge publicly her half-sister, Janet. She had resolved with her husband that the illegitimacy of her sister, an illegitimacy secured by her race,[33] precludes any obligation on the part of Olivia toward Janet or her child. The description of the burning of the will joins semantically two aspects of the issue of responsibility in the odd reiteration of the word residue, which reinforces the relationship between the two sisters as one deriving from love, and involving responsibility and debt.[34] The first mention of residue describes what is leftover from the fire's consumption of the "offending" paper. The true story of the offense, or the story of the true offense, resists consumption by the fire, and produces Janet as a residue or remainder. (She is described on page 263 as the "daughter [who] remained.") Janet is the residue that is, rather than money or land, the true legacy that Merkell leaves behind to his daughter Olivia. The distinction between legacy and heritage, on the one hand, associated with and guaranteed by law, and residue, on the other hand, is the distinction between what is left (as in left to) and what is left over, between what is legally transmitted and what escapes determination by the law.

Olivia understands that the reference to a first wife is an acknowledgment of a second wife, Janet's mother, Julia, and leads her to investigate further the envelope that contained the will. In the envelope is a letter in which Merkell confesses his marriage to Julia and their love for one another. The legacy, the confession, and Olivia's attempts to deny the past and her relationship to Janet put her in a moral dilemma; she cannot resolve what she owes Janet and why.

> [T]he woman [Julia] had *not* been white, and the same rules of moral conduct . . . *could* not . . . apply, as between white people! For if this were not so, slavery had been, not only an economic mistake, but a great crime against humanity. If it had been such a crime, as for a moment she dimly perceived it might have been, then through the long centuries there had been piled up a catalogue of wrong and outrage, which, if the law of compensation be a law of nature, must for some time, somewhere, in some way be atoned for. She herself had not escaped the penalty. (266)

Olivia cannot resolve what the novel calls her "moral pocket" (an expression that links economic debt to the moral debt) leading her to become physically ill. Neither can the novel's closure resolve its own moral pocket. At the end of the novel, during a race riot that has resulted in the deaths of many black people, including Janet's young son, Olivia's own son becomes ill and Janet's physician husband, Dr. Miller, is the only one who can cure him (as all the white doctors are absent). When Olivia comes to the Millers' home seeking help for her son, she is directed to Janet, who is keeping a vigil over her own dead son's body. The narrator reinforces Dr. Miller's first impression of the striking resemblance between the two women, who could stand in one for the other, as they both weep for their sons. The physical likeness of the two sisters is paralleled by the likeness of their situations, which creates the expectation for the reader of an identification that Olivia waits for, having confessed all she knows.

In the cannibalistic structure of identification that this scene between the two women enacts, Olivia, as the white sister, expects to incorporate her sister. Olivia believes that Janet should put herself inside Olivia and be identified with her. That Olivia might identify with Janet, the black sister, in this way — that Janet could take her in — is not entertained as a possibility. To the extent that Olivia can be read as America, identification can only take place in one direction. Janet, however, resists. She rejects the identification: "I throw back your father's name, your father's wealth, your sisterly recognition. I want none of them — they are bought too dear!" (329), but she sends her husband to treat her sister's son. Although the novel closes with Miller's arrival at the Carteret home while the child is still alive, the novel does not guarantee any positive statement of resolution. The pursuit and establishment of an ethical relationship would require an identification that would be the undoing of identity and of difference, an option so unacceptable that it can neither be assumed by Janet or Olivia, nor promoted by narrative. The other option, modeled by their husbands, of rejecting any possibility of a relationship "between the races" is equally intolerable.

The scene between the sisters mirrors and revises another account of a failed identification, this one between the husbands of these two women. Olivia comes to the Millers' home to beg for Dodie's life only after her husband informs her that he has unsuccessfully petitioned the doctor. When Major Carteret had asked Miller to operate on his son, Miller responded by opening the door wider so that Carteret could witness the spectacle of Janet weeping by their son's dead body:

> Carteret possessed a narrow, but a logical mind, and except when confused and blinded by his prejudices, had always tried to be a just man. In the agony of his own predicament, — in the horror of the situation at Miller's house, — for a moment the veil of race prejudice was rent in twain, and he saw things as they were, in their correct proportions and relations, — saw clearly and convincingly that he had no

standing here, in the presence of death, in the home of this stricken family. Miller's refusal to go with him was pure elemental justice; he could not blame the doctor for his stand. He was indeed conscious of a certain involuntary admiration for a man who held in his hands the power of life and death, and could use it, with strict justice, to avenge his own wrongs. *In Dr. Miller's place,* he would have done the same thing. Miller had spoken the truth, — as he had sown, so must he reap! He could not expect, could not ask, this father to leave his own household at such a moment. Pressing his lips together with grim courage, and bowing mechanically, as though to Fate rather than the physician, Carteret turned and left the house. (320–21, my emphasis)

In a moment of understanding that rips aside the veil (anticipating Du Bois), Carteret puts himself in Miller's place. As a result of this identification, Carteret walks away, accepting fatalistically that there will be complete separation between them. He reasserts his white identity.

According to Freud, a healthy ego will only admit (to) what corresponds to its organization, without remainders. But what happens to what will not or cannot be admitted into consciousness? Freud responds that the ego creates a symptom.[35] The symptom is a creation of the psyche's anxiety relative to that which it has produced: its remainder. The symptom allows us to recognize the other is/as our fiction. The importance of the symptom is that it marks a presence and an absence; it marks what can never be known. The self has no language to make the remainder known to itself, because to know the remainder is to annihilate the self as it has been produced. The political implication of this formulation is the *opposite* of what is claimed for (racial) democracy. This is the power of Janet's refusal of identification with Olivia at the end of *The Marrow of Tradition.* She refuses to identify with her sister and blocks (if it were possible) her sister's identification with her, yet she sends her husband to save the child. This scene suggests a posture that would free one to act, to act with humility, not knowing and unknown. Janet does not ask Olivia to identify with her, to cease being a white Southern aristocratic woman, before she acts. Janet does not desire that Olivia know her or that she know Olivia before acting for their community.

From Janet's perspective, the approach to overcoming the racial division of their community through identification would come at too high a cost. The politics of identification in its aim toward unity, wholeness, and peace is, in fact, violent; it always requires a death, the loss of the unknown. This violence, expressed in the metaphors of incorporation that structure the ego and the notion of (racial) democracy, could be felt more productively by the self as its remainder. The ego or any other identity formation, in living on less comfortable terms with its symptom, would have a greater possibility for producing remainders that are various rather than disavowed. Janet models this possibility by resisting for herself and for Olivia the need for each to know the other (the kind of thinking that informs proclamations such as "if you are not [with] us, you are against us) before acting. While Janet's action does not reduce her suffering, it does preserve her position as a resistant remainder, one that has refused the choice of being only inside or only outside.

FOUR

The New Negro and the Turn to South America

He would not Africanize America, for America has too much to teach the world and Africa. He would not bleach his Negro soul in a flood of white Americanism, for he knows that Negro blood has a message for the world. He simply wishes to make it possible for a man to be both a Negro and an American.

—W. E. B. Du Bois, *The Souls of Black Folk*

"There is absolutely no color line": Democratic Models and Destinations

"It was with secret thrills of a peculiar and inexpressible joy that I, at last, on the third day of last February, accompanied by my wife, sailed from the port of New York for a visit to the South American republics. It was the opening chapter in the realization of a golden dream long cherished."[1] So began the first in a series of articles that appeared in the *Chicago Defender,* in which Robert Abbott, the newspaper's founder and publisher, chronicled his 1923 tour. Abbott's stated goals in undertaking this trip were many: to see the Negro in a "modern society" located in an environment similar to that of Africa; to compare the effect of "Latin-European" racial attitudes to those of North America on democratic participation; to uncover the outlines of South America's "future ethnic homogeneity"; and to provide a sense of the economic and social opportunities "for that enlightened and growing group of North American Negroes, who so recently are beginning to look to the South American continent as, after all, the most likely haven for a solution of their individual problems" (24 April 1923). Abbott informed his readers that as a result of his trip, he was "more determined than ever to fight to make our country, like Brazil, like the Argentine, lands of true democracy, rather than a country of mock democracy" (26 May 1923).

The son of formerly enslaved parents, Robert Abbott had studied printing at Virginia's Hampton Institute and law at Chicago's Kent College of
Law. On 5 May 1905, he founded the *Chicago Defender*, which would
almost immediately become the United States' most widely read black periodical. The newspaper's motto was "American Race Prejudice Must Be
Destroyed."[2] Initially focused on local news, the paper quickly expanded
its reporting and readership. Since Chicago was a railroad center of the
United States at the beginning of the twentieth century, the porters, railroad
men, waiters, and stage performers who regularly rode the trains carried the
paper across the country and guaranteed its expanding popularity and influence. Rail workers would take copies of the *Chicago Defender* and return
with out-of-town papers and magazines for the paper's editors. Entertain-
ers on tour would collect news, obtain subscriptions, and recruit agents to
distribute papers. Consequently, the paper soon reflected a national set of
concerns. It became an outlet for denouncing racism and inequalities and
for promoting opportunities to improve the political and economic situation of its readers.

Ship workers supplemented the work of rail workers in expanding the
paper's range of influence by delivering the newspaper to ports around the
world. Before long, the pages of the *Chicago Defender* included numerous
articles on issues affecting people of color, both domestically and internationally. In 1915, Abbott opened offices in New York and London, enabling
the paper to address its growing readership's broad concerns. The paper's
circulation rose dramatically. By 1918, circulation reached 100,000 and by
1920 had nearly tripled to 285,571. Two-thirds of sales were made outside
of Chicago and 23,000 copies were sold in New York City alone. The paper's
2,359 agents ensured that its circulation would continue to increase.

The *Chicago Defender* played a crucial and well-documented role in the
Great Migration. At the beginning of the twentieth century, many factors
impelled thousands of black people to leave the South for the northern cities. These included the failure of Reconstruction following the Civil War, the
increasing poverty among Blacks who were less and less able to eke out a living as sharecroppers, the effects of the Mississippi River floods in 1912 and
1913, a boll weevil epidemic, the institution of segregation, and racist violence in the form of beatings, murders, rapes, and lynchings. These factors,
combined with the curiosity inspired by the numbers already heading North
and free train tickets provided by factory owners anxious to increase ranks

depleted by the Great War, propelled Blacks northward in search of employment and freedom from the violence and oppressive conditions of the South. In 1917, W. E. B. Du Bois speculated that more than 250,000 "colored workmen" had moved to the North.[3] Between 1915 and 1920, Chicago's black population increased by 148 percent. Articles in the *Defender* contributed to this upsurge. After a series of *Chicago Defender* articles emphasized the advantages of moving to the North, the Chicago Urban League received 940 letters inquiring on conditions in Chicago. The newspaper even provided for excursions and group fare rates to support the migration to the North.

While the black press promoted migration as a relief from the effects of racism in the South, the advent of World War I introduced another set of concerns. The black press, including the *Chicago Defender*, supported the war effort, yet called attention to the duplicity of a nation that required black soldiers to die in defense of a democracy in which they did not fully share. Initially, Blacks saw participation in the First World War as a conduit to the benefits of full citizenship in the United States: "Is there a man anywhere in the world that would deny to the race that these men represent, since they fought for the freedom of the world, their own freedom in every thing that relates to full citizenship?"[4] The black press in the United States reported overwhelming evidence to answer the question in the affirmative, noting that "while Colored soldiers have been bravely fighting to establish a world-wide democracy, . . . Judge Lynch and his followers have been busy in mobbing, lynching and burning colored men, women and children at the stakes in America."[5] Many argued that when the government allowed lynching to proceed unchecked, it undermined the credibility of the United States abroad. In an open letter to President Wilson, Kelly Miller, dean of Howard University, avowed:

> Mr. President, you have sounded the trumpet of democratization of the nations, which shall never call retreat. But Mr. President, a chain is no stronger than its weakest link. A doctrine that breaks down at home is not fit to be propagated abroad. One is reminded of the pious slaveholder who became deeply impressed with the plea for foreign missions that he sold one of his slaves to contribute liberally to the cause. Why democratize the nations of the earth, if it leads them to delight in the burning of human beings after the manner of Springfield, Waco, Memphis, and East St. Louis while the nation looks helplessly on?[6]

Significantly, Miller excludes Brazil from his catalogue of nations that could be susceptible to exulting at the public spectacle of the death of human beings because in Brazil, "under a Latin dispensation, where a more complex racial situation exists than in the United States, racial peace and good-will prevail" (148–49).

The hostility of the United States was contrasted to the welcoming attitude of Europeans, especially the French, toward black soldiers from the United States and from the colonies. In the pages of *The Crisis,* W. E. B. Du Bois reported on the recognition France had accorded black soldiers: "It was France — almighty and never-dying France leading the world again. . . . Men of Africa! How fine a thing to be a black Frenchman in 1919 — imagine such a celebration in America!"[7] Days later in another editorial, Du Bois would assert that the democracy for which black soldiers so valiantly had fought could be found in Europe rather than in the United States. "Fellow blacks," he proclaimed, "we must join the democracy of Europe."[8]

Europe, at first, was held up as the model of democracy for people of African descent throughout the world. African American leaders, however, soon found themselves compelled to take into account the full range of negative actions taken by France, Belgium, and England as colonial powers in Africa, Asia, and the Caribbean. At the 1919 Pan-African Conference in Paris organized by Du Bois, delegates testified to widespread and persistent atrocities committed by colonial powers.[9] The terrible treatment of black soldiers in Europe was quickly shown to rival that of black soldiers returning to the United States. Black veterans, for example, were not allowed to participate in Britain's Victory Celebrations of 19 July 1919. These veterans as well as students from Africa and the Caribbean, who also refused the government's repatriation initiative and instead opted to remain in Britain after the end of the war, were subjected to vicious attacks in the streets and at home. Cardiff, Liverpool, and other seaports experienced violent riots against black servicemen.[10] Although the white press reported on the riots, it was the black British press that called attention to the hypocrisy of the British attitude: "They [black soldiers] were drowned, butchered in cold blood and terribly maltreated and maimed. . . . Every ounce of strength was put into the struggle by the Black man. . . . He fought with the White man to save the White man's home . . . and the War was won. . . . Black men all over the world are asking . . . What are we going to get out of it all?"[11]

The factors that eventually complicated the idealization of Europe and even Africa and the Caribbean as possible democratic models and destinations are absent from the discussions of South America. African American

writers did not generally perceive Argentina and Brazil as colonial powers nor did they perceive these nations as beset with the internal political
and ideological struggles for power that marked the colonized and formerly
colonized nations of the Caribbean and Africa. These perceptions, coupled
with the idea that South American nations were free of racial prejudice, led
African American writers, journalists, and activists of varying political and
ideological positions to invoke South America as a positive example in their
writings and speeches on citizenship and democracy.

In the first two decades of the twentieth century, a number of books on
Brazil appeared that had a significant impact on the way that Brazil was
conceived of in discussions that addressed the relationship between race and
democracy. In 1910, the British colonialist and explorer, Sir Harry Johnston, published the extensively illustrated *The Negro in the New World*, an
"idiosyncratic" work, which, in many ways, anticipates Gilberto Freyre's
Casa Grande e Senzala.[12] This work, based on a research trip promoted by
President Theodore Roosevelt, was cited by Chesnutt, Du Bois (whose visit
to London in 1911 to attend the Universal Races Conference was facili-
tated by Johnston; Johnston's subsequent ill health prompted him to ask
Du Bois to represent him at the conference[13]), and Booker T. Washington
(who was interviewed by Johnston for his book and who reviewed the finished product for *The Journal of the African Society*). Kelly Miller also
reviewed *The Negro in the New World* in 1914.[14] The publication of Johnston's study was preceded by former Governor of Jamaica (and Secretary of
State of India) Lord Sydney Olivier's *White Capital and Coloured Labor*
(1906),[15] which included several chapters on "The Transplanted Negro" in
the Americas and followed in 1914 by the British historian and politician
James Bryce's *South America: Observations and Impressions*.[16] These last
two works served as important sources for the Chesnutt essays discussed in
the last chapter.

In 1926, Roy Nash published *The Conquest of Brazil*.[17] A favorable, unsigned review of it in *The Crisis* begins with the observation that
many American writers had characterized Brazil as a white country or at
least one that is "emerging white." These studies ignored black and indigenous people except to speak of them as "slaves or peons." The reviewer
observes, however, that the white sociologist Nash, the third secretary of
the NAACP, had refused to write such a book. Following a format similar to that used by Johnston and Bryce, and one that would be used by

Freyre, Nash discusses the interactions among and the contributions of the "Portuguese, Negroes and Indians" to Brazil, and the "Negroid strain of the Portuguese themselves" that predisposed them to be "more color-blind than any other people in Europe. They are so color-blind that they will look straight at a black man and see only a man." The passages the reviewer quotes from the book highlight its racial aspects rather than the extensive chapters on the environment or the economy, including one that has Nash echoing the familiar notion that "Destiny has erected in Brazil a social laboratory which shall reveal the significance of 'race.'" Nash predicts that the world will watch to see if Brazil's experiment fails, giving fodder to those who bemoan the "rising tide of color" or "yellow peril" (these are references to white supremacist Lothrop Stoddard's 1920 work, *The Rising Tide of Color against White World Supremacy*), or succeeds in giving the world an example of "a civilization powerful enough to enable her to sit on the bench of equality beside the Powers of the temperate zone who now proclaim themselves Lords of Creation."[18] Nash does not predict the final outcome.

While differing in the level of condescension in tone, these works all share many similarities: They examine the interactions of the "Portuguese, Negroes, and Indians" with each other and the environment; they note the lack of a color line in South America and the Caribbean in contrast to the United States; and they all dispute the inherent criminality of black men that was used as a justification for lynching in the United States, arguing that the nonexistence of rape by black men outside of the United States undermined claims of its existence within it.[19]

These books were accompanied by a spate of articles and speeches published in the *Amsterdam News*, the *Baltimore Afro-American*, *Opportunity*, *Atlanta Independent*, *Philadelphia Tribune*, *Tulsa Star*, the *Crusader*, and the *Chicago Defender*, among others. Although the topics of the articles varied widely, the underlying message to readers did not. For all of these writers, the most significant point was that Brazil had no color line and, furthermore, could provide the United States with a solution to its racial divide. This solution could come either in the form of emigration from the United States to Brazil or in the form of an example of a society in which racial mixture was encouraged and racial discrimination unknown. For many, attention to Brazil was both instructive and opportune.

Underlying the comparisons of the United States and Brazil were perceived differences in race relations between the two nations. The United States was assumed to have a clearly defined and rigorously enforced line between the black and white races, which established that racial mixture could only produce black bodies. The color line was thought to derive from the harshness of U.S. slavery and the hostilities of the Civil War. In contrast, Brazil's apparent absence of a color line was deemed to derive from a relatively mild system of slavery and extension of cordial relations that had led to the abolition of slavery through decree rather than as a result of war.

> [S]lavery was never cruel and harsh in Brazil. The relation of slave to master was much in the nature of a hired servant. They belonged to the same church, observed the same feast days, and often married into the family of the master. Today the same fraternal relationship exists. All celebrate Emancipation Day together. It is a national holiday like our Fourth of July.
>
> The country [Brazil] is fortunate in having no deep wounds to heal. There is no division of the country caused by difference of opinion on the slave question. Thirty-two years ago the slaves were freed by universal common consent without shedding a drop of blood.[20]

In the early decades of the twentieth century, visitor after black visitor to South America generally and Brazil specifically noted with satisfaction that no color line existed to the south of the United States. Contributors to the black press repeatedly proclaimed, "There is absolutely no color line"[21] in Brazil. An excerpt from a 1914 article in the *Philadelphia Tribune* provides one of many examples:

> In Brazil . . . [the] question of color does not exist there, though the date of their enfranchisement is of a more recent date than that of this country. There a man is judged by personal merit. There is no blank wall of a prejudice that faces him. All the opportunities of life are open to him. If there is a failure it is by the individual and not from any prejudice on the part of the dominant class to keep him down or to deny to him the rights of a man and a citizen of Brazil. There is no line of demarcation drawn anywhere in the business world, the mechanic arts, in the artisan class or in the social world.[22]

Many, the historian Carter Woodson among them, credited the high rate of miscegenation for the absence of the color line. Noting the penetration of "Negroid" races into Italy, France, and even Great Britain and Ireland,

Woodson declares that: "[b]ecause of the temperament of the Portugese [sic], this infusion of African blood was still more striking in their country. As the Portugese [sic] are a good-natured people void of race hate they did not dread the miscegenation of the races." This attitude extended to Brazil where the first settlers mixed with the indigenous peoples. Their offspring served to facilitate the "assimilation of Negroes" by intermarrying with them when they came. "After the emancipation in 1888, the already marked tendency toward this fusion of the slaves and the master classes gradually increased."[23]

The twentieth-century characterization of the Brazilian system of slavery as mild would have come as a surprise to nineteenth century readers of the black press in the United States, who had been given a very different view of slavery in Brazil. These readers had been made aware of the deplorable conditions of enslaved Africans in Brazil, of the existence of maroon communities or *quilombos* such as Palmares, and of the events leading up to Brazil's belated abolition of slavery in 1888. In the summer of 1884, for example, the *Cleveland Gazette,* a black weekly, published an article informing its readers of violence against the enslaved in the efforts toward the abolition of slavery in Brazil.

Rio Janeiro [sic] letters to the *New York Herald* tell of the general dissatisfaction prevalent, and the serious trouble growing out of the emancipation movement. In April, a wealthy planter, and the moneyed partner in a coffee commission house, went to his plantation about six miles from Razende, a town in the province of Rio Janeiro [sic]. The morning of the next day he went out to see his slaves on their way to work. The last three in the procession threw themselves upon him, knocked him down, slashed him with knives and billhooks, and in a few moments left him a mangled corpse. Then they proceeded to the town, delivered themselves to the police, and were put in jail. A few days later a mob of four hundred armed men, residents of the province, entered Razende at four o'clock in the morning. They overpowered the guard, entered the jail, forced the keys from the jailer, went to the cells of the three slaves who had murdered their master, dragged them to the public square, and after diabolical acts of brutality literally chopped them to pieces. Then the mob marched off, shouting for justice. The next day telegrams were sent to Rio Janeiro [sic] asking for assistance, as news had come that the slaves of various plantations were to attack the town and destroy it. The police, who immediately left for the town, found the citizens armed and alarmed. But the slaves presumably got wind of the presence of the officers and nothing was done. The abolition propaganda had worked with some success in the province of Rio Grande do Sul, seventy-eight slaves having been freed at one abolition meeting at Uruguayana and twelve at another at Pelotas. Slowly but surely slavery is dying out even in Brazil.

These outbreaks among the enslaved, although at the fearful cost of life, can but hasten their emancipation, and we hope enlist in their cause such men as helped most materially in the emancipation of the American Negro.[24]

While this description calls attention to the role of black Brazilians in their own emancipation and endorses their acts of resistance, it highlights, however, in the account of the lynching, a view of Brazilian slavery that is violent in a very familiar way, linking the experience of black people from the United States to those of Brazil. Given this background, it is not surprising that the reports that circulated only a few short years after the official end of Brazilian slavery attesting to Blacks and Whites living in harmony would have made a strong impression, inviting readers to wonder what had happened in such a short time to distinguish Brazil from the United States. The example of an area of the world that shared with the United States a common past of slavery and, yet, an apparently different present provided for black Americans a compelling argument against the existence of the color line, antimiscegenation laws, Jim Crow, and lynching. If assaults against black safety and citizenship no longer took place in South America, they reasoned, why should they continue in the United States?

Black Internationalism: Bound by Blood and Common Interest

The black press in the United States advanced the image of a South American and a specifically Brazilian racial democracy as a model for the improvement of the racial situation of Blacks from the United States. Even before Robert Abbott's series of articles, titled *My Trip through South America*, in which he wrote of his desire to see Negroes living without the consciousness of a racial difference "so strangely potent in hindering the natural and wholesome evolution of 12 millions of Negroes within the confines of North American society" (56), other journalists and leaders had advocated a Brazilian model of racial democracy: "Brazil offers a present and first hand evidence of the solution of the race problem by intermarriage. This example will not be lost on the American Negro. To him it is becoming plainer and plainer that the longer he remains a group within a group, the longer will the stronger group prey upon the weaker and less numerous."[25] If, in what follows, I focus on Abbott's writings, it is because he is exemplary rather than exceptional.

Once he arrived in Brazil, Abbot described a "perfect political state" thoroughly homogeneous in blood as a result of intermarriage. He made the observation that "Negro people are evident on every hand, enjoying with inconceivable ease the entire facilities of a present day democracy" (68). According to Abbott, Brazil's adherence to a strict notion of democracy, understood as racial democracy, distinguished it from the United States, making it a model and a potential home for African American professionals from the United States. "The idea will be to open up a practical avenue for commercial enterprise and to create a connection in Brazil for the Negro of the United States who may desire to settle in a new country, under conditions more in harmony with his notion of freedom. . . . Neither exploitation nor colonization is involved in this scheme of practical business" (77).

Others had already endorsed this plan. R. W. Merguson, a Pittsburgh journalist, for example, had, in 1915, advocated for it, qualifying, however, the type of emigrant that would be desirable:

> For the ambitious and intelligent colored man, in quest of fairer fields for expansion and growth, for an atmosphere not tainted or permeated by the endless varieties and forms of race prejudice to be found in the United States, it might be well to turn his attention in the direction of Brazil. For the man without capital, the inducements are not alluring. Far from it. But if he has capital, or if a professional man or woman seeks an unrestricted and welcome environment, Brazil offers many inducements. Doctors, dentists, lawyers, teachers and professional men in any line do well.[26] (41)

Significantly, like the books on Brazil that I discussed in the opening of this chapter, Merguson's article contains several photographs of the landscape, architecture, and the people. These images reinforce the idea of Brazil as an agreeable and cosmopolitan country — a "Negro land,"[27] where people of various colors and races easily interact with one another in work and social settings.

This sense of the promise of South America for black business people was also reflected in popular culture. For example, the *Baltimore Afro-American* considered newsworthy the fact that Oscar Micheaux, the prolific black filmmaker, saw opportunities beyond the borders of the United States: "Oscar Micheaux, the film producer," they reported, "dropped by the office last week and told of a planned trip that will include a tour of the West Indies, and South America. The objective of that journey is to place the Micheaux product in those places. A publicity campaign will also be launched to acquaint the citizens with the colored productions."[28] I have not been able to establish yet whether Micheaux actually completed this tour; however, the timing, plot, and cast of his 1927 film, *The Millionaire*, would suggest that he did.[29] This now-lost film, released two years after the announcement of his planned voyage, includes Robert Abbott and his wife in its cast ("they played their parts better than the veteran Charlie Chaplin . . . [and] received $100 a minute"). The film's protagonist is a black man who sought his fortune and relief from racism in South America. Advertised and reviewed in numerous papers, its plot was described in sensationalistic prose:

> *The Millionaire* deals with the adventures of Pelham Guitry, a soldier of fortune, a man who, as a youth, possessing great initiative and a definitive objective, hies himself far from the haunts of his race—thousands of miles away to South America. There, upon the wild, billowy plains of the Argentine, he becomes a sort of "Wild Bull of the Pampas." Fifteen years fly by, and, having amassed a huge fortune, he returns to America, his heart anxious and hungry for that most infinite of all things—woman. In New York he meets Celia Washington, the siren—a woman with an inferiority complex—a beautiful, dazzling talented—but unworthy creature; the concubine of Lizard, a most notorious underworld character in New York, who, in league with Brock, king of the underworld, seek to inveigle him into marriage with the vampire.[30]

The link that Micheaux makes in his film between South America and Harlem is one that I will discuss in more detail at the end of this chapter in relation to its appearance in two Harlem Renaissance novels: *Passing* by Nella Larsen and *Plum Bun* by Jessie Redmon Fauset. The film reinforces how literary and popular visual culture during the New Negro Movement registered the public discussion of the relationship between the United States and South America in general and Brazil in particular as one of opportunity.[31]

In a carefully researched article on the extent to which the United States government and the Brazilian government colluded to undermine the emigration of Blacks to Brazil, Teresa Meade and Gregory Alonso Pirio discuss the history of the colonization syndicates that promoted black settlement outside of the United States. According to the authors, groups of black North Americans responded to a notice that appeared in the black press in the summer of 1920 publicizing Brazil's programs to promote immigration. The Brazilian government had targeted white developers and laborers by this plan, which promised land, free medical care, and free transportation, as well as free food and lodging in Brazil until the immigrant was settled. The groups of black businessmen involved in promoting emigration, however, were unaware that this program expressly barred people of color from entering the country with the goal of settling. Months after the appearance of this notice, a Chicago group incorporated the Brazilian American Colonization Syndicate (BACS) in Delaware. The syndicate advertised its efforts in the leading black papers of the period, including *The Crisis*, the *Baltimore Afro-American*, and the *Chicago Defender*. The ads asked: "Do you want Liberty and Wealth in a Land of Plenty? Then Buy Land in Brazil South America. Unlimited Opportunity and Equality!"[32]

The United States government recognized that Brazilian authorities did not want Blacks to enter the country and cooperated in raising barriers to black emigration. In an unsigned editorial in *The Crisis*, presumably written by Du Bois, the author addresses "the extraordinary effort on the part of the United States to keep Negroes from migrating, especially to Mexico and South America."[33] The article conveys to the readers the response of the American ambassador to Brazil to a request by *The Crisis* for clarification of Brazilian policy regarding black emigration:

> Replying to your letter of January 21, 1927, I beg to say that neither the Brazilian Constitution nor Laws define the word "Negro," but that under the Brazilian Federal law which was promulgated through Executive Decree No. 4, 247, of January 6, 1921, the entry of aliens into national territory is subject to Administrative approval, permission to enter being refused when public order or national interest are considered to be affected. According to the convenience of the moment, restrictions are applied to all foreigners, irrespective of race or color and the restrictions which were formulated in 1921 as to the admission of United States citizens of color were framed as the result of a report to the effect that a syndicate had been formed in the United States to send American Negroes to the states of Matto Grosso and Goyaz for colonization purposes.
>
> The Brazilian Government would probably be willing to allow such American Negroes as desire to visit Brazil for the purposes of travel or business, or who are in transit through that country, to obtain passport visas from such Brazilian officials abroad as are competent to issue them. (132)

The editorial interprets Brazil's reluctance to admit Blacks as the result of propaganda from the United States government and as the usurpation of Brazil's right to oversee migration and recommends that U.S. Blacks "spread some propaganda ourselves among our neighbors to the south who are bound to us by blood and common interests" (132).

The writer of this editorial, like many other writers before and after, failed to recognize Brazil's role in barring the immigration of people of color. Meade and Pirio assert in their article that the extensive efforts Brazil made during the 1920s to prevent any Blacks from entering the country were not just to ensure the "success" of the strategy of whitening the population. Brazilian authorities also feared the entry of ideologies that promoted race consciousness, especially at a time when Blacks were already organizing socially and politically (98). "In fact," assert Meade and Pirio, "whitening would only ultimately succeed as long as no counter-ideology appeared that asserted the equality, or even the superiority, of blackness" (102).

The ambassador's comments, as conveyed by *The Crisis* editorial, imply, furthermore, that it was precisely in keeping with the policy of encouraging white immigration to speed the process of *embranquecimento* that in 1900, 1906, and 1920 the census omitted all color designations. The *Instituto Brasileiro de Geografia e Estatística* (IBGE) had justified the practice by arguing that the classification by color would establish a *linha de cor* (a color line) incompatible with Brazil's newly formed democracy. Sam Adamo has argued, however, that in omitting color distinctions, the IBGE was less concerned with democratic principles than with concealing the high number of Blacks in the Brazilian population.[34]

In fact, Abbot's preparation for his journey with his wife was affected by these policies. In describing the preparations for their trip, he remarks that "[w]e received prompt cordial service from all save the Brazilian consul. Thus, it was only after pressure was brought to bear did I succeed in getting the consul from Brazil to visa our passports. This, it seems, has been the experience of every American Negro during the last few years who has sought entry into Brazil," an experience he attributes to the interference of the United States (58).[35] Even in the face of the refusal of the Brazilian consul to grant a visa, a visa that was ultimately obtained by Abbott's light-skinned, blue-eyed wife, the articles and the speeches he gave in Brazil revealed his determined resolve to present Brazil to North *and* South Americans as an ideal both of racial harmony and of democracy.

The significance of Abbott's trip and speeches was viewed very differently from the perspective of the Afro-Brazilian press. Both his perception of Brazil and his proposal to encourage the emigration of black business people were met with suspicion. Abbott's visit was the subject of many articles and editorials in the Afro-Brazilian newspapers of São Paulo, Rio de

Janeiro, and Campinas, and provided an occasion for a discussion of black Brazilian citizenship.

While the *Chicago Defender* was establishing in the United States, the black press in Brazil was also growing in size and significance. The collection of the Jornais Negros Brasileiros at the Instituto de Estudos Brasileiros at the Universidade de São Paulo includes thirty-one titles published in São Paulo. A number of these papers were linked to social or political clubs. These titles include: *O Menelick, O Bandeirante, O Alfinete, O Getulino* (published in Campinas, São Paulo State), *A Liberdade, O Patrocinio, A Rua, A Sentinela, Auriverde, O Kosmos, Elite, O Xauter, O Progresso, O Clarim*, and *O Clarim da Alvorada*, which all began publication during the twenties. *Chibata, Cultura, Tribuna Negra, A Voz da Raça, O Mundo Negro*, and *O Brasil Novo* began publication in the thirties. *Alvorada, O Novo Horizonte* began publication in the forties, and *Cruzada Cultural, Mundo Novo, O Multirão, O Ebano, A Velha Guarda, Senzala*, and *Níger* began publication in the fifties and sixties.[36]

These papers were founded to address the effects of racism, to build group solidarity, to educate readers about the history of Africans and their descendants in Brazil, and to publicize history and activities of black political, social, and artistic organizations in the United States, the Caribbean, Europe, and Africa. In the early decades of the twentieth century, the papers regularly published articles on the NAACP, Marcus Garvey's Universal Negro Improvement Association, the Pan-African Congresses, the situation of Blacks in South Africa and on independence movements throughout the world. They compared the situation of black people in the United States and Brazil and reported on lynchings and the responses to them by government officials and black communities. The newspapers published poetry, serial fiction, announcements of birthdays, marriages, death, gossip, advertisements, and news — local, national, and international — editorials, photographs, and drawings. The papers were particularly assiduous in their documentation of events in and outside of Brazil that demonstrated the need to combat racism. [37]

Two themes predominated in the articles responding to Abbott's trip: the impact of U.S. black immigration on race relations in Brazil and the correction of Abbott's perception of the state of black Brazilians. In recognition of its significance, I reproduce below in its entirety a translation of an article, otherwise unavailable in English, by Abilio Rodrigues published in the

Kosmos. This article, portions of which were reprinted in other papers, is itself a summary and commentary of an article that was originally published in a black newspaper in Rio de Janeiro and subsequently widely circulated.

Due to the kindness of a friend who, like myself and others, yearns for the well-being of blacks in Brazil, I was offered a copy of the newspaper, *A Patria* [*The Fatherland*], which is published in Rio de Janeiro, dated the 11th of March. Were it not for this kindness, I would not have had the pleasure of reading the article, with José do Patrocinio, Jr.'s byline about the illustrious North American journalist, Dr. Robert S. Abott *[sic]*, "leader" [in English in the original] of the Negro race in Chicago, who, a few days ago, gave a talk at the Trianon Theater in Rio.

José do Patrocinio Jr. begins [the article] by declaring that his absence from that literary meeting was of course noticed, since everyone recognizes him as an [important] person as much for the color of his skin as for the legacy of the name that he bears. [José de Patrocínio, Sr. was a well-known black abolitionist and founder of the Brazilian Anti-Slavery Society[38]]

[As publisher of the paper, Patrocínio, Jr.'s absence was a]ll the more surprising, given that "A Patria" was the only newspaper that had publicized and praised the distinguished journalist.

The theme selected [by Abbott] was: *Brazil's democracy is true democracy, because it is based on principles of human equality.*

According to José do Patrocinio, Jr., Dr. Abott's *[sic]* intention of establishing a favorable comparison between his nation and ours was immensely flattering.

But, the words that should have been heard by the Blacks in Brazil were not those so eloquently proffered by the "leader" [in English in the original]; these words should have been other, more truthful ones. This equality [that he says] exists for blacks here — fantastic — purely fantastic.

One sees in every walk of life that the Black requires three times the effort to achieve a better position. Mediocrity is not tolerated from him and his value is challenged at every step in the desire to make him disappear (*extingui-lo*). This is the degradation that has been his lot since he was given his liberty out of pity thirty-four years ago!

Dr Abott *[sic]* believes "in principles of human equality," certainly due to the illusion provided by his initial impression of contacts between the black and the white in all social interactions, but this is only a superficial [view] because, particularly for the black *from here* [my emphasis], it [the contact] doesn't add up to what it should be or could be. The facts gathered by Dr. Abott *[sic]* would conjure for North American blacks signs of evident happiness, but for the blacks of Brazil [they] would be [signs of] intensely sad disappointment — [signs of] keeping them [Brazilian Blacks] [locked] in the illusion of equality while contempt endures and all achievement is lumped together as useless or barely acknowledged.

What we should have heard from Dr. Abott's *[sic]* lips was a lesson in the energy [that could be harnessed] to dissipate the lethargy that debilitates the black of this land, who believes that life is a dream that evaporates in the grave.[39]

Abilio Rodrigues's article continues:

Abolitionist Propaganda was not directed toward Negroes. The propagandists addressed themselves to whites to prove to them that they were committing an injustice, but they did not teach Blacks to react against this injustice. This is why in his moving speeches, José do Patrocinio, Sr. coined a phrase that became a rallying cry for [black] abolitionist propaganda: *Slavery is robbery!* The victim of a robbery reacts against the robber; he does not beg him or even convince him that he should return to him what he snatched away by force. This [to react] is what is human.

The negro race that was under the whip, the most fecund fount of the importance and wealth of this land, became useless if not noxious to Brazil. Resigned to the piteous disdain of the white who makes him think that the war between the races does not exist among us, [Black people have] never again reached [the heights of] a Viscount of Jequetinha, a Rebouças, a Cotegipe, a Tobias Barreto. Sadly there are those who hide their negro origins for fear of disdain. Why? There are corporations that bar Negroes from positions of status and management. Why? If some mention the mixing together of blood that is the ethnic characteristic of Brazil, it is [to demonstrate that] it is through miscegenation that blacks enter civilization; immediately, however, there rises up a clamor against this offense. Why? Mr. Eloy de Souza is a singular example [as the only Black] in the National Congress. Why? To Mr. Juliano de Moreira and Mr. Evaristo de Moraes,[40] the doors of society unwillingly open, forced apart by the undeniable intellects of these men. Cruz e Souza was the leader of a school that renewed Brazilian poetry. And currently the Metropolitan Soccer League excludes players with dark skin from matches where the team would represent Brazil. At each step we bump up against the prejudice that excludes, that humiliates, that crushes the man of color.

And we continue to be undermined by the illusion that "the real democracy is Brazilian because it is based on the principles of human equality."

Thanks to the kindness of a friend, this, then, is the summary of the article by José de Patrocinio, Jr., because in other circumstances it would have passed me by as it certainly did the majority of blacks in Brazil.

What saddens me most of all [however] is that after our illustrious speaker [Abbott] arrived in São Paulo and checked into one of our hotels, "The Palace Hotel," he, upon his return from an outing, was asked by the proprietor to leave the hotel because the room had already been taken by another. Why? The fact that some white North Americans, who were lodged at the hotel, forced the hotel owner to kick out his black guest.

Even here in a foreign land, they want to impose these old prejudices that exist in North America. Nevertheless, what was the attitude of the hotel owner *as a Brazilian* [my emphasis]? It was to attend to the request made by the North Americans. And this is the equality pointed to as the pattern for the true Brazilian democracy?"

Illusion . . . pure illusion.[41]

The fact that Abilio Rodrigues's article was reprinted numerous times and that others appeared discussing the implications of Abbott's visit highlights the visit's importance in crystallizing the link between race and democracy in Brazil. Rodrigues's article sympathizes with Abbott's desire to see a place where democracy could include black people; nevertheless, he faults Abbott for not recognizing the high cost of the inclusion — the disappearance of black people *as such*.

Abbott was severely criticized in the Afro-Brazilian press for the speeches and articles outlining his impressions of what he saw once he arrived in Brazil. He celebrated the black people he saw in positions of responsibility and in all strata of society. Black Brazilian journalists and commentators, however, blamed him for not taking into account that the visible is always mediated, that one *learns* to see. They blamed him for not understanding that the black people that he saw and with whom he wanted to identify *as* black people were not really black people. Most of all, they blamed Abbott for not understanding that although there were many black people in Brazil, a majority in fact, they were as invisible to him, Abbott, who did not make an effort to meet with them,[42] as Blacks were to the Brazilian state, to official representation. Journalists, like Abilio Rodrigues, refused to oppose Brazil to the United States in a simplistic way. From their perspective, the rhetoric of racial democracy, which depended on whitening and the eventual disappearance of black people, allowed racism to remain in place in the guise of doing away with racialization.

Abbott's determination to see Brazilian democracy as a true democracy regardless of his experiences was evidenced in the columns he published in the *Chicago Defender*. When they were put out of their hotels in Rio de Janeiro and in São Paulo, Abbott blamed "American Color Prejudice" (64) rather than the hypocritical Brazilian attitude pointed out by Rodrigues, an attitude that polices a color line, even as it denies its viability in Brazil. This contradiction, as articulated in Abbott's article, reinforces the extent to which the United States and Brazil are mutually imbricated. If black North Americans needed Brazil to provide the possibility of a racial democracy, however "illusionary" it might be, Brazil similarly needed the United States to cover for Brazilian racism.

These proofs of Abbott's resolve to ignore the implications of what he saw and underwent are provided not only by the accounts in the reaction to his trip in the black Brazilian press but also those in his wife Helen's diary. According to Abbott's biographer, Roi Ottley, Helen was gravely offended by the reaction that she and her husband occasioned in Brazil. She told her sister, Idalee Magill that they were scrutinized as if they were an act in a "sideshow," perhaps because, to the Brazilians, she was white and her husband black. Her insistence on being Black would have been perceived as a rejection of the discourse of *embranquecimento,* making her a most dangerous resistant remainder. She claimed that her husband embarrassed her by not paying attention to the obvious signs of displeasure on the part of their hosts, insisting on going where he was clearly not welcomed. The incidents of discrimination were so frequent that she appeared less and less in public. She also reported that after being forced to leave the Palace Hotel, they were allowed to check into another hotel. The hotelier, however, prevented them from eating in the restaurant, directing them instead to a nearby "Negro" restaurant. They left the hotel when the hotel's porters declined to carry their bags.[43]

Abbott's speeches advocating the emigration of middle-class African Americans coincided with debates surrounding Brazil's immigration policies. In an article from the black press titled "Echos do Projeto Fidelis Reis," the journalist T. Comargo drew attention to immigration legislation introduced by the statesmen Fidelis Reis and Cincinato Braga, which promised disaster for the "millions" of Brazilians who have "black skins": "a Camara Alta que acaba de votar a Lei que será o opprobrio inexoravelmente lançado em face de tantos brasileiros, continuará consciente de que cumprio o seu dever"[44] (And the Upper House of Congress, which has just voted in a law that will represent opprobrium inexorably thrown into the face of so many Brazilians, will feel confident that it has only fulfilled its duty). The law called for the cessation of immigration of people of color from Africa and Asia, and incentives to increase European immigration in order to promote the policy of *embranquecimento.* Not coincidentally, the law had the support of the National Academy of Medicine.[45]

While Comargo acknowledges that an increase in the number of Blacks through immigration could only add to the misery in which Brazilian Blacks already live, he states that the greater danger for Blacks is the selection of words that Fidelis Reis used to justify his project: "Sim, por toda uma eternidade vae ficar patente que o sangue negro é uma corrupção, que o elemento negro é uma desordem na formação do caracter ethnologico brasileiro" (1)

(Indeed, for all time it will be clear that black blood is a corruption, that the black element is a deviation in the formation of the Brazilian ethnological character). This selection of words reinforces the connection between pathology and blackness so familiar to the newspaper's readers.

Comargo worries furthermore that in the future all Brazilians and, indeed, the whole world will curse:

> . . . esse negro que fez o Brasil agrícola com os seus braços, que fez o Brasil intellectual com o sangue das suas esposas as quaes aleitaram com tanto carinho os grandes vultos que hoje sentem praser em se tornaram os nossos mais encarniçados inimigos. (1)

> . . . this black who made agricultural Brazil with his hands, who made intellectual Brazil with the blood of his wives who breastfed with so much affection those great men of consequence who now take pleasure in becoming our most blood-thirsty enemies.

Abbott's comments about Brazil and silence about the United States would have been particularly offensive to a readership well-informed about events taking place in the United States as well as knowledgeable and critical of the situation in Brazil.

As a follow-up to an article on the banning of immigration by people of color encoded in the Fidelis Reis law, black journalist Evaristo de Moraes points out that one of the reasons commonly given for preventing the immigration of black North Americans is that they would bring with them their hatred of whites and that their predisposition to a race war would ensure that they would disturb the domestic peace. The author offers a criticism of this view by asking "Como é possivel prezar a quem nos menospreza?" (How is it possible to esteem those who put us down?). He catalogues for the reader the contributions black people have made to the United States: 400,000 men and $225 million to the war, the black colleges and universities, the institutions, farms, banks, newspapers, factories. He calls attention to the legal assaults against black people in the form of prohibitions against intermarriage, annulment of interracial marriages that ultimately punish the children, and the flouting of the Fourteenth and Fifteenth Amendments to the constitution, as well as noting the violence of the Ku Klux Klan and lynching. He concludes that the anger of Blacks toward the whites given these circumstances is understandable. Were the environment changed, so too would the attitudes. He implies that if Brazil were truly confident about its racial democracy, the rightful anger felt by U.S. Blacks would have no reason for expression in Brazil. Moraes qualifies this last observation by warning that those who are prejudiced in Brazil could still manage to convince other Brazilians that all people of color from the United States who wish to come to Brazil are undesirables.[46]

Afro-Brazilian newspaper editor Benedicto Florencio acknowledged that for those who come from the United States, where black people are regularly lynched, Brazil must seem like an ideal place, given its lack of this type of violence.

> De facto, quem chega aqui ás préssas e vê a mistura por cima sem conhecer das substancias componenetes, illude-se facilmente com a côr da chita. Mas, se o visitante é portador de uma missão diplomatica, de cujos resultados depende de uma séria orientação a tomar, elle será sempre um leviano quando sem conhecer a verdadeira situação do que está vendo superficialmente, se abalança a elogiar garantindo e afirmando coisas que no fundo não são verdadeiras.[47]

> Of course, he who comes for a short while and sees the mixture (of races) superficially without knowing the true facts, easily has the wool pulled over his eyes [literally, "is fooled by the colorfulness of the cloth"]. But, if the visitor is on a diplomatic mission the outcome of which depends on serious study, he will be a stubborn fool, if without knowing the truth of the situation that he is seeing superficially, he dares to go about praising, vouching for, and affirming things that are fundamentally not true.

If Abbott intended to return to the United States to tell "our North American brothers" that in Brazil there existed true human equality, that there were no prejudices, that the law was rigorous in the equality of its application, he would be very wrong: "Nós, porém, os negros brasileiros não endossamos de fórma alguma o sugestivos enthusiasmos do Sr. Abbot [sic], porque ninguem mais apto para falar da injustiça do que a propria victima" (We, however, the black Brazilians, do not in any way endorse Abbott's flights of fancy, because no one is more able to speak of injustice than its victims).

Many journalists may have rejected Abbott's interpretation of the present situation of black Brazilians. Others, however, focused on their perception of threat that that a mass immigration of black North Americans would pose: "A vinda dos negros norte-americanos será o golpe de morte para aquella obra mathematica do desapparecimento gradativo da raça negra no Brasil"[48] (The coming of black North Americans will be the deathblow for the mathematical formula leading to the gradual disappearance of the black race in Brazil). Theodore Roosevelt, reflecting on his own visit to Brazil in 1913, thus summarized this ideology: "In Brazil, on the contrary, the idea looked forward to is the disappearance of the Negro question through the disappearance of the Negro himself— that is through his gradual absorption into the white race" (410).[49]

This phrase "disappearance of the Negro question through the disappearance of the Negro," threads together several themes. The notion of racial democracy—which depends on a narrative of assimilation in which the "black race" is incorporated into the white race—forecloses the possibility of a political life of plurality and difference. Its consequences for black citizenship cannot be overstated. The articles in the Afro-Brazilian press make clear that the putative choice to participate in the racial democracy necessitates, in fact, for black people, the remaindering of blackness in the "racial" of racial democracy. Michael Hanchard has posited that "In Brazil, the absence of racial or ethnic 'givens' is more profound than in other polities, but this is a matter of *degree* of instability with regard to racial or ethnic identifications, rather than the case of one polity containing 'timeless' features of racial inequalities and antagonisms, with another polity—in contrast—having no identifiable patterns of dominance or subordination informed by race."[50]

While Hanchard frames the question in terms of stable and unstable, or givens and degrees, I would frame the question somewhat differently. Blackness, in terms of racial democracy, is the name given to that which exceeds it and makes it visible—it is the remainder that makes the notion of racial democracy possible and sustainable, yet always destined to fail. As a narrative, it serves to shore up a specifically *American* (North *and* South) notion of citizenship.

"It is South America that attracts him":
Brazil in the Harlem Renaissance

In August 1928, Nella Larsen completed the manuscript for her second novel. The title, *Nig,* not only recalled *Nigger Heaven,* the title of her friend and mentor Carl Van Vechten's controversial novel about Harlem, but also foregrounds the character Clare Kendry in its reference to her husband's nickname for her, "Nig." According to Thadious Davis, a

Larsen biographer, the title was deemed too inflammatory for a novel by an "unproven" author, leading the publisher to substitute *Passing* in order to attract interest and attention without giving offense.[51]

The novel opens as Irene Redfield, from whose perspective the story is told, reads a letter from Clare Kendry, a childhood acquaintance. The letter, on foreign paper, "with its almost illegible scrawl seemed almost out of place and alien" (143). It initiates Irene's recollection of their encounter two years before, when they met by chance on a Chicago terrace, and sets in motion the intertwining of their lives that provides the plot of *Passing*. In an exchange of confidences, Clare had revealed to Irene that she passes for white always and everywhere, even — if not especially — with her husband, Jack. Raised by her father's white aunts, Clare followed their command that she keep secret that her mother was a "negro girl." Clare explains to Irene: "When the chance came to get away [from the aunts], that omission was of great value to me. When Jack, a schoolboy acquaintance of some people in the neighborhood, turned up from South America with untold gold, there was no one to tell him I was colored. . . . You can guess the rest" (189). They married. Having made his fortune in South America, Jack has no desire to return to the place that would be a fine place, if, as he claims, "they ever get the niggers out of it" (203).

Jack Bellew provides this assessment of Brazil during a conversation with Irene. Irene has met Clare's husband at their hotel suite, where she has joined Clare and Gertrude, another childhood acquaintance, for tea. Before Jack's arrival, the three women catch up on their lives since high school — Clare has had a daughter with Jack and neither knows that she is passing; Gertrude has married Fred, their former classmate, and his family keeps secret the fact that she is passing. When Jack finally enters the room to greet the women, he sees nothing to challenge his assumption that they are all white. He quickly shocks Irene and Gertrude with the use of his pet name for his wife — Nig — and by the explanation that Clare prompts him to give her guests: The use of the name relies on Jack's belief in the comedy of the endearment, "Nig," for his blonde wife. This is clear enough, as is the reason for the ensuing laughter as Clare, Gertrude, and Irene (and the reader) recognize the irony of the moment, since each is passing for white. What perhaps is not so clear is that the nickname provides one link in a signifying chain that joins Clare and Brazil each to the other, with ultimately disastrous consequences for the characters in the novel. The nickname

"Nig," so shocking in its immediate context, a drawing room in Chicago, is not at all shocking—is, in fact, so common as to scarcely draw attention to itself in another context, the very South American context that is the source of Bellew's wealth. Nig is the English translation of the Spanish and Portuguese, *negra, nega,* a common term of endearment, frequently, if not necessarily, detached from any direct identification of race (except, as in the case of *Passing,* by contrast) in that it is often used among South Americans who consider themselves white. In a display of its roots in slavery, this term is often accompanied by the possessive—*mi* or *minha*—my nig.

In addition to the overt irony provided by the fact that Clare sees herself as precisely that which Jack names as an impossibility, there is also the irony of Jack's adoption of this term. The capacity of language to overdetermine and exceed its speaker undermines Jack's own claim to be immune to racial mixture. In answer to Clare's query as to what difference it could possibly make if he were to discover that she was 1 or 2 percent colored, he declares: "Oh, no, Nig, nothing like that with me. I know you're no nigger, so it's all right. You can get as black as you please as far as I'm concerned, since I know you're no nigger. I draw the line at that. No niggers in my family. Never have been and never will be" (201).

As a discursive system in which cultural, linguistic, and biological transmission is precisely a process of mixture and contamination, South America speaks Jack as much as he speaks it. The symptom, his adoption of the term *Nig,* betrays as much. South America endures in and through him because it contains within itself a realization that national purity/racial purity is impossible. That Jack—the character who should be unambiguously white for the novel's other characters as well as for its readers—transmits this point serves to make it all the more fruitfully. There is an effect of translation here that mimics not only miscegenation, but also the ambivalence surrounding it, expressed, for example, in Chesnutt's essays. When Brazil is invoked, it stands as an ideal of racial democracy through "amalgamation," yet when it is "imported" it becomes a symptom of the failure of that ideal in its insistence on the disappearance of the Negro. The ideal means differently in and out of place.[52]

As Jack, Clare's husband, is associated with South America, so too is Irene's husband, Brian. In his case, for the very reason that it disgusts Jack, South America makes Brian feel, instead, disgust for his own country. Early in their marriage, Irene had fought with Brian to remain in the United States, but she "knew, had always known, that his dissatisfaction had continued, as had his dislike and disgust for his profession and his country" (218). Brian's disgust for his profession and his country is unacceptable to Irene, who sees his disgust in terms of its implications for her citizenship. "She would not go to Brazil. She belonged in this land of rising towers. She was an American. She grew from this soil, and would not be uprooted" (267). Brian's desire to move to Brazil derives from his hatred of segregation and racial violence as well as his perception that Brazil, in contrast to the United States, could provide a safe home for African Americans. Given his social and professional standing, Brian certainly would have read the books and articles I have discussed in this chapter. On an occasion when Irene and Brian disagree about the extent to which they should discuss with their children the realities of racism and racist violence, the long-buried source of the tension that structures their marriage returns to the surface. Brian tells Irene that if she had wanted him to keep secret from their sons the violence that could touch their lives, she should have allowed the family to move to Brazil, where presumably her desire for silence on the subject of racism could be reasonably justified. Brian's resentment and Irene's insistence on opposing a move to Brazil lead her to watch him and think:

> "It isn't fair, it isn't fair." After all these years to still blame her like this. Hadn't his success proved that she'd been right in insisting that he stick to his profession right there in New York? Couldn't he see, even now, that it *had* been best? Not for her, oh no, not for her—she had never really considered herself—but for him and the boys. Was she never to be free of it, that fear which crouched, always down deep within her, stealing away the sense of security, the feeling of permanence, from the life which she had so admirably arranged for them all, and desired so ardently to have remain as it was? That strange, and to her fantastic, notion of Brian's going off to Brazil, which, though unmentioned, yet lived within him; how it frightened her, and—yes, angered her! (217)

In Irene's first conversation with Jack, he asks her about Brian. Irene tells him that her husband is a physician and Jack replies that it must be trying on her nerves, having a husband with lady patients. Irene claims, however, that she does not fear lady patients; she fears rather Brian's desire for Brazil/South America: "Brian doesn't care for ladies, especially sick ones. I sometimes wish he did. It's South America that attracts him" (203). Irene fears that Brian will leave her for Brazil and substitute a place—that place—for her, a black woman. Later, this initial fear is itself displaced by fear that

Brian is having an affair with Clare. Brazil, then, comes to stand in not only for a nonracist society (where one could forget race), but also as and for a secret (the effects of race and racism), as well as a placeholder for the object of an impossible, utopic desire (to be black and yet not black, to be black and American, which is not the same as overcoming double consciousness, to be white) and, eventually, as a double for Clare. Irene and Brian never speak about his desire for Brazil and it is only in her extraordinary efforts to produce a "substitution" (this is Irene's word to indicate her sense that she must compensate Brian for remaining in the United States) that Brazil, as a secret desire, comes to be seen: "Were all her efforts, all her labors, to make up to him that one loss, all her silent strivings to prove to him that her way had been best, all her ministrations to him, all her outward sinking of self, to count for nothing?" (224). So, one substitution leads to another and Irene cannot, in the end, be sure that the substitution has been complete or even merely sufficient because she comes face to face with the logic of the remainder:

> Then why worry? The thing, this discontent which had exploded into words, would surely die, flicker out, at last. True, she had in the past often been tempted to believe that it had died, only to become conscious, in some instinctive subtle way, that she had been merely deceiving herself for a while and that it still lived. But it *would* die. Of that she was certain. She only had to direct and guide her man, to keep him going in the right direction. (218)

Irene ultimately decides that Clare would be a good substitute for Brazil if a relationship with Clare would keep Brian in the United States. If Irene keeps Clare's secret—that she is passing—Brian may pursue the affair and, out of deference to the children, remain at home with Irene in a show of a continuing marriage. That is, the substitution would permit the conservation of her "negro family," which could exist as such only in the United States and not in Brazil. "Now that she had relieved herself of what was almost like a guilty knowledge, admitted that which by some sixth sense she had long known, she could again reach out for plans. Could think again of ways to keep Brian by her side, and in New York. For she would not go to Brazil. She belonged in this land of rising towers. She was an American. She grew from this soil, and would not be uprooted. Not even because of Clare Kendry, or a hundred Clare Kendrys" (267).

Clare is like Brazil—she simultaneously threatens and makes sense of passing in the United States. In Irene's mind, Clare, with her mysterious and unreadable smiles, becomes a sign of Irene's inability to know and control. This inability insinuates itself into Irene's relationship with her husband, leading Irene to link the two threats—perhaps to her marriage, but certainly to her security as a well-to-do American *Negro* woman: "Brian again. Unhappy, restless, withdrawn. And she, who had prided herself on knowing his moods, their causes and their remedies, had found it at first unthinkable, and then intolerable, that this, so like and yet so unlike those other spasmodic restlessnesses of his, should be to her incomprehensible and elusive" (246). Like Brazil, Clare introduces, ironically, "self-consciousness." Clare, as one who passes, and "Brazil," as the space that "erases" race, become reminders of dissatisfaction and division. Irene blames Clare for the introduction of doubt, of proof of the inability to know another, and of unwanted desire (further described as an unwanted desire for desire), all of which threaten her security: "Security. Was it just a word? If not, then was it only by the sacrifice of other things, happiness, love, or some wild ecstasy that she had never known, that it could be obtained? And did too much striving, too much faith in safety and permanence, unfit one for these other things?" (267). Clare, therefore, like Brian's dream of Brazil, must die, directed and guided, perhaps—the narrative leaves open all possibilities—by Irene's hand, to keep her, Clare, like Brian, going in the right direction.

Clare's death, linked, through the image of a dying flame and through the image of Irene's direction and guidance, to the death of Brian's dream of moving to Brazil, provides a final instance in which Clare and Brazil can and will substitute for the other. In the course of the novel, each becomes a placeholder—a reminder—for the object of an impossible, utopic desire. In the wake of the Great War, of the northern migrations, of the urban riots, when the failure of northern opportunity to fulfill the promise of the South has become apparent, Larsen, in conversation with her peers, offers up a phantasmatic Brazil as a South that is beyond the South, not as a counterpart to the North, but as an apotheosis of Southernness. In this context *embranquecimento* would be the ultimate expression of racism, in that it requires the death of blackness. This offer is all the more compelling in light of the other alternative to the American North Larsen had offered in her novel *Quicksand*, published the year before *Passing*. In *Quicksand*, the alternative is the North of the North—Denmark—to which Helga Crane "escapes" before returning to an ultimately disastrous life in the southern United States. It appears that Larsen rejects not so much the South of the past but the South of the stereotypically understood future American. *Passing* uncovers the politics of amalgamation. If amalgamation requires a death, *Passing* will not permit that it should be the death of blackness — an impossible death, in any case, not least because Clare, like Mrs. Abbott, is a resistant remainder.

The South (the South of the United States and the South of America — Brazil) is given an equally complex expression in *Plum Bun,* the 1928 novel by Larsen's friend and contemporary, Jessie Redmon Fauset, the literary editor of *The Crisis.* In Fauset's novel, Angela Murray is introduced to the reader as a young Philadelphia student living with her mother, who, like Angela is light enough to pass, and her father and sister, who are not. The issue of who can claim to be American and in what way is presented early in the novel in a conversation that Angela has in school with a fellow student who thinks that Angela is white. Angela's talent lies in her ability to paint portraits, and she is particularly interested in representing (racial) "types":

> Angela took the sketch of Hetty Daniels to school. "What an interesting type!" said Gertrude Quale, the girl next to her "Such cosmic and tragic unhappiness in that face. What is she, not an American?"
>
> "Oh yes she is. She's an old colored woman who's worked in our family for years and she was born right here in Philadelphia."
>
> "Oh coloured! Well, of course I suppose you would call her an American though I never think of darkies as Americans. Coloured, — yes that accounts for that unhappiness in her face. I suppose they all mind it awfully."[53] (70)

Because she does mind, Angela moves to New York to be an art student, changes her name to the foreign-sounding Angèle Mory, and passes for white. She becomes involved with the wealthy, racist Roger Fielding, but soon falls in love with Anthony, a fellow art student whom Angela believes is white and from Brazil. Anthony has changed his last name from Cruz — "because no American would ever pronounce the z right" (95) — to Cross, the name emphasizing his racial, linguistic, and national crossings. Anthony's father, John Hall, who was black, had been a sailor. John's own father was a skilled Georgia farmer whose wealth was the envy of the poor whites around him. In the course of his wanderings, John arrived in Rio de Janeiro where he met Maria Cruz, "who had the blood of many races in her veins, even though she looked white. She looked favorably on the young sailor whose brown color was like that of her own father" (290). After marrying, the couple traveled to different countries before settling in Georgia. Upon his father's death, John inherited the property. The resentment of the white men in the neighborhood at John's wealth was compounded by their jealousy of his marriage to the beautiful Maria. One of these men, mocked by his friends for showing a preference for a "nigger wench" insulted her with some words of Spanish he had picked up in his own wanderings. She slapped him and in return Hall was lynched and all the property burned.

After this, according to Anthony, Maria lives her life in fear of black people. "She believes that we, particularly the dark ones, are cursed, otherwise why should we be so abused, so hounded. Two years after my father's death she married a white man, not an American—that was spared me,—but a German, who, I believe, treats her very kindly. I was still a little boy but I begged and pleaded with her to leave the whole race alone" (290). In Anthony's account of the lynching, he notes that Maria, as a Brazilian, was necessarily an innocent regarding the jealousy and racism that led to her husband's death. She did not interpret the advances of the white neighbor's as potentially dangerous to herself and to her family or understand the certainty of being punished for "uppity ways" (282). The refusal to be seen as a representative of the black race drives Maria to "join" the white race as a foreigner, a symbolic embrace of *embranquecimento*. Her son, however, who retains her name in an Americanized form, vows "always to hate [white people] with a perfect hate" (291).

Anthony tells Angela this story to explain why, although they love each other, they cannot be together. Earlier in the novel, Angela had realized that Anthony had some secret from his past, a secret that prevented him from returning to Brazil ("No . . . I'm never going back to Brazil. I couldn't"). Angela had assumed the secret must have to do with "some hot feud, a matter of hot blood and ready knives" (141). Anthony instead informs her that because he is "coloured" and because he believes Angela to be a "damned American," he must separate from her. Learning his secret, Angela is anxious to restore his belief in "human goodness" and keeps her racial background from him. Even so, the "blood" that keeps them apart is not only racial but also familial. By the time that Angela reveals herself, Anthony, determined to live as a black man, and unbeknownst to any involved, has engaged himself to Jinny, Angela's brown sister.

Angela must suffer and embrace her suffering before "passing back" into her black community as Angela Murray and out of her "foreignness" as Angèle Mory.

More than once the thought came to her of dying. But she hated to give up; something innate, something of the sprit stronger than her bodily will, set up a dogged fight, and she was too bruised and sore to combat it. "All right,' she said to herself wearily, "I'll keep on living." She thought then of black people, of the race of her parents and all the odds against living which a cruel relentless fate had called on them to endure. And she saw them as a people powerfully, almost overwhelmingly endowed with the essence of life. They had to persist, had to survive because they did not know how to die.

The Brazilian model of a racial democracy embodied by Maria Cruz fails in the U.S. context as an example that Anthony and Angela can embrace, but neither is any positive statement of their place in America made at the end of the novel. The novel's resolution takes place in Paris, as Angela, now living abroad, meets Anthony, who was sent as a surprise Christmas gift from Jinny and her true first love, the brown Matthew Henson.

Neither *Plum Bun* nor *Passing* resolves the contradiction between being black and being American. Each author provides a setting in which the United States is defined in relation to a phantasmatic Latin America and its corresponding utopian ideal of racial democracy. It is within this setting that we can fully appreciate not only the ambiguity of Irene's role in Clare's death but also the ambiguity of Jack's final words to Clare: "Nig! My God! Nig!" (239). This cry of horror and agony (in which he calls her by the pet name "Nig" rather than "nigger" as he had when he entered) at the disappearance of Nig/Clare could be read as an ambivalent response to Roosevelt's description of Brazil's approach to eliminating racial discrimination and as the mourning of the loss of an object of a utopian desire. Even the ambiguity of the end[54]—the police declare Clare's death an accident, yet return to examine the windowsill—provides a focus on that which must be remaindered in order to sustain the social, racial, and sexual order that America (North and South) is so invested in.

FIVE

The Remainder Is a Reminder
Cannibalizing the Remains of the Past

Seen from the point of view of death, the product of the corpse is life. It is not only in the loss of limbs, not only in the changes of the aging body, but in all the processes of elimination and purification that everything corpse-like falls away from the body piece by piece. It is no accident that precisely the nails and hair, which are cut away as dead matter from the living body, continue to grow on the corpse.

—Walter Benjamin, *The Origins of German Tragic Drama*

"Loving our children to death": Identification and the African Diaspora

MY STUDY has explored the tangled network of allusions to the figure of the remainder in the United States and Brazil. As I have demonstrated, the remainder is signaled in African American writing with surprising frequency through references to Brazil (or a generalized South America) and to the metaphor of cannibalism. In what follows, I will show that issues related to race and the remainder are not localized in a single historical moment nor limited to the contexts of the United States and Brazil. These issues, furthermore, have implications for the constitution of an African Diaspora. Although the late twentieth-century images and texts from the United States, Cuba, Jamaica, Guyana, and Brazil that I will analyze in this final chapter do not follow the chronology of my discussion up to this point, they reveal a continued investment in the terms of the earlier discussions I have examined. These works indicate the persistence of a problem that exceeds the moment of its most overt articulation at the beginning of the twentieth century and highlight the insistent timeliness of questions that have not yet been satisfactorily addressed.

The perpetuation of cannibalism as an important metaphor is suggested its appearance at a noteworthy moment in August Wilson's play *Ma*

Rainey's Black Bottom, in which we are asked to think about the politics of cannibalism: Who is eating whom? What happens to the remainder? Wilson's treatment of consumption demonstrates how the figure of cannibalism changes as it migrates geographically. The play also mirrors the chronology of *Cannibal Democracy,* in that it takes place in 1927 and was first performed in 1984. *Ma Rainey's Black Bottom* is the second in a ten-play cycle that explores the U.S. black experience throughout the twentieth century. According to Wilson, each play considers a series of issues significant to one decade, but placed within the context of the "400 year old autobiography"[1] of black people in the United States. Set in 1927 Chicago, *Ma Rainey's Black Bottom* brings together a group of musicians who will provide backup for the historical blues singer, Ma Rainey, in a fictional recording session. The stage directions establish the combative mood of the play, set up its historical and social background, and provide a bird's-eye-view description of the city that narrows in scope to focus on the black population, which, in a mere ten years from 1910 to 1920, had almost tripled as a result of the Great Migration.

The play opens as the white owner of the studio, Sturdyvant, and Ma Rainey's manager, Irvin, argue over the singer's delayed arrival, while the musicians pass the time in a room below debating rather than practicing the music they have been instructed to play. Their talk ranges over topics that contrast old ways and new, the South and the North, Toledo's "sharecropper" brogans and Levee's new city shoes, Ma's own blues arrangement of *Ma Rainey's Black Bottom* and Levee's modern jazz arrangement of the song. In the course of the discussion, the musicians — Cutler, the leader of the band, Slow Drag, and Levee — listen to Toledo's monologue, which, as the longest speech by far of the play, demands attention:

> That's what you is. That is all we is. A leftover from history. . . . Now, I'm gonna show you how this goes . . . where you just a leftover from history. Everybody come from different places in Africa, right? Come from different tribes and things. Soonawhile they begin to make one big stew. You had the carrots, the peas, and potatoes, and whatnot over here. And over there you had the meat, the nuts, the okra, the corn . . . and then you mix it up and you let it cook right through to get the flavors flowing together . . . then you got one thing. You got a stew.
>
> Now you take and eat the stew. You take and make your history with that stew. All right. Now it's over. Your history is over and you done ate the stew. But you look around and you see some carrots over here, some potatoes over there. That stew's still there. You done made your history and it is still there. You can't eat it

all. So what you got? You got some leftovers and you can't do nothing with it. You already making you another history . . . cooking you another meal, and you don't need them leftovers no more. What to do?

See we's the leftovers. The colored man is the leftovers. Now, what's the colored man gonna do with himself? That's what we waiting to find out. But first we gotta know we the leftovers. Now, who knows that? You find me a nigger that knows that and I'll turn any whichaway you want me to. I'll bend over for you. You ain't gonna find that. And that's what the problem is. The problem ain't with the white man. The whiteman knows you just a leftover. 'Cause he the one who done the eating and he know what he done ate. But we don't know that we been took and made history out of. Done went and filled the white man's belly and now he's full and tired and wants you to get out the way and let him be by himself. Now, I know what I am talking about. And if you wanna find out, you just ask Mr. Irvin what he had for supper yesterday. And if he's an honest white man . . . which is asking for a heap of a lot . . . he'll tell you *he done ate your black ass* and if you please I'm full up with you . . . so go on and get off the plate and let me eat something else.[2] (my emphasis)

On one level, this passage summarizes Toledo's position on the problem plaguing the characters in the play. Each character expresses the awareness that he or she is being exploited by Sturdyvant and Irvin for the profit that they will make on this recording. According to Kim Pereira: "These men and these women — whose forefathers strived to bring America into the twentieth century — are now dispensable commodities in a country hurrying to the top of the international ladder. . . . They have served their purpose, and white America would like nothing better than to close its eyes and hope they just disappear."[3] Toledo's cannibalism metaphor converges with and yet diverges from the theme of the commodification of black people noted by Pereira, expanding its sense to embrace a reconsideration of black citizenship.

Although the play goes to great lengths to present the black characters as consumers, it also shows that this would be a detrimental path for them. The stage directions point out that Ma Rainey, her entourage, and the band are all well dressed and throughout the play they discuss in detail hoped-for future purchases. One has the sense that Dussie Mae's attachment to Ma Rainey could be measured in dresses and shoes. The disastrous consequences of their activities as consumers — a dispute about Levee's purchase of Florsheim shoes leads to Toledo's death, Ma's insistence on buying a Coca Cola exacerbates the conflicts in the studio and her possession of a luxury car nearly leads to her arrest when a policeman claims not to believe it is hers — bring these characters face to face with the forces of the capitalist system, but from a position of weakness due to the effects of racism, showing that consumerism is, at best, a complicated path. The play explores consumerism, not merely as a pun, but as a way of becoming American. The promise of a consumer society is, for Wilson's black characters, a promise of destruction and disappearance because in America they are, after all, as Toledo points out, set up to be the eaten and not the eaters.

The studio is also a site of production and for competing attitudes toward production.[4] Sturdyvant and Irvin are representatives of capitalism as a system in which "there is never a loss; everything, even war, always results in an accumulation of value, a re-investment. This is the secret of capitalism as compared with other systems, its inexorable growth."[5] Ma Rainey's willful wastefulness, therefore, forces everyone involved in the production of the record to confront the implications of Toledo's speech. Ma Rainey knows that she is the leftover: "They don't care nothing about me. All they want is my voice. . . . As soon as they get my voice down on them recording machines, then it is just like if I'd be some whore and they roll over and put their pants on" (79). Ma Rainey does not deny that position, as Levee will to his detriment, not only, however, because she has a market for her music that is invisible to Sturdyvant and Irvin. Rather, she counters the economy that refuses the remainder with an economy of the remainder; she wastes time, money, and opportunity in order to assert a remainder that won't be disavowed, that "won't get off the plate," and that cannot be reinvested.

The slippery ambiguity of the pronouns and adverbs in the speech–you, they, we, here, there — make Toledo's allegory at first seem like another version of the American melting pot, more often descriptive of the immigrant experience than of the experience of slavery. It is the work of the reference to cannibalism, with its primary connotation of savagery and barbarism, to distinguish between these two experiences. Toledo's interpretation of the analogy, in its overt evocation of cannibalism, highlights the politics of this consumption; whites consume, and "black" is what is left over. An ambiguity also attaches to the use of the word leftover. In the first paragraph, the leftover refers to that which has not yet been incorporated, but could one day be — the African. This leftover would correspond to a vision of democracy that excludes the foreigner — the African — but does not produce blackness — embodied instead in the "colored man," who, in corresponding to the remainder, is an effect of the creation of America. Significantly, the setting of the first meal is "over there" in Africa, where the leftover is just a leftover and not a remainder. The last paragraph of the speech, however, implies a temporal and spatial shift. This new meal is apparently taking place in the post–Middle Passage (no longer African but "colored" or "nigger") present in the American space ("his plate") occupied by the musicians and Irvin. The leftovers are now produced through a process of cannibalization ("he done ate your black ass") and function, not as a sign of democracy's failure, but of a racial democracy's success in constituting itself through its remaindering of blackness.

The first stew is made in Africa, of Africans. In the context of the first part of the speech, all eat and all make their own, albeit intertwined, history. In America, however, Blacks are consumed to make an American history. Nowhere in the speech, however, does Toledo argue against the process of incorporation. It is, after all, how America, as America, comes into being. The speech uses a model of cannibalism to suggest that as a process of identity formation in the wake of slavery, cannibalism may be a necessary process. Significantly, the speech does not argue that Blacks should instead become the consumers; as I have indicated, Wilson makes that a tragic option throughout the play. The passage, in addition, in its insistence on leftovers, highlights the idea that blackness is an effect of history, one sedimented as a disciplined and disciplining repetition that neither preexists this process nor exists as an accident of a system that is not working correctly.

The critical weight of this passage lies in Toledo's exhortation that Blacks recognize and embrace the fact that "we's the leftovers." Involved in this recognition is the negation of the desire "simply" to make democracy work better for Blacks, since this desire would presuppose a democratic formation capable of consolidating itself without leftovers. A politics of leftovers or remainders suggested in Toledo's speech might well lead us to explore the idea of citizenship practices and their possibilities in a way that also speaks to the gap illuminated by the Brazilian census I discussed in the introduction to this book in that black citizenship practices are not always state-centered; they do not necessarily engage the state, nor are they always managed by it.

Striking in Toledo's interpretation of his own cannibalistic metaphor is the refusal of any ethical relationship to the leftover, expressed in the last paragraph of the speech. As I have demonstrated, most literary and nonliterary texts that involve even obliquely a reference to cannibalism, its structure, and its remainders are far more ambivalent than *Ma Rainey's Black*

Bottom, introducing into their plots or arguments the idea that there could be (from every position) a relationship to what is leftover as remainder—a relationship of love, of guilt, of responsibility, of loss, of reparation.

In the introduction to *The Black Atlantic: Modernity and Double Consciousness,* Paul Gilroy addresses the double consciousness and cultural intermixture that distinguish those defined through the African Diaspora. He looks to African American thinkers to challenge what he calls the "narrowness of vision which is content with the merely national." According to Gilroy, these thinkers "were prepared to renounce the easy claims of African American exceptionalism in favour of a global coalitional politics in which anti-imperialism and anti-racism might be seen to interact if not to fuse."[6] My examination of the real and imagined exchanges that took place between African Americans and Afro-Brazilians during the early decades of the twentieth century indicates how complex these coalitional politics can be and continue to be, especially where the African Diaspora is concerned.

I ended the last chapter with a discussion of Nella Larsen's novel, *Passing,* which is framed by the question of an African Diaspora. This interest in the African Diaspora is introduced by the novel's epigraph taken from Countée Cullen's poem, "Heritage":

> One three centuries removed
> From the Scenes his fathers loved
> Spicy grove, cinnamon tree
> What is Africa to me?[7]

These lines provide an only apparently odd epigraph for a novel that seems to address nothing more than the situation of upper-middle-class African Americans in New York and Chicago. The novel, however, does indeed explore what it means to be a diasporic black people in America through its references to South America and the Caribbean. The turn to America in a work that "starts out" in Africa invites a consideration of the Middle Passage, of slavery and its legacy.

The question—What is Africa to me?—that opens Nella Larsen's *Passing* in the form of its epigraph finds an echo in Nobel Prize–winning author Toni Morrison's *Paradise.* This 1997 novel recounts the relationship between Ruby, a black town in Oklahoma, and a previously abandoned convent on its outskirts now occupied by women of various races who are both loved and feared by the town's inhabitants. In the middle of the novel,

Ruby's schoolteacher and historian, Pat Best, enters into a discussion with one of the town's religious leaders, the Reverend Misner as they both watch the schoolchildren perform the Christmas nativity play. Misner has been wondering if Pat's history lessons have been too narrow, when, as if divining his thoughts, she asks him:

> "You think what I teach them isn't good enough?"
>
> Had she read his mind? "Of course it's good. It is just not enough. The world is big, and we're part of that bigness. They want to know about Africa—"
>
> "Oh, please, Reverend. Don't go sentimental on me."
>
> "If you cut yourself off from the roots, you wither."
>
> "Roots that ignore the branches turn into termite dust."
>
> "Pat," he said with mild surprise. "You despise Africa."
>
> "No, I don't. It just don't mean anything to me."[8]

The nativity play is an allegory for Ruby's founding and for the way that the population has sealed itself off from the outside world. For Misner, this isolation is Ruby's most troubling quality. For Ruby's founders and leaders, however, this very isolation is the sole guarantor of the town's strength and immortality because it protects Ruby from the threat that outsiders, particularly whites and light-skinned Blacks, represent. As they continue their conversation, Pat acknowledges Misner's impatience at the zeal with which the town's elders also use this isolation to preserve the darkness of their black skins, which they prize, for it gives no sign of the taint of slavery that lighter skins evidence.[9] Pat points out to Misner that he, unwittingly perhaps, aligns himself with the desire of the town's elders to deny the shameful legacy of slavery when he nostalgically reaches back in time and across space to Africa:

> "Africa is our home, Pat, whether you like it or not."
>
> "I'm really not interested, Richard. You want some foreign Negroes to identify with, why not South America? . . . Or is it just some kind of past with no slavery in it you're looking for?"
>
> "Why not? There was a whole lot of life before slavery. And we ought to know what it is. If we're going to get rid of the slave mentality, that is."
>
> "You're wrong, and if that's your field you're plowing wet. Slavery *is* our past. Nothing can change that, certainly not Africa."
>
> "We live in the world, Pat. The whole world. Separating us, isolating us—that's always been their weapon. Isolation kills generations. It has no future."
>
> "You think they don't love their children?"
>
> " . . . I think they love them to death." (210)[10]

This passage suggests that Africa might be a place one returns to or flees from. It might even be a place experienced variously and ambivalently as betrayed and betraying by both those who left and by those who didn't. Regardless of how one interprets Africa's significance, however, the conversation between Pat Best and Reverend Misner implies that its significance for America cannot be understood without taking slavery into account.

I first will turn to the work of two contemporary visual artists: María Magdalena Campos-Pons and Keith Piper. Because they both address in their art the legacy of slavery and the work of recollection before a scattered and shattered past, they allow me to address the framing issues of this chapter in relation to the visual that is so confounding and important in discussions of blackness in an international frame. These two artists, like the writers I will address, are not interested in preserving a false integrity of the past; their fissured work of recollection — as distinguished from the completion implied in a work of remembering — relies on fragments, transparency, contingency, and technology.

The three novels that I address in the second half of this chapter: Toni Morrison's *Paradise*, Erna Brodber's *Louisiana*, and Marilene Felinto's *As Mulheres de Tijucopapo* (*The Women of Tijucopapo*) all explore the ways in which slavery and the accompanying scattering of people necessitate an unsettling examination of how we form our black communities internationally. *Louisiana* is concerned with diaspora, in this case the ties between the United States and Jamaica. Ella, a character reminiscent of Zora Neale Hurston, has been sent to the South to interview Mammy Grant King for a Works Progress Administration (WPA) project. Ella's recordings seem to be blank until she learns how to hear in a different way, allowing her to uncover the history of an interwoven St. Mary's, Louisiana, United States, and St. Mary's, Louisiana, Jamaica. This history revolves around the complex figure of Marcus Garvey. Risia, the protagonist of *The Women of Tijucopapo*, yearns for a revolution that won't leave her behind, one that will address the loveless life she has had in a harsh land. Each of these novels addresses the formation of community, the violence that this formation entails, and the losses that derive from these formations — losses that are variously figured as corpses, as excrement, and as other remainders.

In the last chapter, I discussed how the publisher of the *Chicago Defender*, Robert Abbott, was severely criticized in the Afro-Brazilian press for speeches and articles outlining his impressions of what he saw once he arrived in

Brazil. Abbott's misrecognition of and failed identification with Blacks in Brazil invites us to ask what, in fact, does it mean to be constituted in and through the African Diaspora — to identify ourselves with one another as a diasporic black community? I have argued throughout this study that identification, in the psychoanalytic sense, as the narcissistic form of incorporation, secures identity,[11] and promotes its fantasy of wholeness and an ethical valuing of peace. Identity incorporates alterity or otherness, while simultaneously obscuring the history of that incorporation, making it seem that the identity is given, not made. The remain(ders)s of identity's past losses and exclusions are encrypted and silenced. If this is so, how then do those who are remaindered from this process of Americanization, those whom the visual artist María Magdalena Campos-Pons calls "the sons and daughters of those who made the long involuntary journey and who remember where [in a reference to slavery and the Middle Passage] the pain starts" deal with their own losses and exclusions? If identification figured as cannibalism has secured American identity, what then are we to make of the identity of the African Diaspora? Do these sons and daughters of those who made the long journey have an alternative to cannibalizing the remains of the past?

Although *Paradise*, *The Women of Tijucopapo*, and *Louisiana* speak to the difficult question raised in the last lines of the conversation between Pat Best and Reverend Misner quoted above, when Misner tells Pat Best that isolation kills generations, he makes a comment that also begs to be examined in light of the novel *Corregidora's*[12] insistent refrain that the Corregidora women make generations to bear witness to the brutality of slavery. This refrain from Gayl Jones's novel — a novel that complicates the relations between slavery and freedom, love and hate, isolation and community, death and/in life — could be seen to influence Misner's response to Pat Best's question. His response, when she asks him if he believed that they didn't love their children, resonates through each of the novels that I examine in this chapter. In the "Afterward" to her translation of *The Women of Tijucopapo*, Irene Matthews puts forward her own version of Pat's question as the one that drives Risia, the novel's protagonist: "Risia asks a three-part but fundamentally inseparable question: Can a perfect act of love procreate and, if so, should *only* a perfect act of love procreate and, if so, how can you justify, ratify, the existence of a child not born out of love?" (125). Each of the novels links this question as it pertains to individuals to the formation of a people formed through the violence of slavery. Would the justification,

ratification—most often understood as political and psychological reparation—of a diasporic black community necessarily entail, as Reverend Misner fears, loving our children to death?

"Relocating the Remains": Visualizing a Diasporic Blackness

María Magdalena Campos-Pons was born in Cuba and has resided in Boston since 1990. Her installations combine large-scale Polaroid photography, videotape, performance, painting, and sculpture. Many of her projects,
especially the three-part series *History of a People Who Were Not Heroes*
(1997–2000), on which I will focus as an example, address the history of
the artist's family and other families like hers, the current inhabitants of a
town in Matanzas, Cuba. Campos-Pons's family home stands on the site
of the slave quarters that had housed her great-grandfather, an enslaved
Yoruba, and is the subject of the first part of *History*, titled "A Town Portrait" (1994/1997). Included in this installation are photographs of family
members, the slave quarters, and the sugar plantation's bell tower, now in
decay; a reconstructed fountain, a freestanding doorway, and a wall that
evokes the Cuban site. A sound track plays the artist's voice singing nursery
rhymes, and a video shows her stringing flowers as she remembers childhood rituals.

"Spoken Softly with Mama" (1998), the second part of the series, contains glass irons and trivets, embroidered sheets, and wooden ironing boards,
whose shape recalls iconic representations of slave ships. On piles of sheets
and on the walls are projected images of the artist embroidering, shaking
out sheets, and scattering pearls across a polished floor, as pictures of relatives flash in the background and sounds of feminine conversation fill the
room. This part of the exhibit honors the intimate work and living spaces of
the women of Campos-Pons's family, who supported themselves by sewing,
washing, and ironing. The artist uses fine materials to exalt their labor.

The third part of the series, "Meanwhile the Girls Were Playing," is
based on the artist's youthful relationship with her sisters in Cuba, conveyed through mounds of colored glass that suggest swirling skirts, the artist's dance performance, video, and sound. Many of the components of the
series, reminiscent of the sugar plantation economy of her birthplace, were
produced or collected in Cuba with the collaboration with the artist's sister and mother, who still reside there. Campos-Pons composed some of the

photographs in the United States, which were then taken, according to her directions, by her sister or a friend in Cuba. The series' elements — even the glass, a seeming emblem of transparency, is textured, colored, and glued where broken to highlight fractures in time — historicize and fragment the integrity of that memory-identity and present the past, not as *the* past, but as a mediated past.

Keith Piper's work, like that of Campos-Pons's, considers the relationship of history to current discussions of identity and culture. Of Caribbean descent, Piper was born in Malta and raised in Birmingham, England. Piper joined Eddie Chambers, Claudette Johson, and Donald Rodney to form the BLK Art Group. In 1981 and 1982, the group mounted a series of provocative exhibitions titled *The Pan African Connection*. The exhibitions challenged the accepted view of a national English aesthetic culture linked to British modernism by exploring the relationship between black political struggles and contemporary artistic practices. After the BLK Art Group disbanded, Piper expanded his interest in appropriated images to multimedia installations that brought together painting, sculpture, texts, textiles, and music. Piper shifted to computer-based technology in the late eighties in order to create a space in his collage for the viewer's associations and interpretations of the ever-shifting digital layers of his work. The collaboration of the artist and viewer allows for a contingent and unfolding collective narrative that defies a linear recounting.

Piper's *Relocating the Remains* was commissioned by InIVA (The Insitute of International Visual Arts) and exhibited in London in 1997. It is also available as an interactive CD-ROM and as an interactive Web site. Its three sections, titled "Unmapped," "Unrecorded," "Unclassified," reprise Piper's earlier work and reflect his enduring concern with the effects of slavery, colonization, and industrialization on "the geography of black bodies as alternatively a vessel, a commodity, a symbol of colonial expansionism."[13] According to Piper, "'Unmapped' [is] an investigation of the various perceptions of the black body as defined beneath the dominant gaze. 'Unrecorded' examines the gaps in historical narratives which continue to distort and obscure black presence. 'Unclassified' centers around an examination of the impact of new technologies on surveillance and policing, especially in relation to notions of community, nation and cultural difference."[14]

Scholars of photography have called attention to the way that the rhetoric of photography's transparency has made claims for its truth that have made it a preferred technology for surveillance and categorization, not least in colonial contexts. Their critique of photographic transparency uncovers a mutually sustaining relationship in which the state, buttressed by the knowledge and control photographic evidence provides, invests photography with an authority that cannot be reduced to its technical and semiotic properties. While the work of Piper and Campos-Pons is in conversation with this critique, their interest in transparency contains another set of concerns related to an aesthetic and ethical investment in the African Diaspora.

Prior to undertaking the series *History of a People Who Were Not Heroes*, María Magdalena Campos-Pons had addressed the Middle Passage in a work titled *Tra* (1991). The installation revolves around the relationships among three generations of a black Cuban family in the sugar-growing region of Matanzas. It is composed of three large T shapes covered with photographic transfers on cloth, bits of wood, and glass and contains carved and engraved text. Each T shape is titled; the first is "Travesia" (Middle Passage), the second "Trata" (slave trade), and the third "Tragedia" (tragedy). Each T is inscribed with a poem, and the group is flanked on either side by large pieces of wood that call to mind slave ships. The poem that accompanies "Travesia" reads:

> It was a long involuntary journey
> Like ripping up a tree and scattering its roots.
> Not everyone made it.
> We are the children of those that remember
> Only where the pain began.

The title of the installation links, through the repetition of the first three letters, the various concerns of the piece: *travesia, trata, tragedia* (Middle Passage, slave trade, tragedy). The title also suggests a series of words indicative of imprisonment: *trampa* (trap) and movement: *traducción* (translation — from one place to another as well as from one language to another) and *transparencia* (transparency). Campos-Pons links transparency — a persistent theme of her work, as a technique and a concept — to the in-between:

> When I was doing *History of a People Who Were Not Heroes*, I think that the transparency is a very, very, very important concept. . . . Transparency is about memory. Also, I think transparency [is] about displacement. When you are [a displaced person] you are always in this space that is in-between, in-between physical and not seeing, but they are there.[15]

Tra also evokes the Cuban anthropologist Fernando Ortiz's notion of trans-culturation. His study of the history of Cuba from the perspective of the cultivation of sugarcane and tobacco must be an important point of reference for Campos-Pons's work. Ortiz's familiar neologism, coined to describe the results of first contact among distinct cultures in what would become Cuba, distinguishes itself from acculturation, which is the unidirectional translation from one culture to another. For Ortiz, transculturation aims to memorialize mutual transformation.

> I am of the opinion that the word transculturation better expresses the different phases of the process of transition from one culture to another culture, which is what the English word acculturation really implies, but the process also necessarily involves the loss or uprooting of a previous culture, which could be defined as deculturation. In addition it carries the idea of the consequent creation of new cultural phenomena, which could be called neoculturation. In the end, as the school of Malinowski's followers maintains, the result of every union of cultures is similar to that of the reproduction of individuals: the offspring always has something of both parents but is different from each of them.[16]

It is this definition of transculturation that generally finds its way into discussions of hybridity and diaspora in the redemptive, celebratory mode. The idea that cultural contact is procreative and analogous to sexual contact, and that the American offspring would be a miscegenated child is not a new one. Ortiz's neologism, however, is not so much an attempt to account for a New World, as it was conventionally understood, as for a new set of uncertainties and accumulated losses deriving from the violence of the encounter in Cuba. As Oswald de Andrade had before him, Ortiz points out that from the perspective of America, Europe is the New World rather than the Old World:

> If the Indies of the America were a new world for the Europeans, Europe was a far newer world for the people of America. They were two worlds that discovered each other and collided head-on. The impact of the two on each other was terrible. One of them perished as though struck by lightning. It was a transculturation that *failed* as far as the natives were concerned, and was profound and cruel for the new arrivals. The aboriginal human base of society was destroyed in Cuba, and it was necessary to bring in a complete new population, both of masters and servants. This is one of the strange social features of Cuba, that since the sixteenth century all its classes, races and cultures have all been exogenous and have all been torn from their places of origin, suffering the shock of their first uprooting and a harsh transplanting. (100, my emphasis)

One must argue against Ortiz's narrative disappearance of indigenous peoples and against his narrative of the disappearance of indigenous people. This perspective describes loss and exclusion in such a way as to account only for the descendents of Europeans and/or Africans. Furthermore, this passage makes clear that transculturation does not automatically result from every encounter in the "contact zone."[17] In Ortiz's description, African and indigenous peoples can only experience acculturation or failed transculturation (disappearance).

> The Negro brought with their bodies their souls. . . . They, the most uprooted of all, were herded together . . . always in a state of impotent rage, always filled with a longing for flight, freedom, change and always having to adopt a defensive attitude of submission, pretense and acculturation to the new world. Under these conditions of mutilation and social amputation, thousands and thousands of human beings were brought into Cuba year after year and century after century. . . . And all in the painful process of transculturation. (101–2)

Cuban national identity is secured not only through the successful transculturation of the Europeans but also by those whose actual death and whose social death[18] in life derives from their incorporation as an other. Transculturation, in its description and its practice, produces the remains of those who could not or would not be incorporated into a Cuban identity. The effect is that African and indigenous people can never be "Cuban," as this identity can only result from successful transculturation, a process that Ortiz's description forecloses for them. Transculturation, then, cannot be understood apart from death — from death figured in/as its remains as a corpse.

In a compelling essay published in the catalogue for Keith Piper's *Relocating the Remains,* Kobena Mercer argues for an aesthetics of black necrophilia. This idea derives from an interview that the filmmaker, John Akomfrah, gave on black British cinema. In the interview, when Akomfrah was asked about the omnipresence of corpses in black films, he suggests that, "necrophilia is at the heart of black filmmaking." For Akomfrah, necrophilia entails "feeding off the dead." He points out that the "desire shifts from melancholia to necrophilia almost. You almost begin to desire these figures precisely because they are irretrievable, impossible to capture, therefore dead."[19] Taking as a point of departure Akomfrah's suggestive formulation, one could conclude that in a melancholic relation to the dead, the dead live by feeding off the living, while in a necrophilic relation to the dead, the living live by feeding off the dead.

This formulation finds support in an observation made by Nicholas Abraham and Maria Torok in *The Shell and the Kernel*. Abraham and Torok allow that there is a relationship to loss that does not fall into the dyad incorporation/introjection, both of which are related to identification. While incorporation denies the trauma of loss by encrypting the lost object and silencing it, introjection gives language to the trauma of loss, thereby adjusting to and then overcoming it. Neither option, as we will see in this chapter, is satisfactory for the former objects of slavery—now diasporic subjects of the legacy of slavery, and its remainders. Necrophilia/necrophagia, however, provides a more interesting set of possibilities:

> An imaginary [ritualistic] meal eaten in the company of the deceased may be seen as a protection against the danger of incorporation. . . . Necrophagia, always a collective practice, is also distinct from incorporation. Even though it might well be born of a phantasy, necrophagia constitutes a form of language because it is a group activity. By acting out the fantasy of incorporation, the actual eating of the corpse symbolizes both the impossibility of introjecting the loss and the fact that the loss has already occurred. Eating the corpse results in the exorcism of the survivor's potential tendency for psychic incorporation after death. Necrophagia is therefore not at all a variety of incorporation but a preventive measure of anti-incorporation. (129–30)

Necrophilia/necrophagia, unlike either introjection or incorporation, can acknowledge, at the same time, both the trauma of loss and the impossibility of overcoming the trauma of loss.

I would argue that an engagement with necrophilia, if not necrophagia, links the works of Erna Brodber, Marilene Felinto, and Toni Morrison, each of which struggles with how to relate to remain(der)s.[20] The temptation is as great as it is perilous, when faced with the desire for an ethical relationship to one's remain(der)s, to express this relationship through reparations: to name the unnamed, to represent the unrepresented, to give voice to the silent, to make the invisible visible. One might assume that this is what lies behind the doors of Piper's installation *Relocating the Remains*, marked "Unmapped," "Unrecorded," "Unclassified." Yet, behind the doors is a proliferation of ways of naming and categorizing. Piper fragments these images with their emphasis on categorization and control and asks us to consider identity—both black and white—through its mediated representation. The fragmentary, shifting, and layered images of Piper's work expose the history of the mediated image.[21] His installation suggests that to repair the fragment, in other words, to offer a counter-discourse of healing wholeness and repaired identity, is to offer a solution that reasserts the problem—the enforcement of identity. Piper's work, with its valuing of chance and contingency, promotes relocation rather than reincorporation of the remain(der)s.

The frontispiece to this book is a photograph from Campos-Pons's series, *When I Am Not Here / Estoy alla,* that comments directly on these issues of selfhood and identity. The photograph, originally in color, is of the upper torso of the artist covered with mud, in which are traced the words, "Identity could be a tragedy." The face is stippled so that it recalls an African mask, and the frontal pose of the life-sized image of the artist invites the viewer to lock eyes with her in a gesture of sympathy and identification. Yet, the eyes are not open. They are shut but painted in such a way as to appear open. Evocative of Wilson Harris's "dead seeing eye" and "living closed eye,"[22] the presentation of the eyes inscribes the violence of identifying with another. The photograph shuttles the viewer back and forth between an other that one cannot recognize (recognition being the political form of identification) and the self, which, in the face of the refusal of that recognition, can no longer be so sure of itself. This photograph, which seems to be about identity, creates the in-between space,[23] a space of a relationship to an other that is not, or not yet, appropriative. This space is a space of not knowing and of not being driven to know.

The words written on the body of the artist are also significant. If one were to emphasize the last word, the sentence, "Identity could be a *tragedy*" seems to be a warning. The sentence, could, however, be fruitfully read as a statement of possibility. Bonnie Honig suggests in *Political Theory and the Displacement of Politics* that tragedy is the appropriate genre for acknowledging the remainder, for tragedy revolves around the forced recognition that there can be no remainderless choice. In this case: "Identity *could* be a tragedy."

The refusal of identity marks the work of both María Magdalena Campos-Pons and Keith Piper. This refusal is not an end in and of itself. It is a political strategy, a relocation of the remains rather than a re-incorporation that aims to redeem them. Relocation leaves the remains as remainders that would be reminders not of something but of some way, an unsettling and uncomfortable, perhaps, way of living with the remains of what can never be made whole.

Sites of Entanglement

Erna Brodber's *Louisiana* addresses the connections among the descendents of Africans in Africa, Europe, the Caribbean, and the United States. Ella, the novel's central character is the daughter of West Indian parents, whose heritage was hidden from her. Ella leaves her home in New York to conduct ethnographic research in the South. When her informant, Mammy Sue Ann Grant King, dies before she can record her oral history, Ella feels driven by duty to the WPA and to her graduate advisor in the Anthropology department at Columbia University to give an account of her informant's life. In her efforts to know and to record a life according to the conventions of her training, she fails. The tape recorder she brought with her from the university is soon replaced by Ella's own body, which becomes a medium for Mammy and her best friend, Louise. After death, they want to convey to her information they had concealed in life to protect their own safety and that of their colleagues. Through her service as a medium, the secret of Marcus Garvey's association with Mammy, her lover Silas and her friend, Louise, also known as Lowly is revealed, as are Ella's own familial associations to Garvey's hometown in Jamaica. Through her perilous incorporation of Mammy and Louise, Ella comes to embody the African Diaspora:

> I am the link between the shores washed by the Caribbean sea. . . . I join the past with the present. In me Louise and Sue Ann are joined. Say Suzie Anna as Louise calls Mammy. Do you hear Louisiana there? Now say Lowly as Mammy calls Louise and follow that with Anna as Louise calls Mammy. Do you hear Louisiana there? Now say Lowly as Mammy calls Louise and follow that with Anna as Louise sometimes calls Mammy. Lowly-Anna. There's Louisiana again, particularly if you are lisp-tongued as you well could be. Or you could be Spanish and speak of those two venerable sisters as Louise y Anna. I was called in Louisiana, a state in the USA. Sue Ann lived in St. Mary, Louisiana and Louise in St. Mary, Louisiana, Jamaica. Ben is from there too. I am Louisiana. I wear a solid pendant with a hole through its center. I look through this hole and I can see things. Still I am Mrs. Ella

Kohl, married to a half-caste Congolese reared in Antwerp by a fairy godfather. I wear long loose fitting white dresses in summer and long black robes over them in winter. I am Louisiana. I give people their history. I serve God and the venerable sisters.[24] (124–25)

Ella, desirous of telling a coherent story, initially had refused to accept that the full range of the entanglement (to use Edouard Glissant's apt term) that is the African Diaspora will not be conveyed in a way that does away with mystery, pain, confusion, or division. Her early refusal to engage with all of the experiences of those who survived slavery derives from the shame she has inherited from her parents who aspire to the American Dream and to the middle class. Her refusal also leaves her vulnerable to the demand that she, as a medium, passively serve the dead, who, in death, feed on her after having, in life, fed on the dead. As she grows weaker and thinner while channeling Louise/Lowly, Ella discovers that Lowly also had dealt melan-cholically with the losses of her family members by incorporating them. "If it was not possible [for Louise/Lowly] to keep earthly touch with her kin and the spot where they had grown her, she could lock them in her heart and feed on them. Well-masticated, digested material was what Lowly gave me. This intense child nibbling intensely on memories" (122).

This description of cannibalism is echoed in the description of Mam-my's family. Mammy grew up with her grandmother, who represented for the townspeople a reminder of the remainders of the constitution of their community:

This is the family culture in which Mammy grew — punished resistance. She grew up with her grandmother, truly a woman of sorrows who by this sad fact achieved some notoriety in the area. No one wanted to add to her martyrdom, if it could at all be helped. They resented her status. No one wanted to see another resistance and another punishment in that family. The village and its leading lights did not want their shame to resurface every generation. *This family was living proof of their cannibalism.* (152, my emphasis)

The people of the town know that the stability of their community comes at the cost of Mammy's family. Mammy's mother was an organizer in the sugarcane fields. She was the third person in the family to be killed for political activities; her father and stepfather were lynched. Mammy comes from a long line of people who resist. That they remain is a sign to the other accommodating residents of their town of the price they have paid for the semblance of peace. The town, however, tired of the remainder that is the reminder of how they constituted their community, facilitates Mammy's departure. The nature of Mammy's resistance remains mysterious to Ella until Ella relinquishes the effort to redeem it through language, to *know* and to identify (with) it. The narrative discredits this effort to know as appropriative and argues that there must be a space for and value in what cannot be understood.

Risia, the protagonist of *As Mulheres de Tijucopapo* (*The Women of Tijucopapo*), also searches to know a traumatic past. She embarks on a reverse migration from the city of São Paulo north to Recife, Pernambuco, the home she and her family left years earlier as part of a mass migration south of Northeasterners attempting to escape the crushing poverty of their drought-ridden region. In the course of her journey, she recalls the events of her life that have left her feeling ashamed and abject. She struggles to find the strength to be the resisting remainder rather than just the remainder that is resisted (the abject). Betrayed, rejected, submissive, Risia's mother represents everything that is shameful, and, as a consequence of her own expulsion from the maternal line — "Mama is a shit" — she has cut Risia off from the heroic past of her ancestors, the women of Tijucopapo — the mud mouth women.[25]

The historical context of the novel is established by two significant dates in recent Brazilian history. The first, 1964, marks the institution of the dictatorship, and the second, 1968, the passage of particularly repressive laws, calculated to put down all resistance to the dictatorship. These dates also mark the failures of Risia's own personal revolt undertaken to create a space for herself in her family and in her nation. The impediments to achieving this place are crystallized in a series of experiences that are intertwined in her memory. One takes place during a school trip to a country club: "In Manjopi I learned how different I was. Manjopi — my hair looked like a hangman's ropes kneaded [duma força amaciada (literally, smoothed out by force)][26] with brilliantine mama put on it and that the sun melted at midday" (72). Unlike her plump, white classmates, "the daughters of rich sergeants," Risia is a poor, dark, and skinny scholarship student, whose mother is a born-again Christian and whose father is a womanizer. The incident at Manjopi was crucial in making her experience herself as abject. "In Manjopi I died a little. Manjopi. Big shit. I hadn't made it. How many Manjopis did I have to spend before I made it to where I am today — capable of arranging a face that can put up with a party with sergeants' daughters? In the end, that's the shit you get, the shit of a face that can put up with anything" (60).

Having lost her lover and tired of commuting from the poor suburbs of São Paulo where she lives to the center of the city to join her intellectual friends at lavish parties, she decides to go to Tijucopapo. No longer willing to be part of "São Paulo, [where] the world takes place in the gullet, in gulps and eructions" (89), Risia sets out to discover the source of her shame by determining who is to blame for the fact that her mother was given away by her own mother, described as a "heavy Negress": "Mama's last native link died out . . . when she was given away. Everything about Mama is adopted and adoptive. My mother has no origins; in reality my mother doesn't exist" (22–23). Risia's mother was left "in Poti, a moon-town, where I [Risia] was born and where I know my grandfather was an Indian. Sometimes I look at myself in the mirror and I tell myself I come from Indians and blacks, dark-skinned people, and I feel like a tree, I feel rooted, a manioc plant coming out of the ground. Then I remember that I am nothing" (23–24).

Risia's sense that she is nothing derives from her failed attempts to identify with the structures of power that exclude her — the dictatorship, the Brazilian nation, the flag, the white elite, the wealthy, the patriarchal family, São Paulo. She is filled with consuming anger and resentment. She remembers a time in her childhood when she still thought it would be possible to achieve the sense of inclusion she desires. She describes how she felt as she practiced for her anticipated participation in a patriotic parade:

> Behind me was the long slab of cement concealing the shit my brothers and sisters shat. . . . And in the evening I'd join the parade [to commemorate Brazilian independence] proud of myself in my gala dress. "Go to hell with my pinworms, papa and mama, with my roundworms, with my *Giardias.*" I would march proudly to the noise of the brass band, the big drum thundering boom de boom up there in front. Boom boom, boom boom, boom boom. Go to shit, to dung, to pellets of caca. . . . Me stepping firmly in place. On the shit, on the dung, on the pellets of caca. . . . Me feeling proud of myself. And me forgetting . . . that papa was a shit, that mama hadn't hugged me. . . . Behind me a slab of cement I banged my head on as I slipped off the stool . . .
>
> I fell into an abyss, my head banged against the slab full of shit that was not, definitely not, mine. Was the shit supposed to be for me, Nema? So I was under-

going the most serious of my falls, the most undignified—on the very day of the
parade. . . .When I came to there were women around the bed . . . (108–9)

When Risia is forced to acknowledge that she is the remainder of Brazilian
national identity, she wakes up to embrace and be embraced by the women
of Tijucopapo, the women who choose to resist. When she reaches the end
of her quest, she is the resistant remainder that is both visible and invisible
(since shadows do not appear under the midday sun) as a Brazilian—"What
I made was a thought. The women of Tijucopapo were, finally, like me
casting shade on the ground, at midday, under a burning sun, on the BR
[a highway that is the main migratory route from North to South], on the
road" (120).

As she nears Tijucopapo, Risia is physically transformed to more closely
resemble the women of Tijucopapo—"my skin gets darker and darker, I'll
arrive in Tijocopapo black, sweating like a black" [suando como um negro
sua] (literally, sweating like a black man sweats) (94, 81)—and she becomes
an agent of representation. Risia's journey involves learning to acknowledge rather than to forget or lie about herself, her mother, and their condition and to see the cause of their suffering not in their abjection but in the
forces that created the conditions that result in their painful choices. "I am
traveling to paint the revolution that won't knock my one and only whole
Guarana down from the counter" (83), but instead of aligning herself with
"those guilty of all the lovelessness I suffered and of all the poverty in which
I lived. I'm going to tell all the wretched workers in the factory that they
are unhappy wretches because these are brightly lighted parties taking place
in São Paulo. And, if they wanted to, they would drink a whole Guaraná
because there in São Paulo life keeps happening in gulps and gullets and
eructions" (91).

Throughout the novel, Risia says that she wants to tell her story in the
form of a letter in English to her mother. She wants to escape into another
language, one that could give her the Hollywood happy ending denied her
in her own language. The irony is that Risia starts, yet does not succeed
in completing the letter in English. The novel ends, significantly, with the
hope, expressed in the subjunctive, for a happy ending or at least one that
will work out well for her. This hope is conveyed in the Brazilian Portuguese
rather than in English: "Eu quero que tudo me termine bem" (133).

A Gift to the Citizens of Ruby

The dangers of identifications that disavow the remainder also are explored in *Paradise*. Desirous of giving a "gift to the citizens of Ruby" (187), Patricia Best decides to record Ruby's past. This gift, which should have involved all the citizens in the process of telling their story soon becomes an occasion for resentment. The women of Ruby, used to keeping secrets, outright refuse to participate in the project precisely when the subject turns to marriage certificates. These very documents would have revealed a fundamental contradiction. They would have given evidence of ratification by the State that Ruby abjures in its isolation. Yet the refusal of the women also reveals a sense of propriety that is derived from the very culture that has denied them and that they are, despite their insistence to the contrary, still tied to. They did not want to reveal stories of incest, illegitimacy, thwarted love, and hate. As the doors to the true story of Ruby close to her, Pat realizes how much had been blotted out of their official history. "It got to the point where the small m [married] period was a joke, a dream, a violation of law" (187). Pat is the child of one of these marriages. Her father loved her mother—an outsider. Her mother's light skin testified to the past of slavery and racism that the town's elders would repress, forever barring her daughter from being considered a full member of Ruby. Pat neither identifies with nor completely rejects the town's founding families nor their goals. This gives her a more dispassionate view of Ruby's past.

The official story of Ruby is the story of its founding, rooted in the "Disallowing." The first "Disallowing" took place as a small band of freedmen traveled from Louisiana and Mississippi to Fairly, Oklahoma, in search of a new life after the failures of the Reconstruction. Fairly's light-skinned black inhabitants refused them entrance to the town and so the nine excluded families established their own town, which they called Haven. After the Second World War, returning veterans found their town impoverished and assaulted by lynching mobs. The descendants of the first nine families moved the town to a more remote location and renamed it Ruby. The inhabitants of the town brought with them a cherished oven and placed it in the middle of the town. The original inscription over the Oven fractured in the move from Haven to Ruby, leaving the interpretation of the remaining words, "the Furrow of His Brow," open to community debate.

While the Oven provides the ostensible center of the town, Pat's investigations soon reveal to her the true center of the town: her mother's grave on its margins, where Ruby's secrets lie encrypted. The Oven is a substitute that permits the disavowal of the town's remain(der)s. No one had died in Ruby: "Well, crazy as it sounds, I believe the claim of immortality is this town's rebuke against Daddy's mortuary business. . . . They think Daddy deserves rebuke because he broke the blood rule first, and I wouldn't put it past them to refuse to die just to keep Daddy from success" (199).

Pat's emotional distance makes her aware of the fragments of stories, as well as the stories of the fragments that those who had been "thrown out and cast away in Fairly" deny in the interest of the official story of their town's integrity. As Elizabeth Yukins points out, it is not a coincidence that Steward Morgan, who will be the leader of the attack on the women of the Convent, makes the strongest statement in favor of Ruby's exclusionary and static past: "If you, any one of you, ignore, change, take away, or add to the words in the mouth of that Oven, I will blow your head off just like you was a hood-eyed snake" (87).[27]

The first Disallowing took place when Zechariah, the patriarch of the band, wounded in the foot, remained behind while his son approached the town of Fairly:

> It was the wound that forced him to stay behind and let his friend and his sons speak in his stead. It proved, however, to be a blessing because he missed the actual Disallowing; and missed hearing disbelievable words formed in the mouths of men to other men, men like them in all ways but one. Afterwards the people were no longer nine families and some more. They became a tight band of wayfarers bound by the enormity of what happened to them. Their horror of whites was convulsive but abstract. They saved the clarity of their hatred for the men who had insulted them in ways too confounding for language: first by excluding them, then by offering them staples to exist in that very exclusion. Everything anybody wanted to know about the citizens of Haven and Ruby lay in the ramifications of that one rebuff out of many. But the ramifications of those ramifications were another story. (189)

The narrative abruptly shifts at this point from the story of the Disallowing to a description of Pat lifting the window and glancing at her mother's grave. The first Disallowing was by light-skinned black people ("Blue-eyed, gray-eyed yellowmen in good suits") who took up a collection, offered food and blankets, but did not permit their dark-skinned brothers to stay in the town. This resulted in the institution of the "unspoken" blood rule. No one of mixed blood could join Ruby. Pat's father, Roger Best, was the first to violate the blood rule. Menus was the second, with a "sandy-haired girl from Virginia" (195).

> So the rule was set and lived a quietly throbbing life because it was never spoken of, except for the hint in the words Zechariah forged for the Oven. More than a rule. A conundrum: "Beware the Furrow of His Brow," in which the "You" (understood), vocative case, was not a command to believers but a threat to those who had disallowed them. . . . So the teenagers Misner organized who wanted to change it to "Be the Furrow of His Brow" they were more insightful than they knew. They were the agents rather than God—they made Menus give back his girl. (195)

Zechariah, who was not present at the Disallowing to hear the "disbelievable words" and or to experience the insult "too confounding for language," establishes the unspoken blood rule. He mobilizes the community around the words engraved on the oven and works to turn Ruby's attention from the remainders of the constitution of its community. Pat remembers the reaction of the town when she arrived with her mother, Delia:

> Their jaws must have dropped when we arrived, but other than Steward nobody said anything directly. They didn't have to. Olive took to her bed. Fulton kept grunting and rubbing his knees. Only Steward had the gall to say out loud, "He's bringing the *dung* we leaving behind. Dovey shushed him. Soane too. But Fairy DuPres cursed him, saying, "God don't love ugly ways. Watch out he don't deny you what you love too." A remark Dovey must have thought a lot about until 1964, when the curse was completed. But they were just women, and what they said was easily ignored by good brave men on their way to Paradise. They got there, too, and eventually had the satisfaction of seeing the *dung* buried. Most of it anyway. Some of it is still aboveground, instructing their grandchildren in a level of intelligence their elders will never acquire. (201–2, my emphasis)

Pat's mother is the "dung," the remainder and the reminder of the 8 Rock's disavowal of the history of slavery and its role in constituting them as black Americans.

If the ramifications of Pat's mother's death from the blood rule are displaced and disavowed in the Oven, they are clarified and embraced in the Convent. The nine women of the Convent are the remainders, linked through the images of excrement and detritus to Pat's mother (and Pat), that are reminders that won't keep the peace. According to the men of Ruby:

> They [the women of the Convent] don't need men and they don't need God. Can't say they haven't been warned. Asked first and then warned. If they stayed to them-

selves, that'd be something. But they don't. They meddle. Drawing people out there like flies to shit and everyone who goes near them is maimed somehow and the mess is seeping back into *our* homes, *our* families. We can't have it, you all. Can't have it at all. (276)

On the day of the massacre at the Convent, the men of Ruby demonstrate that they prefer to kill rather than acknowledge their own remainders:

> Earlier, when they blew open the Convent door, the nature of their mission made them giddy. But the target, after all, is detritus: throwaway people that sometimes blow back into the room after being swept out the door. So the venom is manageable now. Shooting the first woman (the white one has clarified it like butter: the pure oil of hatred on top, its hardness stabilized below). (4)

The women of the Convent, unlike the men of Ruby, embrace the remainder without taking it in. Each of the women comes to the Convent with an understanding of herself as abject. This understanding is fostered by the society that the men of Ruby represent. As they gather to plan the assault on the Convent, the men discuss, "with gratitude" what they have sacrificed to live in Ruby. Their discussion demonstrates how the men have made the Convent the repository of the remainders of their sacrifices:

> "What have you [the residents of Ruby] given up to live here?" [Reverend Cary, one of the leaders of the massacre and Misner's nemesis,] asked, hitting "up" like a soprano. "What sacrifice do you make *every* day to live here in God's beauty, His bounty, His peace? . . . Picture shows, filthy music." He continued with fingers from his left hand. "Wickedness in the streets, theft in the night, murder in the morning. That's what you have given up."
>
> Each item drew sighs and moans of sorrow. Suffused with gratitude for having refused and escaped the sordid, the cruel, the ungodly, all of the up-to-date evils disguised as pleasure, each member of the congregation could feel his or her heart swell with pity for those who wrestled with those "sacrifices."
>
> But there was no pity here. Here [at the Convent], when the men spoke of the ruination that was upon them—how Ruby was changing in intolerable ways—they did not think to fix it by extending a hand in fellowship or love. They mapped defense instead and honed evidence for its need, till each piece fit an already polished groove. (275)

The men feel pity for those who have not made the same sacrifices they have, yet feel no pity for the remainders of those very sacrifices. The relation to the remainder inexorably divides the men of Ruby from the women of the Convent. The women of the Convent learn to feel pity and compassion for the remainder, while the men of Ruby kill in the interest of preserving the illusion of a remainderless world.

When the men enter the Convent with the intention of killing all the inhabitants, they find on the floor chalk outlines that the women had made of their own bodies. In and around these outlines they had represented all that had made them dead to themselves before their arrival at the Convent. "Down below under long slow beams of a Black & Decker, Steward, Deek and K. D. observe defilement and violence and perversions beyond imagination. Lovingly drawn filth carpets the stone floor" (287). Steward's reaction is to reject (again) what he sees and to deny any relationship to it: "The evil is in this house," said Steward. "Go down in that cellar and see for yourself" (291). Deek, however, recognizes the remainder, if only briefly: "My brother is lying. This is our doing. Ours alone. And we bear the responsibility" (291).

The women of the convent have drawn their bodies on the floor at Consolata's urging. To understand the full significance of her gesture, we must unpack this section's references to Brazil. As a child, Consolata was rescued by the Reverend Mother, Mary Magna, and brought to the United States to be educated in the Convent. Consolata tells the story of her rescue as part of the ritual of exposing the remainders' remainders, of which the drawings are a part:

> My child body, hurt and soil [with dirt, excrement] leaps into the arms of a woman who teach me my body nothing my spirit everything. I agreed her until I met another. My flesh is so hungry for itself it ate him. When he fell away the woman rescue me from my body again. Twice she saves it. When her body sicken I care for it in everyway flesh works. I hold it in my arms and between my legs. Clean it, rock it, enter it to keep it breath. After she is dead I can not get past that. My bones on hers the only good thing. Not spirit. Bones. No different from the man. My bones on his the only true thing. So I wondering where is the spirit lost in this? It is true, like bones. It is good like bones. One sweet, one bitter. Where is it lost? Hear me, listen. Never break them in two. But never put one above the other. Eve is Mary's mother. Mary is the daughter of Eve. (263)

Consolata had an affair with Deek. She expresses that love through a desire to cannibalize him. She lost him when she "was bent on eating him like a meal" (239), which turns out to be her big mistake (237). "Dear Lord, I didn't want to eat him. I just wanted to go home . . . she wanted to say . . . *he and I are the same*" (241, my emphasis). Before she can help the other women in the Convent, Consolata, having lost Deek and Mary Magda, must learn a different way to love. She learns, through an exercise of shared feeling, of pity and compassion, to let the other remain.

Consolata[28] invokes the Virgin Mary in her speech to the suffering women of the Convent and immediately links her to Iemanjá, who though not named as such, is a central figure in *Paradise*'s ritual of understanding: "Then she told them about Piedade, who sang but never said a word" (264). Consolata describes for the women how Piedade had cared for her:

> We sat on the shorewalk. She bathed me in emerald water. Her voice made proud women weep in the street. . . . Piedade had songs that could still a wave, make it pause in its curl listening to language it had not heard since the sea opened. . . . At night she took the stars out of her hair and wrapped me in its wool. Her breath smelled of pineapples and cashews. . . .

Worshipped by many titles, including the Pietà, and Mater Dolorosa, Mary's name has its roots in the Hebrew word *marah* meaning "bitterness" or "bitter sea."[29] In Brazil, Iemanjá is syncretized with Mary as Nossa Senhora de Piedade (Our Lady of Pity or Compassion), Nossa Senhora do Rosario (Our Lady the Rosary), Nossa Senhora das Candeias (Our Lady of the Candles), Nossa Senhora da Conceição (Our Lady of the Immaculate Conception), Nossa Senhora dos Navegantes (Our Lady of the Sailors), and Nossa Senhora das Dores (Our Lady of Sorrows).[30] Iemanjá, Yemayá, Yemanji are names given to the American embodiment of Yemojà, a Yoruba river deity. She is said to be the mother of the majority of the Orixás, with Exú, the messenger, as the notable exception. Because Iemanjá is associated with motherhood and loves all children, she is believed to have accompanied her enslaved sons and daughters from Africa to the Americas. In the process, she transformed herself from a river deity into a deity of the sea in order to better protect her enslaved children. Iemanjá's name is derived from the Yoruba, Yèyé omo ejá (mother of the children that are fish). In Brazil, she is often represented as a mermaid with hair that undulates with the water, a crown of pearls, shells, and sea stones. Her colors are light blue, white, and transparent crystal; her attributes are a fan and beaded necklaces. She can be referred to by names that reflect this aspect: Mãe da água (Mother of the Water), Rainha do Mar (Queen of the Sea), Princesa do Mar (Princess of the Sea), Sereia do Mar (Mermaid of the Sea), and Dona Janaína (syncretized with indigenous water deity).

Like Mary, with whom she is syncretized in the Catholic tradition, Iemanjá protects sailors. For example, on the beachfront of Jabotão dos Guararapes in the northeast of Brazil, a statue of Iemanjá stands before the entrance to the Church of Nossa Senhora de Piedade. Mary and Iemanjá are often worshipped together and share feast days. Iemanjá's followers regale her with candles, flowers, coins, shiny ornaments, bits of mirrors and glass, blue and white bead necklaces and bracelets tossed into the sea from rowboats.

Paradise ends with an extended invocation of Iemanjá/Piedade. This description conflates the figures of the Convent women with the figure of Iemanjá. In the flow of the sea, entangled in one another, surrounded by the remainders of the Middle Passage, they wait to embrace those who have most recently arrived:

> In ocean hush a woman black as firewood is singing. Next to her is a younger woman whose head rests on the singing woman's lap. Ruined fingers troll the tea brown hair. All the colors of the seashells — wheat, roses, pearl — fuse in the younger woman's face. Her emerald eyes adore the black face framed in cerulean blue. Around them on the beach sea trash gleams. Discarded bottle caps sparkle near a broken sandal. A small dead radio plays in the quiet surf.
>
> There is nothing to beat this solace which is what Piedade's song is about, although the words evoke memories neither one has ever had: of reaching age in the company of the other; of speech shared and divided bread smoking from the fire; the unambivalent bliss of going home to be at home — the ease of coming back to love begun.
>
> When the ocean heaves sending rhythms of water ashore, Piedade looks to see what has come. Another ship, perhaps, but different, heading to port, crew and passengers, lost and saved, atremble, for they have been disconsolate for some time. Now they will rest before shouldering the endless work they were created to do down here in paradise. (318)

Throughout *Paradise,* the inhabitants of Ruby and its remainders have modeled the dangers to a diasporic black community that refuses its remainders. Iemanjá, both black and brown, models an ethical way of loving what remains, of accompanying rather than taking in, embracing rather than incorporating, of feeling *with* rather than feeling *for.*

Epilogue

*Wishrop is curiously sliced in two—webbed enemy-in-the-other, webbed
other in the enemy . . .*

— Wilson Harris, *Palace of the Peacock*

TONI MORRISON'S *Paradise* closes with an appeal to those created through slavery to shoulder the work of reparation "down here in paradise." These words recall the closing of Alejo Carpentier's *The Kingdom of This World.* This 1949 novel by the Cuban author recounts the Haitian Revolution according to the literary practice of *lo real maravilloso* (the marvelous real) that he had defined in the preface to the Spanish edition to that work:[1]

> In the Kingdom of Heaven there is no grandeur to be won, inasmuch as there all is an established hierarchy, the unknown is revealed, existence is infinite, there is no possibility of sacrifice, all is rest and joy. For this reason, bowed down by suffering and duties, beautiful in the midst of his misery, capable of loving in the face of afflictions and trials, man finds his greatness, his fullest measure, only in the Kingdom of this World.[2]

If the final lines from *Paradise* recall these lines from *The Kingdom of This World,* they also resonate with Wilson Harris's evocation of paradise in his introduction to *The Guyana Quartet. Palace of the Peacock,* the first of the novellas collected in this very dense work, tells the story from the disintegrating perspective of the Narrator/Dreamer of a boat journey from the coast of Guyana to the interior. Donne, the narrator's brother, leads the *El Doradonne* crew in search of the laboring folk of Mariella mission, who have escaped inland where they are bound to conduct a series of rituals. Mariella, Donne's violently mistreated mistress, leads the folk. The crew's journey is a repetition of several previous journeys: a journey by Donne when he captured Mariella, a journey by a previously drowned crew

having the same names and appearance as this one, the colonialist March of
El Dorado, and Marlow's voyage in *Heart of Darkness*. At the end of the
novella, Carroll, a character who has survived the journey only to plunge to
his death in a fatal attempt to climb a waterfall, plays a flute whose music
"impl[ies] a paradise in which the infernal deeds of the *El Doradonne* crew
are so ingrained that nothing has apparently changed since the hanged/shot/
drowned horseman [Donne as dreamed by the narrator] appears to fall in
the opening phases of *Palace* and to foreshadow more than one death for
the crew. . . . Nothing has changed in Carroll's paradise save for 'the second death' that re-opens or revisits every blind deed in the past."[3] Harris's
evocation of paradise confirms a desire to seek the possibility of change in
the kingdom of this world rather than the next. This paradise is brought
about through "an art of fiction where the agents of time begin to subsist
upon the real reverses the human spirit has endured, the real chasm of pain
it has entered, rather than the apparent consolidation, victories and battles
it has won."[4]

Morrison, Carpentier, and Harris, as well as the other writers that I
addressed in the last chapter of this study, attempt to devise a form of writing that could account for what was left behind as a remainder of the legacy
of slavery. For Harris, the history of lost origins said to be the tragedy of
the Caribbean, or for that matter, the tragedy of the children of slavery, is
tragic only when this loss is experienced as the deprivation of a final destiny
rather than as a comedy of the evasion of a final destiny — death. According
to Samuel Durrant, the *El Doradonne* crew gains on its journey:

> an awareness [that] is not simply a rational understanding of the cycle of repeti-
> tion in which they are trapped, for such an understanding would merely satisfy the
> desire for "cynical truth" by leading to a nihilistic acceptance of their inability to
> alter their fate. Rather, it is a *revelation* of existence in which the world-weariness
> of being is transformed into the innocence of becoming, a revelation that goes
> beyond the nihilism of historical determinism in so far as it opens up for the crew
> "the ghost of a chance" of discarding their inherited nature . . . [I]t is not simply a
> question of discarding one nature for another, of becoming a more moral or ethical
> subject. This would merely be to repeat the bourgeois novel of education, centered
> around the progress of the individual subject, that Harris claims to move beyond.
> To abandon the "lust to rule" is in fact to abandon subjectivity itself. The goal of
> the Harrisian narrative is the dissolution rather than the education of the individual
> subject, the revelation of what he dubs our "complex mutuality."

The "lust to rule" inheres in the demand for identification and in the violence of that demand. A "complex mutuality" would provide an alternative and Harris's preferred metaphor for this alternative is the Carib bone flute.

In the introduction to *The Guyana Quartet,* Harris states that his research into the bone flute after the publication of *Palace of the Peacock* reinforced his intuitive understanding of its significance as a validation of his fiction, "a fiction that seeks to consume its own biases." This validation came to Harris when he discovered that the Carib/cannibal bone flute had a long history in Guyana (9).

To describe the bone flute, Harris refers to the work of Michael Swan. In an appendix titled "The Caribs" to an account of his travels to the interior of Guyana, Swan discussed the frequent accusations of cannibalism against the Caribs. Turning to the authority of ethnographer Richard Schomburgk, Swan quotes him at length to defend the Caribs:

> Although [he says] the Caribs in the Colony are generally accused of cannibalism, especially by the Negroes, who still relate with horror what their parents told them about their eating the flesh of the fallen during the quelling of the Negro uprising in 1763, this was distinctly denied not only by my own chief but all others from whom I made enquiry. The former told me the following about it. After a victory gained, their forefathers usually brought back to the settlement an arm or leg of the slaughtered enemy as a trophy, which would then be cooked to so as to get the flesh more easily off the bone; a flute was made out of this to be used as an instrument on the next war expedition. One still frequently finds in the Carib camps such flutes made from human bones.[5]

Swan points out that the ritual surrounding the production of the bone flute could include ingestion of a morsel of the flesh of the enemy if individual participants so chose. The significance of the ritual was to produce an instrument that in Harris's conception provides an alternative to cannibalizing the remains of the enemy, to cannibalizing the remains of the past. The music of the flute derives from and provides for a relation, that of the "webbed enemy-in-the-other, webbed other in the enemy," a relation not of incorporation but of mutual embrace, an embrace that acknowledges without insisting on incorporating the other in the name of knowledge, understanding, and peace.

Notes

Preface

I have reproduced all Portuguese quotations as they are in the original, including archaic orthography, idiosyncrasies, and errors.

1. Shelly Fisher Fishkin, "Crossroads of Cultures: The Transnational Turn in American Studies — Presidential Address to the American Studies Association, November 12, 2004," *American Quarterly* 57.1 (Spring 2005): 17–58 (21).

2. J. B. Clarke, comp., New York (State) Emancipation Proclamation Commission, *A Memento of the Emancipation Proclamation Exposition of the State of New York* (New York: Robert N. Wood, 1913).

3. José Clarana, "Getting Off the Color Line," *The Crisis* (September 1913): 244–46.

4. Jessie Faucet *[sic]* and Cezar Pinto, "The Emanicipator of Brazil," *The Crisis* (March 1921): 208–9.

5. Robert M. Levine and John J. Crocitti, eds., *The Brazil Reader: History, Culture, Politics* (Durham, N.C.: Duke University Press, 1999), 354.

6. *The Crisis,* (December 1916): 92.

7. Cornell University, Cornell Alumni Directory 1922, 13, no. 12 (1922): 120.

8. William Edgar Easton, *Christophe: A Tragedy in Prose of Imperial Haiti* (Los Angeles: Press Grafton, 1911).

9. "Satisfied that her honored friend had reasonable ground to congratulate the grandson of Queen Victoria on his coronation, Miss Miller assured Aunt Harriet [Tubman] that she could send a letter to the King of England, but that she would ask me [Clarke] to write it for, as a British subject from the West Indies, I might be more familiar with the proper form of address. And Aunt Harriet immediately replied, 'I know where he came from as soon as I heard him speak.'" J. B. Clarke, "An Hour with Harriet Tubman" in Easton, *Christophe,* 115–22 (117–18).

10. James B. Clarke, "Race Prejudice at Cornell," *Cornell Era* 43, no. 5 (March 1911): 196–202; Easton, *Christophe,* 107.

11. Appended to *America the Peacemaker,* published under the name Jaime C(larana) Gil, is a series of letters criticizing outbreaks of violence against Asians and Filipinos that justified themselves as defenses against "the yellow peril" and one to the Jewish Tribune criticizing their coverage of an impending discussion in France's parliament on racism

in France. Jaime C. Gil, *America the Peacemaker* (New York: Veritas, 1924). As José Clarana, he also published and editorial, "Haitian Support of Bolivar," *New York Times*, 21 Apr 1921.

12. Jaime C. Gil, "Race Feeling in France," *New York Times* editorial, 8 July 1923.

13. José Clarana, "Plácido—Poet and Martyr," *The Crisis* (July 1913): 82.

14. José Clarana, "The Schooling of the Negro," *The Crisis* (July 1913): 133–36.

15. José Clarana, "The Colored Creoles of Louisiana," *The Crisis* (February 1916): 192–93.

16. James B. Clarke, "The Negro and the Immigrant in the Two Americas," *Annals of the American Academy of Political and Social Science* 49 (September 1913): 32–37. Articles include "Professional and Skilled Occupations," by Howard University philosopher and dean, Kelly Miller; "Industrial Education and the Public Schools," by Booker T. Washington; and "The Negro in Literature and Art," by W. E. B. Du Bois.

17. George Lakoff and Mark Johnson, *Metaphors We Live By* (Chicago: University of Chicago Press, 1980), 12–13. See also pp. 1–6.

18. Paul Gilroy, *The Black Atlantic: Modernity and Double Consciousness* (Cambridge, Mass.: Harvard University Press), 4.

19. It could be pointed out, for example, that the decades bridging the opening and the close of the twentieth century mark two moments of assessing the goals of racial inclusion in both Brazil and United States. The assessment at the opening of the twentieth century was provoked, in the United States, by the end of Reconstruction, the rise in lynching, and increased (legal) barriers to full citizenship. In Brazil, the impetus was the abolition of slavery in 1888 that made citizens of the formerly enslaved and the failure of the First Republic established in 1889. During the 1920s, both Brazil and the United States experienced modernist movements, *Modernismo* and the Harlem Renaissance, respectively, that looked to the space of culture to resolve issues of race and national specificity and to foster revolution in aesthetics—linked in many cases to anthropological research—which would signal a break with the past. Central to both movements was the attempt to racially define the Brazilian, the American.

The assessment at the end of the twentieth century was spurred by the incomplete fulfillment of the promise of the civil rights movement in the United States and of the reaction against the dictatorship in Brazil. Both nations experienced renewed faith in the space of culture, particularly among filmmakers and women writers, who mined the modernist movements of the 1920s for themes, metaphors, and heroes. In addition, recent academic scholarship, fiction, and media reports describe an inversion of the images of Brazil and the United States, as the United States is described as becoming "brown" and as Brazil institutes more radical affirmative action policies. See, for example, Howard Winant, *Racial Condition: Politics, Theory, Comparisons* (Minneapolis: University of Minnesota Press, 1994), and Edward Telles, *Race in Another America: the Significance of Race in Brazil* (Princeton: Princeton University Press, 2004). I hope, furthermore, that other scholars will be interested in extending my discussion through the midcentury, where there is a rich vein of material to consider.

Introduction

1. These organizations included the Instituto Brasileiro de Análises Sociais e Econômicos, Instituto de Pesquisa das Culturas Negras, Agentes de Pastoral Negros, Instituto de Estudos da Religião, Núcleo da Cor, IFCS/UFRJ, Jornal Maioria Falante, Centro de Articulação de Populações Marginalizadas, Centro de Estudos Afro-Asiáticos, Instituto Palmares de Direitos Humanos, Centro de Referência Negromestiça, Ford Foundation, and TerraNova.

2. Text from the back of the poster underwritten by the organizations cited above.

3. Thomas E. Skidmore, *Black into White: Race and Nationality in Brazilian Thought* (New York: Oxford University Press, 1974), 64.

4. Philip D. Curtin, *The African Slave Trade: A Census* (Madison: University of Wisconsin Press, 1969), 47–49. There is debate about the number of enslaved Africans who were brought by force to Brazil. The Brazilian historian Afonso d'E. Taunay estimates a total of 3,600,000 slaves: 100,000 in the sixteenth century; 600,000 in the seventeenth century; 1,300,000 in the eighteenth century; 1,600,000 between 1800 and 1852. *Subsídios para a história do tráfico africano no Brasil* (São Paulo: Melhoramentos, 1941), 305. The historian Caio Prado Jr. places the figure even higher at five to six million before the massive increase in traffic during the first half of the nineteenth century. *Formação do Brasil contemporâneo* (São Paulo: Brasiliense, 1973), 32–34.

5. Mary C. Karasch, *Slave Life in Rio de Janeiro, 1808–1850* (Princeton, N.J.: Princeton University Press, 1987).

6. Frederico Leopoldo Cezar Burlamaque, *Memoria Analytica á Cerca do Commercio d'Escravos e á Cerca dos Males da Escravidão Domestica* (Rio de Janeiro: Comercial Fluminense, 1837), cited by Celia Maria Marinho de Azevedo, *Onda negra, medo branco: o negro no imaginário das elites século XIX* (Rio de Janeiro: Paz e Terra, 1987), 43, my translation.

7. Silvio Romero, *A Litteratura Brazileira e a Critica Moderna* (1880), cited by Celia Maria Marinho de Azevedo, *Onda negra,* 71, my translation.

8. Roberto Ventura, *Estilo tropical: história cultural e polêmicas literárias no Brasil* (São Paulo: Companhia das Letras, 1991), 63.

9. Nancy Leys Stepan, "Race and Gender: The Role of Analogy in Science," in *The "Racial" Economy of Science: Toward a Democratic Future,* ed. Sandra Harding (Bloomington: Indiana University Press, 1993), 365. Expressing a similar idea, Florestan Fernandes states that Blacks are the: "elementos residuais do sistema social (residual elements of the social system)." Florestan Fernandes, *A integração do negro na sociedade de classes* (São Paulo: Ática, 1978), my translation. See also Nancy Leys Stepan, *The Hour of Eugenics* (Ithaca, N.Y.: Cornell University Press, 1991), in which Stepan analyzes the influence of positivism on debates about Brazil's fitness to embrace modernity.

10. Among these many studies are: Skidmore, *Black into White;* Stepan, *Hour of Eugenics;* Anthony W. Marx, *Making Race and Nation: A Comparison of South Africa, the United States, and Brazil* (New York: Cambridge University Press, 1998); Azevedo, *Onda negra;* Dante Moreira Leite, *O caráter nacional brasileiro* (São Paulo: Pioneira, 1983); Lilia Moritz Schwarz, *O espetáculo das raças: cientistas, instituições, e a questão*

racial no Brasil 1870–1930 (São Paulo: Companhia das Letras, 1993); Ventura, *Estilo tropical;* Jurandir Freire Costa, *Ordem médica e norma familiar* (Rio de Janeiro: Graal, 1979; Abdias do Nascimento, *O genocídio do negro brasileiro: processo de um racismo mascarado* (Rio de Janeiro: Paz e Terra, 1978); Clóvis Moura, *O negro: de bom escravo a mau cidadão?* (Rio de Janeiro: Conquista, 1977); Thales de Azevedo, *Democracia racial: ideologia e realidade* (Petrópolis, Brasil: Editora Vozes, 1975); Melissa Nobles, *Shades of Citizenship: Race and the Census in Modern Politics* (Palo Alto, Calif.: Stanford University Press, 2000); Howard Winant, *Racial Conditions: Politics, Theory, Comparisons* (Minneapolis: University of Minnesota Press, 1994); Robert Stam, *Tropical Multiculturalism: A Comparative History of Race in Brazilian Cinema and Culture* (Durham, N.C.: Duke University Press, 1997); George Reid Andrews, "Brazilian Racial Democracy, 1900–90: An American Counterpoint," *Journal of American History* 31, no. 3 (July 1996): 483–507; Michael Hanchard, *Orpheus and Power: The Movimento Negro of Rio de Janeiro and São Paulo, Brazil, 1945–1988* (Princeton, N.J.: Princeton University Press, 1994).

11. Wilson Martins, *The Modernist Idea* (1965), trans. Jack E. Tomlins (New York: New York University Press, 1970).

12. Nobles, *Shades.*

13. David T. Haberly, *Three Sad Races: Racial Identity and National Consciousness in Brazilian Literature* (New York: Cambridge University Press, 1983), 70–98.

14. Bonnie Honig, *Political Theory and the Displacement of Politics* (Ithaca, N.Y.: Cornell University Press, 1993), 127. I have taken this useful quotation out of its original context. In the chapter from which it is taken, "Rawls and the Remainder of Politics," Honig analyzes John Rawls's theories of justice and democracy.

15. Carl Schmitt, *The Crisis of Parliamentary Democracy* (1926), trans. Ellen Kennedy (Cambridge, Mass.: MIT Press, 1985), 9–10.

16. Louis Althusser, *"Lenin and Philosophy" and Other Essays,* trans. Ben Brewster (New York: Monthly Review Press, 2001), 117–18.

17. Chantal Mouffe, *The Democratic Paradox* (New York: Verso, 2000), 40.

18. Honig, *Political Theory,* 49.

19. Cordiality as a quality distinguishing Brazilian race relations during and after slavery is intimately linked with the discourse of racial democracy. See Leite, *Caráter nacional,* 317–30, and Sérgio Buarque de Hollanda, *Raízes do Brasil* (Rio de Janeiro: José Olympio, 1969).

20. The Association for International Conciliation, which would soon become part of the Carnegie Endowment for Peace, published an antiwar document in 1917 titled "A Defense of Cannibalism." The essay's introduction was presumably written by the translator, Preston William Slosson, a Columbia University History Ph.D., State Department employee, and assistant to the American Commission to Negotiate Peace. In it, he states the relation of the document to the war then underway: "The following curious argument, which first appeared in *La Revue* of February 15, 1909, over the signature of B. Beau, will remind the reader of certain books and articles now written to prove that war is inevitable and that the hope of international peace is essentially chimerical" (3). The essay is presented as a speech of a "Carib medicine man" to the warriors who have been

influenced by a Christian missionary preaching against cannibalism. Rehearsing arguments, even the most cynical, that had been made in support of the war, the medicine man concludes: "The essential difference between a compatriot and an enemy is that it is a right and often a duty to eat the latter. To suppress this difference is to enfeeble the bond that unites the tribe. It will be still further enfeebled if we are made to believe that the day will come when one can go among strangers without risk of being eaten by them. If this doctrine spreads it will, therefore, be at the expense of the love that is due to the tribe." This document not only testifies to the pervasiveness of the metaphor of cannibalism in discussions of democracy but to the role of this metaphor in articulating how identities are constructed.

21. Honig, *Political Theory*, 127.

22. Oswald de Andrade, "Manifesto de Antropofagia," in *Vanguarda Europeia e Modernismo Brasileiro*, ed. Gilberto Mendonça Telles (Petrópolis, Brasil: Editora Vozes, 1976), 357.

23. Mário de Andrade, *71 cartas de Mário de Andrade* (Rio de Janeiro: São José, sd), 31, my translation.

24. Karl Abraham, M.D., "A Short Study of the Development of the Libido, Viewed in the Light of Mental Disorders," in *Selected Papers of Karl Abraham, M.D.* (1927), trans. Douglas Bryan and Alix Strachey (New York: Basic Books, 1953), esp. 418–501. See also Melanie Klein, "Love, Guilt and Reparation," in *Love, Hate and Reparations* (New York: Norton, 1964).

25. I thank John Noyes for this observation.

26. Sigmund Freud, *Totem and Taboo* (1913), trans. James Strachey (New York: W. W. Norton & Co., 1950), 141–43.

27. Sigmund Freud, *Three Essays on the Theory of Sexuality* (1905), trans. James Strachey (New York: Basic, 1964), 64.

28. In *New Introductory Lectures on Psychoanalysis*, Freud states that self-fashioning involves "the assimilation of one ego to another, as a result of which the first ego behaves like the second in certain respects, imitates it and in a sense takes it up into itself. Identification has not been unsuitably compared with oral, cannibalistic incorporation of the other person." The qualification—"in certain respects—shows how this theory symptomatically notes yet disavows its own remainders. Psychoanalysis in its reliance on a metaphor, historicized as it is in my discussion, is limited by its anthropological sources and its own process of becoming and reveals itself not as a master discourse but as a discourse of (failed) mastery." Sigmund Freud, *New Introductory Lectures on Psychoanalysis* (1915–1916), trans. James Strachey (New York: Norton, 1977), 63.

29. "The residual, by definition, has been effectively formed in the past, but it is still active in the cultural process, not only and often not at all as an element of the present. Thus certain experiences, meanings, and values which cannot be expressed or substantially verified in terms of the dominant culture, are nevertheless lived and practiced on the basis of the residue—cultural as well as social—of some previous social and cultural institution or formation." Raymond Williams, *Marxism and Literature* (New York: Oxford University Press, 1977), 122.

30. Another way of thinking of the remainder is through the process of mathematical

division implied in pi, in which the remainder is infinite and infinitely produced. See also Honig's description of the remainder, which has been indispensible in helping me to articulate my argument. Honig, *Political Theory*, 213, note 1.

31. Winant, *Racial Conditions*, 61.

32. Alexander Crummell, "The Race-Problem in America,"in *Africa and America: Addresses and Discourses*, 37–57 (New York: Negro Universities Press, 1969), 41. Crummell gives past and present cases of absorption, amalgamation, and separate coexistence. Of the latter, he gives the example of the Papuan and Malay in the Pacific; the Welsh, English, and Scotch in Britain; and the Indian, the Spaniard, and the Negro in Brazil.

33. Kelly Miller, "Amalgamation Again," *The Amsterdam News*, 30 November 1927.

34. Theodore Roosevelt, "Brazil and the Negro," *The Outlook* 106, no. 8, 21 February 1914: 409–11.

35. There is a vast bibliography on this subject. See, for example, Peter H. Schuck and Rogers M. Smith, *Citizenship without Consent* (New Haven, Conn.: Yale University Press, 1985).

36. Philip Ainsworth Means, *Racial Factors in Democracy* (Boston: Marshall Jones, 1919), 151. Means also discusses these ideas in the article, "Race and Democracy in Latin America," *The Nation* 109, no. 28 (1 November 1919): 560–62.

37. Cited by David A. Brading, "Manuel Gamio and Official Indigenismo in Mexico," *Bulletin of Latin American Research* 7, no. 1 (1988): 82.

38. Brading, "Indigenismo," 88.

39. Race appreciation is also an ethical position: "In a word, race appreciation is a doctrine or policy shot through with a spirit of kindliness and generosity; it was eager to find good and useful elements among all people wherever and whenever possible and, on finding them, employ them for the benefit of mankind in general" (Means, *Racial Factors*, 52). Although indigenous people are often included in descriptions of the processes that produce the remainder, they are not remainders in the way that I am using the term to describe blackness because they were already in America. While there are similarities, this difference does not allow a sustained consideration of indigenous people in my study.

40. W. E. B. Du Bois, "The Negro Takes Stock," *New Republic* 37, no. 474 (2 January 1924): 143–45, my emphasis. These eight points were: "1. A voice in their own government. 2. The right to access to the land and its resources. 3. Trial by juries of their peers. 4. Free elementary education for all; broad training in modern industrial technique; and higher training of selected talent. 5. The development of Africa for Africans, and not merely for the profit of Europeans. 6. The abolition of the slave trade and of liquor traffic. 7. World disarmament and the abolition of war; but failing this, and as long as white folk bear arms against black folk, the rights of blacks to bear arms in their own defense. 8. The organization of commerce and industry so as to make the main objects of capital and labor the welfare of the many, rather than enriching the few." Among the specific cases were demands for home rule in West Africa and the West Indies; native law in Nigeria and Uganda; representation for colonies in the French Parliament; recognition of the black majority in South Africa; the end of economic exploitation in the Belgian Congo, Haiti, Liberia, Abyssinia, and Portuguese Africa; and the end to lynching and barriers to full citizenship in the United States.

41. Abilio Rodrigues, "Preto e branco"*Kosmos* 18 de setembro de 1923, np.

42. W. E. B. Du Bois, *The Conservation of Races* (NewYork: Arno Press, 1969).

43. Eugene C. Harter, *The Lost Colony of the Confederacy* (Jackson: University of Mississippi, 1985), 117.

44. Charles Mills, *The Racial Contract* (Ithaca: Cornell University Press, 1997), 12.

45. Cyrus B. Dawsey and James B. Dawsey, *The Confederados: Old South Immigrants in Brazil,* ed. Cyrus B. Dawsey and James B. Dawsey (Tuscaloosa: University of Alabama Press, 1995), 241, fn 82.

46. Winant, *Racial Conditions,* 167–68. Winant's important work has served as the shadowed touchstone throughout this section of my discussion of racial democracy.

47. Scholars working on black movements in Brazil include: George Reid Andrews, *Blacks and Whites in São Paulo, Brazil, 1888–1988* (Madison: University of Wisconsin Press, 1991); Kim D. Butler, *Freedoms Given, Freedoms Won* (New Brunswick, N.J.: Rutgers University Press, 1998); Nobles, *Shades;* Edward Telles, *Race in Another America: The Significance of Race in Brazil* (Princeton, N.J.: Princeton University Press, 2004); *Racism in a Racial Democracy: The Maintenance of White Supremacy in Brazil* (New Brunswick, N.J.: Rutgers University Press, 1998); Winant, *Racial Conditions;* João José Reis e Eduardo Silva, *Negociação conflito: a resistência negra no Brasil escravista* (São Paulo: Companhia das Letras, 1989); Clóvis Moura, *Brasil: as raízes do protesto negro* (São Paulo: Global, 1983); Ana Lúcia E. F. Valente, *Ser negro no Brasil hoje* (São Paulo: Editora Moderna, 1991).

1. United by Anthropophagism

1. Menotti del Picchia, cited by Daniel Pécault, *Os intelectuais e a política no Brasil* (São Paulo: Atica, 1990), 27. For general discussions of Brazilian modernism, see Aracy Amaral, *Artes plásticas na Semana de 22* (São Paulo: Perspectiva-Edusp, 1972); Mário de Andrade, *O movimento modernista* (Rio de Janeiro: Casa do Estudante do Brasil, 1942); Affonso Ávila, ed., *O Modernismo* (São Paulo: Editora Perspectiva, 1975); Alfredo Bosi, *Historia concisa da literatura brasileira* (São Paulo: Editora Cultrix, 1981); Mário da Silva Brito, *História do modernismo brasileiro: antecedentes da Semana de Arte Moderna* (Rio de Janeiro: Civilização Brasileira, 1978); Lucia Helena, *Modernismo brasileiro e vanguardia* (São Paulo: Editora Atica, 1986); Jorge Schwartz, *Vanguardas latino-americanas: polêmicas, manifestos, e textos críticos* (São Paulo: Edusp, 1995); Gilberto Mendonça Teles, *Vanguardia européia e modernismo brasileiro: apresentaçâo dos principais poemas, manifestos, prefácios e conferências vanguardistas de 1857 a 1972* (Petrópolis, RJ, Brasil: Editora Vozes, 1982); Wilson Martins, (1965), *The Modernist Idea: A Critical Survey of Brazilian Writing in the Twentieth Century,* trans. Jack E. Tomlins (New York: New York University Press, 1970); Robert Stam, *Tropical Multiculturalism: A Comparative History of Race in Brazilian Cinema and Culture* (Durham, N.C.: Duke University Press, 1997).

2. Carlos de Moraes Andrade, cited by Moacir Werneck de Castro, *Mário de Andrade: exílio no Rio,* (Rio de Janeiro: Rocco, 1989), 64. Unless otherwise noted, all translations in this chapter are my own.

3. Martins, *Modernist Idea,* 52.

4. Mário de Andrade, "Modernismo e Ação" *Jornal do Comércio* (24 de maio de 1925): s.p.

5. José Bento Monteiro Lobato (1882–1948) was a novelist, journalist, editor, and publisher. As the author of enormously popular novels, including *Urupês* (1918), republished in nine editions between 1918 and 1923, Lobato was seen as a precursor to modernism. His relationship to the modernists was complex. They viewed him as a leader in the renovation of Brazilian letters, yet distrusted his faith in the techniques of late nineteenth-century literary realism. As director of the most important journal, *Revista do Brasil*, as well as owner of his own eponymous publishing house, Lobato was a very important and influential literary figure.

6. For more information, see M. Cavalcanti Proença, *Roteiro de Macunaíma* (Rio de Janeiro: Civilização Brasileira, 1969) and Luís de Câmara Cascudo, *Antologia do folclore brasileiro* (São Paulo: Martins, 1965).

7. Mário da Silva Brito, *História*, 71.

8. For a description of this meeting, see Mário da Silva Brito, *História*, 73.

9. Bosi, *História concisa*, 380.

10. Plinio Barreto, "Academia de Letras," unidentified publication, Recortes Mário de Andrade, Arquivo Mário de Andrade, Instituto de Estudos Brasileiros, Universidade de São Paulo, São Paulo, Brasil.

11. Jorge Schwartz, *Vanguardas*, 117.

12. Oswald de Andrade, "Reforma Literária," *Jornal do Comércio* (19 de maio de 1921), cited in Mário da Silva Brito, *Historia*, 204. In the early twenties, *o grupo dos cinco* (the gang of five) referred to itself as "futurist." When Mário de Andrade complained that the term gave off too "European" an air, they renamed themselves "modernists."

13. Menotti del Picchia, "A Questão Racial," *Correio Paulistano* (10 de maio de 1921): 204. Recortes Mário de Andrade, Arquivo Mário de Andrade, Instituto de Estudos Brasileiros, Universidade de São Paulo, São Paulo, Brasil.

14. Ibid., 204.

15. Ibid., 204–5.

16. Menotti del Picchia, "Capacetes Cossacos . . ." *Correio Paulistano* (15 de julho de 1921). Recortes Mário de Andrade, Arquivo Mário de Andrade, Instituto de Estudos Brasileiros, Universidade de São Paulo, São Paulo, Brasil. In reading this, it is important to remember that Menotti del Picchia, a well-respected journalist with a reputation that extended throughout Brazil, was considered the spokesperson for the modernists, particularly the *grupo dos cinco,* and responsible for the dissemination of their ideas through the press.

17. Roberto Reis, *The Pearl Necklace: Toward an Archaeology of Brazilian Transition Discourse,* trans. Aparedica de Godoy Johnson (Miami: University Press of Florida, 1992), 25.

18. Celia Maria Marinho de Azevedo, *Onda negra, medo branco: o negro no imaginário das elites—século XIX* (Rio de Janeiro: Paz e Terra, 1987), 20.

19. Moacir Werneck de Castro, *Mário de Andrade: exilio no Rio,* 56.

20. Mário de Andrade, "Eu sou trezentos," *Poesias Completas* (São Paulo: Livraria Martins, 1972).

21. Telê Porto Ancona Lopez, *Mário de Andrade: ramais e caminhos* (São Paulo: Duas Cidades, 1972), 226.

22. Mário de Andrade, "Carta a Alceu Amoroso Lima," in *71 Cartas de Mário de Andrade,* ed. Lygia Fernandes (Rio de Janeiro: Editora São José, s/d), 29–32.

23. Sigmund Freud, "The Dissection of the Psychical Personality," in *New Introductory Lectures on Psychoanalysis,* trans. James Strachey (New York: W. W. Norton, 1965), 65. See also the following description: "The first of these is the oral or, as it might be called, pregenital sexual organization. Here sexual activity has not yet been separated from the ingestion of food; nor are opposite currents within the activity differentiated. The *object* of both activities is the same; the sexual *aim* consists in the incorporation of the object—the prototype of a process which, in the form of identification, is later to play such an important psychological part." Sigmund Freud, *Three Essays on the Theory of Sexuality* (1915–1916), trans. James Strachey (New York: Basic Books, 1975), 64.

24. The reference here is to the aim of the sexual instinct, on the one hand, and the aim of the ego instinct (the instinct of self-preservation) on the other hand. Freud points out that the functions of sexuality and nourishment are linked.

25. J. Laplanche and J. B. Pontalis, *The Language of Psycho-analysis* (1967), trans. Donald Nicholson-Smith (New York: Norton, 1973), 211.

26. "O teu cabelo não nega," adaptação de Lamartine Babo sobre motivo da marcha "Mulata" dos Irmãos Valença (Rio de Janeiro: Mangione, Filhos, 1931). I thank Camilo Penna for calling this samba to my attention.

27. Sigmund Freud, *Totem and Taboo,* (1913), trans. James Strachey (New York: W. W. Norton & Co., 1950), 141–43.

28. The word "cannibal" is said to be a deformation of the word Carib. Many scholars have argued that this word informed Shakespeare's choice of name for Caliban, a figure that has been taken up by many Latin American and Caribbean writers as the appropriate figure for this region. See Roberto Fernández Retamar, *Caliban and Other Essays* (1979), trans. Edward Baker, (Minneapolis: University of Minnesota Press, 1989), 6.

29. See W. Arens, *The Man-Eating Myth: Anthropology and Anthropophagy* (New York: Oxford University Press, 1979). Arens notes the irony of the representation of the Tupinamba as devourers of Europeans, when the Tupinamba were all but wiped out by the Europeans. Benedito Nunes makes a similar observation: "Após contribuírem para a composição étnica do Brasil, os aborígenes perdem sua vida objetiva, mas interiorizam-se como espírito nacional" (After having contributed toward Brazil's ethnic composition, the indigenous people lose their own lives but are "interiorized" as the national spirit). Benedito Nunes, *Oswald Canibal* (São Paulo: Editora Perspective, 1979), 35.

30. David W. Forsyth, "The Beginnings of Brazilian Anthropology: Jesuits and Tupinamba Cannibalism," *Journal of Anthropological Research* 39 (Summer 1983): 147–78. Forsyth reviews the writings of Jesuit missionaries on Brazil in order to refute Arens's thesis that the Tupinamba did not practice anthropophagy as had been reported by French and German travelers.

31. Oswald de Andrade, "Manifesto Antropófago" (1928), trans. Leslie Bary "Oswald de Andrade's Cannibalist Manifesto," *Latin American Literary Review* 19 (July–December 1991): 39.

32. Leslie Bary, Robert Stam, and Haroldo de Campos, among others, have proposed this interpretation.

33. Oswald de Andrade, "Manifesto da Poesia Pau-Brasil," 327.

34. Sigmund Freud, *Beyond the Pleasure Principle* (1920), trans. James Strachey (New York: W. W. Norton & Co., 1975), 65.

35. Karl Abraham, M.D., "A Short Study of the Development of the Libido, Viewed in the Light of Mental Disorders," in *Selected Papers of Karl Abraham, M.D.* (1927), trans. Douglas Bryan and Alix Strachey (New York: Basic Books, 1953), 442–53.

36. Melanie Klein, "Some Theoretical Conclusions Regarding the Emotional Life of the Infant," in *Developments in Psycho-analysis*, ed. Joan Rivière (London: Hogarth Press, 1952), 198–236.

37. Sigmund Freud, "Negation" (1925), in *General Psychoanalytic Theory*, ed. Philip Reiff (New York: MacMillan, 1963), 214–15.

38. Nicholas Abraham and Maria Torok, *The Shell and the Kernel*, (1987), trans. and ed. Nicholas T. Rand (Chicago: University of Chicago Press, 1994). I discuss the distinction between incorporation and introjection in greater detail in the next chapter.

39. Jacques Derrida, "Plato's Pharmacy," in *Dissemination* (1972), trans: Barbara Johnson (Chicago: University of Chicago Press, 1981), 128.

40. José de Alencar, *O Demonio Familiar: uma comedia em 4 atos* (Rio de Janeiro: Ministério de Educação e Cultura, 1957).

41. See Thomas Skidmore, *Black into White: Race and National Identity in Brazilian Thought* (New York: Oxford University Press, 1974).

42. Nancy Stepan, *The Hour of Eugenics* (Ithaca, N.Y.: Cornell University Press, 1991), 155–56.

43. This is not to say that in racialized discourse blackness does not then double back to describe the foreign. Nor does this obscure the fact that the remainder also has a remainder. See chapter 5 of this book.

44. Oswald de Andrade cited in Nunes, *Canibal*, 26.

45. See Jean-Claude Blachère, *Le modèle nègre: Aspects littéraires du mythe primitiviste au XXe siècle chez Apollinaire, Cendrars, Tsara* (Dakar, Senegal: Nouvelles Editions Africains, 1981).

46. Nunes, *Canibal*, 13.

47. Mário de Andrade, *Macunaíma: O herói sem nenhum caráter, Edição critica*. Coordenadora: Telê Porto Ancona Lopez (Florianópolis, SC: Editora da UFSG, 1988), 166. Further references will be made in the body of the text. The English translation is from: Mário de Andrade, *Macunaíma*, trans. E. A. Goodland (New York: Random House, 1984), 165. Further references to the novel will be made in the body of the text. Any modifications to the translation will be indicated with brackets.

48. For a discussion of the rhapsody, see Telê Porto Ancona Lopez, "Rapsódia e Resistência," in *Macunaíma* (Edição Crítica), ed. Telê Porto Ancona Lopez (Rio de Janeiro: Edicoes Alumbramento/Livroarte Editora Limitada, 1984).

49. Mário de Andrade, *Prefáciao para Macunaíma*, unpublished. Arquivo Mário de Andrade, Instituto de Estudo Brasileiros, Universidade de São Paulo, São Paulo, Brasil.

50. Mário de Andrade, "Carta a Alceu Amoroso Lima, 19 de maio de 1928," in *Cartas de Mário de Andrade*, ed. Lygia Fernandes (Rio de Janeiro: Editora São José, s/d).

51. Raimundo de Moraes cited by Mário de Andrade, "A Raimundo Moraes" *Diário Nacional,* São Paulo, 20 de setembro de 1931, s.p. Recortes Mário de Andrade, Arquivo Mário de Andrade, Instituto de Estudos Brasileiros, Universidade de São Paulo, São Paulo, Brasil.

52. Ibid.

53. Mário de Andrade, cited by Eneide Maria de Souza, *A Pedra Mágica do Discurso: jogo e linguagem em Macunaíma* (Belo Horizonte: Editora UFMG, 1988), 30.

54. Cocteau, cited by Nunes, *Canibal,* 17.

55. In order to distinguish between Koch-Grünberg's Makunaíma and Mário de Andrade's Macunaíma, I have retained the spelling preferred by each.

56. Teodor Koch-Grünberg, *Del Roraima al Orinoco, Tomo II* (1917), trans. Frederica de Ritter (Caracas: Ernesto Armitano Editor, 1981), 18. I consulted the Spanish translation as well as a translation by Mário de Andrade from the original German to Portuguese. Unpublished manuscript (1929), Arquivo Mário de Andrade, Instituto de Estudos Brasileiros, Universidade de São Paulo, São Paulo, Brasil.

57. Mário de Andrade, "A superstição da cor preta," *Boletim Luso-Africano* (dezembro 1938). This article was based on a talk that Mário gave at a conference commemorating the fiftieth anniversary of the Abolition. He exhorted the audience to recognize the subtle ways the language of color reinforces racism and undermines racial pride for Blacks.

58. Mário de Andrade, "Carta a Augusto Mayer," 17 julho 1928, *Mário de Andrade escreve cartas a Alceu, Meyer e outros,* org. Lygia Fernandes (Rio de Janeiro: ed. do Autor, 1968), 16.

59. Koch-Grünberg, *Del Roraima,* 73. See also Mário de Andrade, *Namoros com a medicina* (São Paulo: Martins, 1980), 99–100.

60. "The novel can be defined as a diversity of social speech types (sometimes even diversity of languages) and a diversity of individual voices, artistically organized. . . . Authorial speech, the speech of narrators, inserted genres, the speech of characters are merely those fundamental compositional unities with whose help heteroglossia can enter the novel; each of them permits a multiplicity of social voices and a wide variety of their links and interrelationships (always more or less dialogized)." M. M. Bakhtin, *The Dialogic Imagination,* ed. Michael Holquist, trans. Caryl Emerson and Michael Holquist (Austin: University of Texas, 1985), 263. For a helpful and informative Bakhtinian reading of *Macunaíma,* see Robert Stam, "Subversive Pleasures," in M. M. Bakhtin, *Cultural Criticism and Film* (Baltimore: Johns Hopkins University Press, 1989), esp. 145–51.

61. Souza, *Pedra,* 47.

62. Mikhail Bakhtin, *Rabelais and His World* (1965), trans. Helen Iswolsky (Cambridge, Mass.: MIT Press, 1968), 281.

63. This word functions much as *sloth* does in English to indicate the name of an animal as well as its defining characteristic.

64. Maria Augusta Fonseca, cited in Mário de Andrade, *Macunaíma,* ed. Lopez, 6.

65. Paulo Prado, *Retrato do Brasil* (Rio de Janeiro: F. Briguiet, 1931), 196–97.

66. Goodland translates this line as: "With fewer ants and better health / Brazil will lead the world in wealth."

67. M. Cavalcanti Proença, *Roteiro de Macunaíma* (Rio de Janeiro: Civilização Brasileira, 1987), 172.

68. "By the second decade of the twentieth century, the appalling misery and ill health of the poor had crystallized in public consciousness as a national issue—as the 'social question.' The group that most agitated physicians, sanitation experts, and reformers in Brazil was largely black and mulatto; these professionals assumed that social ills accumulated at the bottom of the racial and social hierarchy. . . . Racial and class biases thus merged in the language of heredity" Stepan, *Hour,* 37.

69. J. W. Boddam-Whetham, *Roraima and British Guiana* (London: Hurst and Blackett, 1879), 172.

70. John R. Swanton, *Myths and Tales of the Southeastern Indians* (Washington, D.C.: Government Printing Office, n.d.), 75.

71. Fidelis Reis, *País a organizar* (Rio de Janeiro: Coelho Branco, 1931). The document from the Academia Nacional de Medicina is appended to the book.

72. Mário de Andrade, "Prefácio para Macunaíma," Unpublished manuscript. Arquivo Mário de Andrade, Instituto de Estudos Brasileiros, Universidade de São Paulo, São Paulo, Brasil.

73. "Conceber literariamente o Brasil como entidade homogênea = un conceito étnico nacional."

74. Marilene Chauí, cited in Reis, *Pearl Necklace,* 28–29.

75. Mário de Andrade, *Namoros,* 66.

76. Throughout *Cannibal Democracy,* I focus on blackness as a remainder. Although at different moments I discuss the indigenous peoples where the lack of representation of indigenous people as Brazilian coincides with that of black people, I do not see their situations as equivalent. The complex relationship of indigenous peoples to Brazilian identity and how it has changed over time is beyond the scope of this study.

2. Bringing in the Dead

1. Moacir Werneck de Castro, *Mário de Andrade: Exílo no Rio* (Rio de Janeiro: Rocco, 1989). Mário's speech was published in Mário de Andrade, "A expressão Musical dos Estados Unidos," in *Música, doce Música* (São Paulo: Livraria Martins Editôra, 1944), 395–417.

2. Mário de Andrade, "Nova Canção de Dixie," manuscript (25 janeiro 1944), Archivo Mário de Andrade, Instituto de Estudo Brasileiros, Universidade de São Paulo, São Paulo, Brasil. Published posthumously in *Correio Paulistano* (25 fevereiro 1946). Permission Família Mário de Andrade.

3. Jeffrey Needell, "Identity, Race, Gender, and Modernity in the Origins of Gilberto Freyre's *Oevre,*" *American Historical Review* 100, no. 1 (February 1995): 51–57.

4. Not only do these two figures immediately come to mind in any discussion regarding Brazilian culture in the early decades of the twentieth century, but Mário de Andrade and Gilberto Freyre are also associated with the sense of a profound change in the perception of race and national identity during this period. They were, in fact, associated personally with one another. Between the completion and publication of *Macunaíma,* Mário de Andrade made his first trip throughout the Northeast and the Amazon region. While

in Recife, he was escorted on a tour by Gilberto Freyre. A copy of Mário's thank-you letter can be found among Freyre's papers at the Fundação Joaquim Nabuco in Recife, Pernambuco, along with a copy of *Macunaíma*. An edition of *Casa Grande e Senzala*, a gift from Gilberto Freyre, can be found among Mário's papers. It contains Mário's extensive handwritten commentary. Arquivo Mário de Andrade, Instituto de Estudos Brasileiros, Universidade de São Paulo, São Paulo, Brasil.

5. I first saw the unpublished working draft in 1990, when Luís Buarque de Hollanda consulted me on aspects of the text. The screenplay has since been published as Joaquim Pedro de Andrade, *Casa Grande e Cia* (Rio de Janeiro: Aeroplano Editora, 2001). See also Robert Stam, *Tropical Multiculturalism: A Comparative History of Race in Brazilian Cinema and Culture* (Durham, N.C.: Duke University Press, 1997), 13–15.

6. *Quilombolas* were residents of the *quilombos,* maroon communities established by fugitive enslaved people, indigenous people, and other runaways.

7. Stam, *Tropical Multiculturalism*, 13–15.

8. Gilberto Freyre, *Casa Grande e Senzala* (Rio de Janeiro: José Olympio, 1987), lvii. Further citations will be given in the body of the text.

9. Gilberto Freyre, *The Masters and the Slaves* (1933), trans. Samuel Putnam (Berkeley: University of California Press, 1986), xxvi–vii. Further citations will be given in the body of the text. Unless otherwise noted, all translations are Putnam's. Any modifications are placed in brackets.

10. Jurandir Freire Costa, *História da psiquiatria no Brasil: um corte ideológico* (Rio de Janeiro: Editora Campus, 1981), 31–32. See also Roberto Reis, *The Pearl Necklace: Toward an Archeology of Brazilian Transition Discourse*, trans. Aparecida de Godoy Johnson (Miami: University of Florida, 1992), 148, note 8; and Roberto Machado, *Danação da Norma: medicina social e constituição da psiquiatria no Brasil,* (Rio de Janeiro: Graal, 1978), 82–83.

11. Claude Lévi-Strauss, *Tristes Tropiques* (1955), trans. John and Doreen Weightman (New York: Atheneum, 1981), 388.

12. Ernest Renan, "What Is a Nation?" (1882), trans. Martin Thom, in *Nation and Narration,* ed. Homi K. Bhabha (New York: Routledge, 1990), 11.

13. With the independence of Brazil from Portugal in 1822, it was necessary to determine the criteria for citizenship. The constitution of 1824 defined the Empire as "political association of all Brazilian citizens," who "form a free and independent nation." Citizenship was granted Portuguese citizens resident in Brazil. Citizenship was not accorded those born into slavery, who constituted the majority of the population. Freedmen received only limited political rights that stopped short of the right to be electors. Women had no political rights. During the first decades of the nineteenth century, only two percent of the population could vote because of literacy and property ownership requirements. Roderick J. Barman, *Brazil: The Forging of a Nation, 1798–1852* (Stanford, Calif.: Stanford University Press, 1988), 123.

14. José Murilo de Cavalho, *Os Bestializados: o Rio de Janeiro e a República que não foi* (São Paulo: Companhia das Letras, 1987), 115–39.

15. Jurandir Freire Costa, *Ordem médica e norma familiar* (Rio de Janeiro: Graal, 1979), 157.

16. Euclides da Cunha, *Ciclo d'os Sertões* (Rio de Janeiro: José Aguilar, 1966), 166–67.

17. Roberto Ventura, *Estilo tropical: história cultural e polêmicas literárias no Brasil* (São Paulo: Companhia das Letras, 1991), 58.

18. "The method of de-Africanizing the 'new' Negro that was followed here was that of mingling him with the mass of 'ladinos,' or older ones, in such a way that the slave huts became a practical school of Brazilianization." Freyre, *Masters,* trans. Putnam, 375.

19. This dichotomy is also described as the difference between "a historical past mainly European and an anthropological past mainly Amerindian and African." Freyre, *Masters,* trans. Putnam, xxiii.

20. The mulattoes "almost always resulted from the union of the best masculine element—the socially elevated whites of the Big houses—with the best feminine element of the slave huts: the prettiest, healthiest, and freshest of the Negro and mulatto women." Freyre, *Masters,* trans. Putnam, 452.

21. According to Freyre, indigenous women, since their culture was patrilineal, wanted to have children with white colonizers because they recognized that these men belonged to a "superior" race. Freyre, *Masters,* trans. Putnam, 84.

22. Clovis Moura, *Brasil: as raízes do protesto negro* (São Paulo: Global, 1983), 114.

23. *Progresso* (23 de Junho de 1928): s/p.

24. Nina Rodrigues, cited in Moura, *Raízes,* 119.

25. Roberto Machado, Angel Loureiro, Rogério Luz, and Kátia Muricy, *Danação da Norma: medicina social e a constituição da psiquiatria no Brasil* (Rio de Janeiro: Graal, 1978), 353–55.

26. Miscegenation is often marked in *Casa Grande e Senzala* by disease. Gilberto Freyre says that the scar left by syphilis, the "initial ethnic [racial] tare of which Azevedo Amaral speaks, was first of all, a syphilitic tare." Freyre, *Masters,* trans. Putnam, 71. An observation made by Bruno Latour in a different context is helpful: "Both [Freud and Pasteur] announced that they were speaking in the name of the invisible, rejected, terribly dangerous forces that must be listened to if civilization was not to collapse. Like the psychoanalysts, the pasteurians set themselves up as exclusive interpreters of populations to which no one else had access. Bruno Latour, *The Pasteurization of France* (1984), trans. Alan Sheridan and John Law (Cambridge, Mass.: Harvard University Press, 1988), 39.

27. Speaking of priests, he emphasizes "the fact that in the formation of Brazilian society there was not lacking a superior element recruited from the best families and capable of transmitting to its progeny major advantages from the point of view of eugenics and social heritage." Freyre, *Masters,* trans. Putnam, 449.

28. Mário de Andrade satirizes this attitude in *Macunaíma* in the chapter, "Carta pra icamiabas" (Letter to the Icamiabas).

29. Nicholas Abraham and Maria Torok, *The Shell and the Kernel* (1987), trans. and ed. Nicholas T. Rand (Chicago: University of Chicago Press, 1994).

30. Ann Cheng makes the compelling argument that we should think of incorporation and introjection less as opposed and more as stages in the process of mourning. Ann Anlin Cheng, *The Melancholy of Race* (New York: Oxford University Press, 2000), 95–97.

31. This discussion of shame could contribute to an understanding of the shame that the "ex-coloured" man experiences upon witnessing the lynching that will propel him to pass. He so identifies with the dead man that he, too, dies as a black man to live from that moment on as a "mediocre" white man. James Weldon Johnson, *The Autobiography of an Ex-coloured Man* (New York: Vintage Books, 1989).

32. Dante Moreira Leite, *O caráter nacional brasileiro* (São Paulo: Pioneira, 1983).

33. Antônio Sérgio Bueno, *O modernismo em Belo Horizonte: década de vinte,* (Belo Horizonte: PROED, 1982). It is worth noting that *leite* is also a slang word for semen.

34. In a footnote, Freyre refers to Freud in support of his relating love, sex, language, and food to each other as forms of assimilation. For Freyre, one defensible example among many is the word *comer* (eat) that links eating, sex, and obscene language (coprolalia). Freyre, *Masters,* trans. Putnam, 260, footnote 178.

3. The Foreigner and the Remainder

1. W. E. B. Du Bois, *The Conservation of Races* (New York: Arno Press, 1969).

2. James Bryce, *South America: Observations and Impressions* (New York: Macmillan, 1914); Sir Harry Johnston, *The Negro in the New World* (New York: Johnson Reprint Company, 1969); Roy Nash, "The Origin of Negro Slavery in Brazil" *The Crisis,* (October 1923): 264; Roy Nash, *The Conquest of Brazil* (New York: Harcourt, Brace and Company, 1926).

3. George Shepperson, "Introduction," in Johnston, *Negro in the New World.*

4. George Reid Andrews, "Brazilian Racial Democracy, 1900–90: An American Counterpoint," *Journal of American History* 31, no. 3: (July 1996): 483–507.

5. José Clarana, *Os estados unidos pela civilização e a civilização dos Estados Unidos* (Rio de Janeiro, Brasil: Officinas Graficas-do Jornal do Brasil, 1919).

6. José Clarana, "The Schooling of the Negro," *The Crisis* (July 1913): 133–36, my emphasis.

7. W. E. B. Du Bois, *The Souls of Black Folk* (Chicago: McClurg, 1904), 3.

8. Priscilla Wald, *Constituting Americans: Cultural Anxiety and Narrative Form* (Durham, N.C.: Duke University Press, 1995), 176.

9. W. E. B. Du Bois, "The Souls of White Folk," in *Darkwater: Voices from within the Veil* (Mineola, N.Y.: Dover, 1999), 17.

10. Du Bois, Marcus Garvey, James Weldon Johnson, and Zora Neale Hurston all describe their coming to an understanding of their racialized identities in or around a school.

11. Wald, *Constituting,* 190.

12. The fact of miscegenation does not distinguish Brazil from the United States: "There are millions of Negroes in Brazil; amalgamation is as common there now as it was in the southern part of the United States before the War of the Rebellion." "Brazilian Visitors in Norfolk," *Colored American Magazine* (August 1905): 406–7, in *African-American Reflections on Brazil's Racial Paradise,* ed. David Hellwig (Philadelphia: Temple, 1992), 22. The perceived attitude of encouragement of miscegenation makes Brazil notable for these writers.

13. Sallyann H. Ferguson, "Chesnutt's Genuine Blacks and Future Americans," in

Charles Chesnutt: Selected Writings, ed. Sallyann H. Ferguson (Boston: Houghton Mifflin, 2001), 429.

14. Sallyann H. Ferguson, "Rena Walden: Chesnutt's Failed 'Future American,'" in *Critical Essays on Charles Chesnutt,* ed. Joseph R. McElrath Jr. (New York: G. K. Hall, 1999), 205.

15. William Andrews, *The Literary Career of Charles W. Chesnutt* (Baton Rouge: Louisiana State University Press, 1980), 5.

16. Edward W. Knappman, ed., *Great American Trials* (Detroit: Visible Ink, 1994), 218.

17. Charles Lofgren, cited by Eric Sundquist, *To Wake the Nation: Race in the Making of American Literatures* (Cambridge, Mass.: Harvard, 1993), 237. My presentation of the *Plessy* is drawn mainly from Sundquist.

18. Justice Henry Billings Brown, "Majority opinion in *Plessy v. Ferguson,*" in *Desegregation and the Supreme Court,* ed. Benjamin Munn Ziegler (Washington, D.C.: Heath and Company, 1958), 50–51.

19. Thomas Jefferson, "Notes on Virginia," in *Basic Writings of Thomas Jefferson,* ed. Philip Foner (Garden City, N.Y.: Halcyon, 1944), 50–181, esp. 146–47.

20. Bruce Rosen, "Abolition and Colonization: The Years of Conflict, 1829–1834," in *Freedom's Odyssey: African American History Essays from Phylon,* ed. Alexa Benson Henderson and Janice Sumler-Edmond (Atlanta: Clark Atlanta University Press, 1999), 110.

21. Frederick Douglass, "The Present Condition and Future Prospects of the Negro People," in *Frederick Douglass: Selected Speeches and Writings,* ed. Philip S. Foner (Chicago: Lawrence Hill, 1999), 258.

22. Howard H. Bell, "The Negro Emigration Movement: 1849–1854: A Phase of Negro Nationalism," in *Freedom's Odyssey,* ed. Henderson and Edmond.

23. Charles Chesnutt, "A Multitude of Counselors," in *Charles W. Chesnutt: Essays and Speeches,* ed. Joseph R. McElrath Jr., Robert C. Leitz III, and Jesse S. Crisler (Stanford, Calif.: Stanford University, 1999): 80.

24. Cyrus B. Dawsey and James B. Dawsey, "Leaving: The Context of Southern Emigration to Brazil," in *The Confederados: Old South Immigrants in Brazil,* ed. Cyrus B. Dawsey and James B. Dawsey (Tuscaloosa: University of Alabama Press, 1995), 17.

25. These are listed in James M Gravois and Elizabeth J. Weisbrod, "Annotated Bibliography," in *Confederados,* ed. Dawsey and Dawsey, 24–49.

26. Michael L. Coniff, "Forward," in *Confederados,* ed. Dawsey and Dawsey, xii.

27. Sarah Bellona Smith Ferguson, "The Journey: The Narrative of Sarah Bellona Smith Ferguson," in *Confederados,* ed. Dawsey and Dawsey, 24–49.

28. See Frank P. Goldman, *Os pioneiros americanos no Brasil,* trans. Olivia Krähenbühl (São Paulo: Livraria Pioneira Editora, 1972); William Clark Griggs, *The Elusive Eden* (Austin: University of Texas Press, 1997); Alfred Jackson Hanna and Kathryn Abbey Hanna, *Confederate Exiles in Venezuela* (Tuscaloosa, Ala.: Confederate Publishing Company, 1960); Eugene C. Harter, *The Lost Colony of the Confederacy* (Jackson: University of Mississippi: 1985); William B. Hesseltine and Hazel C. Wolf, *The Blue and the Grey on the Nile* (Chicago: University of Chicago Press, 1961); Lawrence Francis Hill, "Confederate Exiles to Brazil," *Hispanic American Historical Review* 7, no. 2 (May

1927), 192–210, and "The Confederate Exodus to South America," *Southwestern Historical Quarterly* 39, no. 3 (1936); Judith MacKnight Jones, *Soldado descansa! uma epopéia norteamericana sob os céus do Brasil* (São Paulo: Jarde, 1967); Betty Antunes de Oliveira, *Movimento de passageiros norte-americanos no porto do Rio de Janeiro, 1865–1890: uma contribuição para a história da imigração norte-americana no Brasil* (Rio de Janeiro: [sn], 1982); Ana Maria Costa de Oliveira, *O destino não-manifesto: os imigrantes norte-americanos no Brasil* (São Paulo: União Cultural Brasil-Estados Unidos, 1995); Andrew W. Rolle, *The Lost Cause: The Confederate Exodus to Mexico* (Norman: University of Oklahoma, 1965); Daniel E. Sutherland, *The Confederate Carpetbaggers* (Baton Rouge: Louisiana State University Press, 1988).

29. Charles Chesnutt, "The Future American: What the Race Is Likely to Become in the Process of Time" (1900), "The Future American: A Stream of Dark Blood in the Veins of Southern Whites" (1900); and "The Future American: A Complete Race Amalgamation Likely to Occur" (1900); in *Chesnutt: Essays,* ed. McElrath Jr., Leitz III, and Crisler, 118–131.

30. Diminishing fractions of blackness create Chesnutt's single homogeneous type. The logic of fractions presupposes remainders.

31. Charles Chesnutt, "What Is a White Man?" (1889), in *Chesnutt: Essays,* ed. McElrath Jr., Leitz III, and Crisler, 68–73. The case referred to is 71 *State v. Davis,* SC 2 Bailey 558 (1831).

32. W. E. B. Du Bois, "Brazil," *The Crisis* (April 1914): 286–87, cited in *Reflections,* ed. Hellwig, 31–34.

33. Chesnutt had used the presumption of the illegitimacy of the children of a black parent and a white parent as an argument against antimiscegenation laws. For him, this presumption associated immorality with all light-skinned black people. "Whatever the wisdom or justice of these laws (prohibiting marriages between whites and people of color), there is one objection to them which is not given sufficient prominence in the consideration of the subject, even where it is discussed at all; they make mixed blood a *prima facie* proof of illegitimacy. It is a fact that at present, in the United States, a colored man or woman whose complexion is white or nearly white is presumed, in the absence of any knowledge of his or her antecedents, to be the offspring of a union not sanctified by law. . . . More than half the people of color in the United States are of mixed blood; they marry and are given in marriage, and they beget children of complexions similar to their own, [but these] laws . . . stamp these children as illegitimate." *Chesnutt: Essays,* ed. McElrath Jr., Leitz III, and Crisler, 72–73.

34. The fire's consumption of the offending paper links this passage to the description of the remainders of a lynching that included the burning of the body, which took place during the race riot. The remainder, then, ties together the novel's two plots: the family romance and the fictionalized account of the Wilmington Riot of 1898.

35. Sigmund Freud, *Inhibitions, Symptoms and Anxiety* (1926), trans. Alix Strachey, rev. and ed. James Strachey (New York: Norton, 1959), 73. I am *not* arguing that blackness is a symptom of whiteness. In historicizing Freud's notions, one of my goals is to show how Freud's location in the modern subject, through his incorporation of a metaphorics of cannibalism, what anthropology relegates to the past, sheds light on the anxieties that attend cannibalism and its remainders. In other words, rather than making of psychoanalysis a

master discourse, I show that the anxieties revealed in the metaphorics of cannibalism and its disavowed remainders are always there, but when they are located in the modern subject, the remainders cease to keep the peace, much as "Freud" would quiet them. I would make a parallel argument to counter any idea that the remainder could be read as abject.

4. The New Negro and the Turn to South America

1. Robert Abbott, "My Trip through South America," in *African-American Reflections on Brazil's Racial Paradise,* ed. David Hellwig (Philadelphia: Temple, 1992), 55–81.

2. My sources for Abbott's biography and for the history of the newspaper are: Roi Ottley, *The Lonely Warrior: The Life and Times of Robert S. Abbott* (Chicago: Henry Regnery, 1955), and Juliet E. K. Walker, "The Promised Land: The *Chicago Defender* and the Black Periodical Press in Illinois, 1862–1970," in *The Black Press in the Middle West, 1865–1985,* ed. Henry Lewis Suggs (Westport, Conn.: Greenwood Press, 1996), 10–49.

3. W. E. B. Du Bois, "The Migration of Negroes" (1923), in *Selections from "The Crisis": 1911–1925,* vol. 1, ed. Herbert Aptheker (Millwood, N.Y.: Krauss-Thomson, 1983), 139.

4. From the *Broad-Ax* newspaper, cited in Walker, *Promised Land,* 28.

5. Ibid. Numerous appeals were made to organizations charged with resolving the aftermath of the war, including "An Appeal to the Nations of the Earth Assembled in the Conference on the Limitation of Armament," which included an exhibit on lynching to reinforce that "Even while this Conference is in session, as late as December 14, 1921, lynchings have occurred. Ten soldiers have been lynched in one year, since returning from service to over seas, where they fought for World Democracy." C. M. Tanner, "An Appeal to the Nations of the Earth Assembled in the Conference on the Limitation of Armament" (Washington, D.C.: Library of Congress, 1921), pamphlet.

6. Kelly Miller, "Disgrace of Democracy" (4 August 1917), in *The Everlasting Stain* (Washington, D.C.: Associated Publishers, 1924), 144–45.

7. W. E. B. Du Bois, "Vive la France!" in Aptheker, *Selections,* 170.

8. W. E. B. Du Bois, "For What?" (1919), in Aptheker, *Selections,* 180.

9. David Levering Lewis, *W. E. B. Du Bois: The Fight for Equality and the American Century, 1919–1963* (New York: Henry Holt, 2000), 47.

10. Ionie Benjamin, *The Black Press in Britain* (Staffordshire: Trentham Books, 1995), 16–17. See also Du Bois, *The Crisis* 19 (January 1920): 107–8, cited in Aptheker, *Selections:* "I have always looked on England as the best administrator of colored peoples and laid her success to her system of Justice. But here, again, I am beginning to waiver. I have talked to Indians, to Egyptians, to West and South Africans, and they have left a great, dull doubt in my mind—a feeling of world apprehension" (251).

11. The *African Telegraph,* cited in Benjamin, *Black Press,* 17.

12. George Shepperson, "Introduction," in Sir Harry Johnston, *The Negro in the New World* (New York: Johnson Reprint, 1969), x-xi.

13. Shepperson, in Johnston, *Negro,* viii. See also David Levering Lewis, *W. E. B. Du Bois: Biography of a Race, 1868–1919* (New York: Henry Holt, 1993), 440.

14. Kelly Miller, "The Negro in the New World and the Conflict of Color" (1914),

in *Out of the House of Bondage* (New York: Neale Publishing, 1914), 187–95. Miller criticized the work for being too impressionistic and for focusing too much on Booker T. Washington and Tuskeegee in its discussion of Negro education. He also faulted it for not giving enough attention to religion.

15. Lord Olivier, *White Capital and Coloured Labour* (1906) (New York: Russell and Russell, 1970). Sir Sydney Olivier hosted Du Bois at a garden party during his visit to Jamaica in 1915. Lewis, *Biography,* 456.

16. James Bryce, *South America: Observations and Impressions* (New York: Macmillan, 1914).

17. Roy Nash, *The Conquest of Brazil* (New York: Harcourt, Brace, 1926). Nash also published articles on Brazil for *The Crisis:* "The Origin of Negro Slavery in Brazil," (October 1923): 146, and "The Origin of Negro Slavery in Brazil,"(April 1927): 264.

18. "Brazil: A Review of 'The Conquest of Brazil' As Told by Roy Nash," *The Crisis* (April 1927): 44–45. Interestingly, an article by Gilberto Freyre lauding Nash's book as one of the best by a foreigner quotes these very passages. See Gilberto Freyre, "O fator racial na política contemporânea," *Ciência & Trópico* 10, no. 1 (1982): 19–36.

19. For example, Olivier argues that because there have been "no terrorism, no special laws, no illegal discriminations against the coloured," white women are as safe in public as in any region of Europe. While this could be shown to be a dubious comparison, as — if not more — dubious, are the grounds for this positive characterization in relation to the United States: "I cannot but surmise that any propensity there may be to such assaults [against white women by black men] in the United States is stimulated by the very character of the attitude of the white towards the coloured poplation. There is maintained a constant storm of suggestion to the most imaginative and uncontrollable of passions in an excitable and imaginative race." Olivier, *White Capital,* 73–74.

20. Associated Negro Press, "Wonderful Opportunities Offered in Brazil for Thrifty People of all Races," *Tulsa Star* (11 December 1920), cited in Hellwig, *Reflections,* 40–43.

21. L. H. Stinson, "South America and Its Prospects in 1920," *Atlanta Independent* (23 December 1920), in Hellwig, *Reflections,* 45. This phrase is repeated throughout most articles on Brazil.

22. "Brazil and the Black Race," *Philadelphia Tribune* (14 March 1914), cited in Hellwig, *Reflections,* 26–30.

23. Carter Godwin Woodson, "The Beginnings of Miscegenation of the Whites and Blacks," *Journal of Negro History* 3, no. 4 (October 1918): 335–53.

24. "Slavery in Brazil," *Cleveland Gazette* (14 June 1884): 2.

25. "Brazil and the Black Race," *Philadelphia Tribune* (14 March 1914), in Hellwig, *Reflections,* 36.

26. R. W. Merguson, "Glimpses of Brazil," *The Crisis* (November 1915): 38–43.

27. "Brazil a Western Negro Land," *The Coloured American Magazine* (September 1906): 144.

28. *Baltimore Afro-American* (12 December 1925): 4.

29. Pearl Bowser, a leading scholar of Micheaux's work, has stated that she is convinced that Micheaux had been to Brazil. (Personal communication, New York, 10 May 2002). For more information on Micheaux and the film, see Pearl Bowser, Jane Gaines, and

Charles Musser, eds., *Oscar Micheaux and His Circle* (Bloomington: Indiana University Press, 2001). See also Thomas Cripps, *Slow Fade to Black* (New York: Oxford University Press, 1977) and Henry T. Sampson, *Blacks in Black and White: A Source Book on Black Films* (Metuchen, N.J.: Scarecrow Press, 1995).

30. "Editor Abbott and Wife Star in the Movies," *Chicago Defender* (19 November 1927): 10A. See also *"The Millionaire,* Drama of Soldier of Fortune, with Race Cast, on Dunbar Screen," *Baltimore Afro-American* (21 January 1928): 7.

31. In the preface to *The Book of American Negro Poetry,* a collection that helped inspire the Harlem Renaissance, another name given to the "New Negro Movement," James Weldon Johnson writes: "Mention of [Paul Lawrence] Dunbar brings up for consideration the fact that, although he is the most outstanding figure in literature among the Aframericans of the United States, he does not stand alone among the Aframericans of the whole Western world. There are Plácido and Manzano in Cuba, Vieux and Durand in Haiti, Machado de Assis in Brazil, Leon Laviaux in Martinique, and others that might be mentioned, who stand on a plane with or even above Dunbar. Plácido and Machado de Assis rank as great in the literatures of their respective countries without any qualifications whatever. . . . Machado de Assis is somewhat handicapped in this respect by having as his tongue and medium the lesser known Portuguese. But Plácido, writing in the language . . . of almost the whole of South America is universally known." Walter White similarly distinguished Machado de Assis and Plácido in *The Negro's Contribution to American Culture: The Sudden Flowering of a Genius-Laden Artistic Movement* (Girard, Kans.: Haldeman-Julius Publications, 1928), 14.

32. Teresa Meade and Gregory Alonso Pirio, "In Search of the Afro-American 'Eldorado': Attempts by North American Blacks to Enter Brazil in the 1920s," *Luso-Brazilian Review* 25, no. 1 (1988): 92–93. This essay also discusses black emigration to other areas of South America, including Mexico, and pays particular attention to the experiences of Cyril Briggs and the followers of Marcus Garvey. The authors describe how the FBI reported the results of their surveillance of Garvey's Universal Negro Improvement Association (UNIA) to the Brazilian government (among others, including that of South Africa) in an effort to halt the spread of black militancy in the United States and abroad.

33. W. E. B. Du Bois, "Keeping Us Home," *The Crisis* (May 1929): 132.

34. Sam Adamo, *The Broken Promise: Race, Health and Justice in Rio de Janeiro, 1890–1940* (Ph.D. diss., University of New Mexico, 1983), cited in Meade and Pirio, *Eldorado,* 104.

35. The difficulty that black North Americans had in obtaining visas to Brazil was also reported in the black press in Brazil. Evaristo de Moraes, "Expansão de um preconceito . . . ou esboço de um protetorado?" *O Getulino* (16 de fevereiro de 1924): s/p.

36. These collections are available to scholars in the United States on microfilm: *The Black Press of Brazil,* ed. Michael Mitchell (Princeton, N.J.: Princeton University, nd) and *A Imprensa Negra,* ed. Miriam Nicolau Ferrara (São Paulo: Instituto de Estudos Brasileiros, 1985) is available on CD-ROM at the University of Maryland, College Park. For a summary of the collection, see also Miriam Nicolau Ferrara, *A Imprensa Negra Paulista (1915–1963)* (São Paulo: FFLCH/USP, 1986).

37. For historical background and discussions of the Brazilian black press in relation to social movements, see Ferrara, *Imprensa negra;* Kim D. Butler, *Freedoms Given, Free-*

doms Won: Afro-Brazilians in Post-Abolition São Paulo and Salvador (New Brunswick, N.J.: Rutgers University Press, 1998); George Reid Andrews, *Blacks and Whites in São Paulo, Brazil, 1888–1988* (Madison: University of Wisconsin Press, 1991); Roger Bastide, *O negro na imprensa e na literatura* (São Paulo: Escola de Comunicação e Artes/USP, 1972); Clovis Moura, *Imprensa negra* (São Paulo: Imprensa Oficial do Estado, 1984).

38. Jessie Redmon Fauset published an article in *The Crisis* detailing José de Patrocinio's biography and his contributions to the abolitionist movement in Brazil. Jessie Faucet *[sic]* and Cézar Pinto, "The Emancipator of Brazil" *The Crisis* (October 1923): 284.

39. Abilio Rodrigues, "Preto e branco," *Kosmos* (18 de setembro de 1923): s/p.

40. Francisco Gomes Brandão, visconde de Jequitinhonha, also known as Francisco Jê Acaiaba Montezuma — a combination of Portuguese, African, Tupi, and Aztec names — was a lawyer, politician, and abolitionist. André Reboucas was an engineer, orator, and abolitionist. João Maurício Wanderley, barão de Cotejipe, was a senator and a key figure in promoting the most significant antislavery legislation. Tobias Barreto was a philospher, poet, and jurist. Juliano Morreira was a pioneering psychiatrist. Evaristo de Moraes was a journalist, historian, founder of the Brazilian Press Association, one of the founders of the Workers Party, and the founder of the Socialist Party. Although he had not yet received his degree, he came to prominence as the lawyer for João Cândido Felisberto, the black leader of the famous 1910 revolt by marines against corporal punishment.

41. Abilio Rodrigues, "Preto e branco," *Kosmos* (18 de setembro de 1923): s/p. For other reports on Abbott's visit, please see Benedicto Florencio's series of three articles, "Cartas de um negro, I," *Getulino* (23 setembro 1923); "Cartas de um negro, II," *Getulino* (30 setembro 1923, reprinted 7 de outubro 1923); and "Cartas de um negro, III," *Getulino* (21 de outubro 1923); and "A questão de Raça" *Auriverde* (abril 1928): s/p.

42. Benedicto Florencio, "Cartas dúm negro," *Getulino* (30 setembro 1923): 1.

43. Ottley, *Lonely Warrior,* 240. Interestingly, the biographer's sympathies are with Abbott, and he treats Helen's views in a condescending manner.

44. Theophilio F. Comargo, "Echos do Projeto F. Reis," *Elite* (20 January 1924): 1. For more discussion of the bill, see Evaristo de Moraes, "Brancos, negros, e mulatos," *Getulino* (30 dezembro 1923); and Theophilio F. Comargo, "O pan-latismos e os negros: a proposta do Projecto F. Reis," *Getulino* (13 janeiro 1924).

45. Fidelis Reis, *Pais a organizar* (Rio de Janeiro: Coelho Branco, 1931). The document from the Academia Nacional de Medicina is appended to the book.

46. Evaristo de Moraes, "Os negros nos Estados Unidos e no Brasil," *Getulino* (13 janeiro 1924): s/p.

47. Benedicto Florencio, "Cartas dúm negro, III" *Getulino* (21 outubro 1923): s/p.

48. Benedicto Florencio, "Cartas dúm negro, II" *Getulino* (30 setembro 1923): s/p.

49. Roosevelt, "Brazil and the Negro," 409–11. This quotation is discussed in Thomas E. Skidmore, *Black into White: Race and Nationality in Brazilian Thought* (New York: Oxford University Press, 1974), 74–75.

50. Michael George Hanchard, *Orpheus and Power* (Princeton, N.J.: Princeton University Press, 1994), 15.

51. Thadious Davis, *Nella Larsen, Novelist of the Harlem Renaissance: A Woman's Life Unveiled* (Baton Rouge: Louisiana State University Press, 1994).

52. See Roberto Schwartz, "As idéias fora do lugar," in *Ao vencedor as batatas —*

forma literária e processo social nos inícios do romance brasileiro (São Paulo: Duas Cidades, 1988), 13–28.

53. Jessie Redmon Fauset, *Plum Bun: A Novel without a Moral* (Boston: Beacon, 1990), 70.

54. This ending was added to the 1971 Macmillan edition of *Passing*.

5. The Remainder Is a Reminder

1. Sandra G. Shannon, "An Interview with August Wilson, " in *The Dramatic Vision of August Wilson* (Washington, D.C.: Howard University Press, 1994), 203.

2. August Wilson, *Ma Rainey's Black Bottom* (New York: Plume, 1985), 57–58.

3. Kim Pereira, *August Wilson and the African-American Odyssey* (Urbana: University of Illinois, 1995), 30.

4. I thank Biodun Jeyifo for calling this aspect of the scene to my attention.

5. Mark Poster, introduction to Jean Baudrillard, *The Mirror of Production* (1973), trans. Mark Poster (St. Louis: Telos, 1975), 11.

6. Paul Gilroy, *The Black Atlantic: Modernity and Double Consciousness* (Cambridge, Mass.: Harvard University Press, 2000), 4.

7. Countée Cullen, "Heritage," in *My Soul's High Song: The Collected Writings of Countée Cullen,* ed. Gerald Early (New York: Anchor, 1991), 104.

8. Toni Morrison, *Paradise* (New York: Plume, 1999), 209. Further reference will be in the body of the text.

9. Valerie Boyd cites a letter from Zora Neale Hurston to her patron Charlotte Mason in which she describes, with pride, Eatonville, her all-black hometown, in similar terms: "Do you know that in more than fifty year's of this town's existence that never has a white man's child been born here? . . . There is no known case of a white-Negro affair around here. No white-Negro prostitution even." Valerie Boyd, *Wrapped in Rainbows: The Life of Zora Neale Hurston* (New York: Scribner, 2003), 236.

10. Morrison had addressed this theme in *Beloved*. In *Paradise,* however, the emphasis on loving one's children to death invites a consideration of community rather than freedom.

11. Nicholas Abraham and Maria Torok, *The Shell and the Kernel* (1987), trans. and ed. Nicholas T. Rand (Chicago: University of Chicago Press, 1994), 111.

12. Gayl Jones, *Corregidora,* (Boston: Beacon, 1986). *Corregidora* traces the story of four generations of women who reproduce themselves in order to preserve on their skins and in their minds the unwritten history of slavery in Brazil. Ursa, the last of the Corregidora woman and the first to be born in the United States, has a hysterectomy as the result of an injury sustained when her husband pushes her down a flight of stairs. She struggles to learn how to ensure the continuity of the story she is enjoined to tell when she cannot produce the next generation. Toni Morrison was Gayl Jones's editor.

13. Dan Cameron, *absolutearts.com.*

14. Keith Piper, *Relocating the Remains* (London: Institute of International Visual Arts, 1997).

15. Michael D. Harris, "Meanwhile the Girls Were Playing: María Magdalena Campos-Pons," *Nka* 13 (Spring/Summer 2001): 52. See also María Magdalena Campos-Pons,

Everything Is Separated by Water, ed. Lisa D. Freiman (Indianapolis and New Haven: Indianapolis Museum of Art, in association with Yale University Press, 2007).

16. Fernando Ortiz, *Cuban Counterpoint: Tobacco and Sugar* (1940), trans. Helen de Onis (New York: Knopf, 1947), 102–3.

17. Mary Louise Pratt provides the term *contact zone* in *Imperial Eyes: Travel Writing and Transculturation* (New York: Routledge, 1992).

18. The term *social death* is Orlando Patterson's. See *Slavery and Social Death: A Comparative Study* (Cambridge, Mass.: Harvard University Press, 1982).

19. Kass Banning, "Feeding off the Dead: Necrophilia and the Black Imaginary, An Interview with John Akomfrah," *Border/Lines* 28/29 (Winter 1993): 33.

20. I am not suggesting that necrophilia/necrophagia would be the only way to conceive of the connections among these works or in the African Diaspora. The complexity of the relation to the past has also been addressed in works that explore historical and cultural continuities.

21. The history of the mediated representation and the pitfalls for the artist are clarified in Marlene Nourbese Philip's meditation on the subject: "*I want to write about kinky hair and flat noses — maybe I should be writing about the language that* kinked *the hair and* flattened *noses, made* jaws prognathous." Marlene Nourbese Philip, "The Absence of Writing or How I Almost Became a Spy," in *She Tries Her Tongue, Her Silence Softly Breaks* (Charlottestown, Canada: Ragweed, 1989), 20.

22. Wilson Harris, *The Guyana Quartet* (Boston: Faber and Faber, 1985), 19.

23. In an interview, Campos-Pons describes how the in-between space is very important to her work. See Michael D. Harris, "Meanwhile," 52.

24. Erna Brodber, *Louisiana* (Jackson: University Press of Mississippi, 1997). Further references will be in the body of the text.

25. Marilene Felinto, *The Women of Tijucopapo,* trans. Irene Matthews (Lincoln: University of Nebraska, 1994). *Tijuco* is mud and *papo* is slang for mouth. The location of the women where the land meets the sea and their association with maternity link them with Iemanjá, an *orixá* that I will discuss in more detail later in this chapter. Irene Matthews notes that the historical women of Tijucopapo, on whom Felinto's fictional women of Tijucopapo are based, played an important role in a revolt against seventeenth-century Dutch invaders (127). Further references will be in the body of the text.

26. Marilene Felinto, *As Mulheres de Tijucopapo* (Rio de Janeiro: Paz e Terra, 1982). I indicate any modifications of Matthews's excellent translation in brackets. Further references will be in the body of the text.

27. Elizabeth Yukins, "Bastard Daughters and the Possession of History in *Corregidora* and *Paradise,*" *Signs* 28 (Autumn 2002): 31.

28. Consolata missionaries dedicate themselves to Mary and to the comfort of the afflicted and abandoned. Interview with Irmã Maria Inês St. Aubyn, Colégio Amor de Deus, Oporto, Portugal, 22 January 2003.

29. I have relied on Anthony Chiffolo, *100 Names of Mary* (Cincinnati, Ohio: St. Anthony's Messenger Press, 2002), for the following information about Mary and Marian worship.

30. Zora A. O. Seljan, *Iemanjá mãe dos orixás* (São Paulo: Ed. Afro-Brasileira, 1973), 39; see also Armando Ayala, *Iemanjá* (Montevideo: Arca, 1993); Pierre Verger, *Notas*

sobre o culto aos orixás e voduns de Bahia de Todas os Santos no Brasil, e na antiga costa dos escravos na África (São Paulo: EDUSP, 1999).

Epilogue

1. "A cada passo hallaba *lo real maravilloso*. Pero pensaba, además, que esa presencia y vigencia de lo real maravilloso no era privilegio único de Haití, sino patrimonio de la América entera. . . . ¿Pero qué es la historia de América toda sino una crónica de lo real-maravilloso? (With each step I encountered the marvelous in the real. But I also thought that the presence and prevalence of the marvelous real was not a privilege unique to Haiti, but the patrimony of the entirety of America . . . For what is the history of Latin America as a whole if not a chronicle of 'the marvelous real'?) Alejo Carpentier, *El reino de este mundo* (la Habana, Cuba: Editorial Pueblo y Educación, 1979), 6–9.

2. *The Kingdom of This World,* trans. Harriet de Onís (New York: Farrar, Straus and Giroux, 1989), 185.

3. Wilson Harris, "A Note on the Genesis of *The Guyana Quartet,"* in *The Guyana Quartet* (Boston: Faber and Faber, 1985), 7–14.

4. Wilson Harris, "Interior of the Novel: Amerindian/African/European Relations," in *Explorations: A Selection of Talks and Articles,* ed. Hena Maes-Jelineck (Mundelstrup, Denmark: Dangaroo, 1981), 13. See also Samuel Durrant, "Hosting History: Wilson Harris's Sacramental Narratives," *Jouvert* 5, no. 1 (2000).

5. Michael Swan, *The Marches of El Dorado: British Guiana, Brazil, Venezuela* (Boston: Beacon Hill, 1958), 284. Swan cites Richard Schomburgk, *Travels in British Guiana, 1840–1844* (1847), vol. 2, trans. Walter E. Roth (Georgetown, Guyana: Daily Chronicle, 1922–1923), 343–44.

Index

Abbott, Helen, 132

Abbott, Robert, 115–16, 123–24, 125, 127–32, 193n1; response of Afro-Brazilian press to trip of, 127–31, 133–34, 152–53, 196n37

abject, 24, 57, 95, 163, 165, 169, 193n35

abolition of slavery (Brazil, 1888), 121, 122, 178n19

Abraham, Karl, 37, 181n24, 186n35

Abraham, Nicholas, xix, 37, 79–82, 159, 186n38, 190n29, 198n11

absorption: amalgamation vs., 16–17, 18; Brazilian method of, 17, 108–9, 110; cannibalism as recurring trope for process of, 17–18; racial democracy requiring consent in, 18–22. *See also* incorporation

Academia Brasileira Das Letras (Brazilian Academy of Letters), 27

acculturation, 157, 158

Adamo, Sam, 127, 196n34

Africa: significance for America, 151–52. *See also* slavery

African Americans: activism of, 91–92; evaluating black citizenship in democratic society, Brazil as enduring reference point for, 15–16, 85; Great Migration, 116–17, 146; professionals, sense of promise of South America for, 124–27, 138

African Diaspora, xvii, 150, 153; double consciousness and cultural intermixture distinguishing those defined through, 150; identification and, 145–54; identity of, 153; sites

of entanglement, 161–65; visualizing diasporic blackness, 154–61

Afro-Brazilian press: growth of, 128; issues addressed by, 127–28; on reasons for preventing immigration of U.S. Blacks, 134–35; response to Abbott's trip to Brazil, 127–31, 133–34, 152–53, 196n37

Akomfrah, John, xix, 158

Aleijadinho (Antônio Francisco Lisboa, artist), 40

Alencar, José de, 38, 186n40

Althusser, Louis, 180n16

Alvarenga, Oneyda de, 43

Alves, Rodrigo, 66

amalgamation, 96, 98, 103–4, 110, 137, 141, 191n12; absorption vs., 16–17, 18

Amaral, Aracy, 183n1

Amaral, Társila de, 14, 27, 40

América Latina (Bomfim), 73

American Colonization Society, 100

American Commission to Negotiate Peace, 180n20

American Studies: importance of placing transnational at center of, xi; shifting terrain from the national to the transnational, xv

America the Peacemaker (Gil), xiii, 177n11

Amsterdam News, The, 15, 120

Analytic Report regarding the Slave Trade and regarding the Evils of Domestic Slavery (Burlamaque), 5

Anchieta, José de, 35

Zita Nunes is associate professor of English and director of the Comparative Literature Program at the University of Maryland, College Park.